IRAQ

OPERATION TELIC 9

FOR THOSE WHO HAVE SERVED AND THEIR FAMILIES SUPPORT

'A soldier takes no honour in taking a life, only the justification that in doing so, it has saved a life.'

Major Carl Gardner

IRAQ

OPERATION TELIC 9

ARNHEM IN BASRA

CARL GARDNER

Pen & Sword
MILITARY
AN IMPRINT OF PEN & SWORD BOOKS LTD.
YORKSHIRE – PHILADELPHIA

First published in Great Britain in 2026 by
PEN AND SWORD MILITARY
An imprint of
Pen & Sword Books Limited
Yorkshire – Philadelphia

Print ISBN 978 1 03619 862 6
ePUB ISBN 978 1 03619 86 40
ePDF ISBN 978 1 03619 865 7

A CIP catalogue record for this book is available from the British Library.

Typeset in Times New Roman 12/16 by
SJmagic DESIGN SERVICES, India.
Printed and bound in the UK by CPI Group (UK) Ltd.

The Publisher's authorised representative in the EU for product safety is
Authorised Rep Compliance Ltd., Ground Floor, 71 Lower Baggot Street,
Dublin D02 P593, Ireland.
www.arccompliance.com

For a complete list of Pen & Sword titles please contact
PEN & SWORD BOOKS LIMITED
George House, Units 12 & 13, Beevor Street, Off Pontefract Road,
Barnsley, South Yorkshire, S71 1HN, England
E-mail: enquiries@pen-and-sword.co.uk
Website: www.pen-and-sword.co.uk

or

PEN AND SWORD BOOKS
1950 Lawrence Rd, Havertown, PA 19083, USA
E-mail: uspen-and-sword@casematepublishers.com
Website: www.penandswordbooks.com

MIX
Paper | Supporting
responsible forestry
FSC® C013604

CONTENTS

LIST OF PLATES

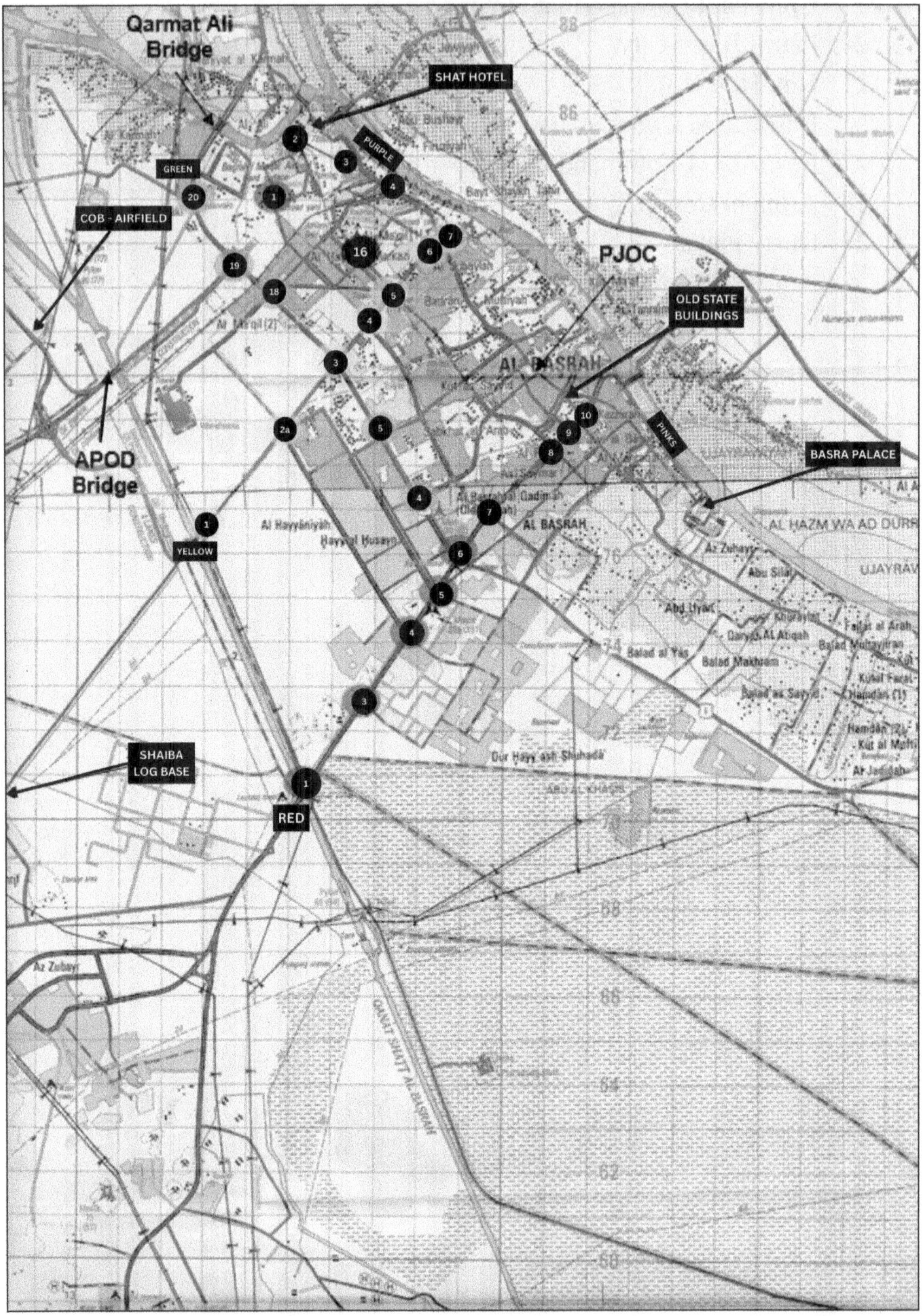

Qarmat Ali Bridge
SHAT HOTEL
PURPLE
GREEN
COB - AIRFIELD
PJOC
OLD STATE BUILDINGS
AL BASRAH
PINKS
BASRA PALACE
APOD Bridge
YELLOW
AL HAZM WA AD DURR
Al Hayyaniyah
Abd Uyan
Dur Hayy ash Shuhada
SHAIBA LOG BASE
RED
Az Zubayr
QANAT SHATT AL BASRAH

INTRODUCTION

The British Army's Warrior fighting vehicles flew over the A-Pod Bridge as part of the sixteen-vehicle armoured patrol. My Warrior had a crew of three, John the commander, me the gunner, Chris the driver and Sam, Wes, Marti, and Croz in the back all armed to the teeth ready to fight if they needed to. The moon shone on the thick steel armour in the Basra City night. I watched as the turrets turned left and right scanning the ground, looking for any signs of the enemy. I was in the gunner's seat, standing with just my shoulders and head sticking out of the turret ready to drop into my seat and engage with the Warrior's high explosive 30mm cannon or 7.62mm chain gun if the enemy dared to open fire on us. The patrol turned left and moved down towards the old Basra Docks. I could feel the cool breeze as the air brushed past my face in the warm Iraqi night.

Everything seemed to slow down as if we were travelling in slow motion. I looked on with pride as the patrol moved down the road with the sunken ship half submerged in the water to our left. The moon glowed, the Warriors and the weapons stood out impressively, dominating the terrain, I felt invincible. I could feel my heart pounding in my body, proud to be a member of the British Army. It is a unique moment only a soldier gets; I call it 'the soldier's moment'.

My brothers in arms have all experienced this throughout the years. In Northern Ireland running out of a patrol base in the city, hard targeting to clear the choke point of the IRA snipers. Running to the helicopter in the fields of South Armagh as it lands to take you back to the barracks. In the hill of Bosnia looking over a dominant force trying to keep civilians safe. Afghanistan, patrolling the green zone, knowing that every step you take could be your last. All soldiers get this feeling where everything slows down. Your surroundings feel unreal, you feel pride, you feel like you can take on the world and you feel like you are part of something special. It really is an exceptional feeling being a soldier. Being part of a band of brothers that would be willing to die for the person to the left and right of them. It is a feeling that no one ever forgets and even when you leave the forces that feeling goes with you and is what cements you to a long and lasting bond with the soldiers and officers with whom you have served.

'CRACK, CRACK, CRACK, CRACK'

I am brought back to reality as the enemy's one in one tracer flies through the air and zips past our Warriors, missing us by inches. I drop from my standing position, hitting my seat hard. It's a well-practised drill, drop, eyes in sights and traverse all in one movement. The turret of my Warrior quickly moves over to the right. I am scanning the ground with the thermal sights searching for the Iraqi insurgents who have ambushed us. I spot movement in an alleyway in the L Shap Flats. The insurgents have been located as they fire another burst of tracer bullets towards our position. Their bullets ping of the metal of our Warrior as they hit their target, us.

I steady the 7.62mm chain gun sights on the enemy and flick the trigger switch to fire. I stamp down on the firing pedal and the Warrior's chain gun spits out its deadly 7.62mm bullets towards the enemy. The area around the insurgents location becomes alive as mine, Wes's, and Marti's bullets from their top cover rifles in the back start ripping the area apart. The threat is gone as John shouts for everyone to cease fire. We stop firing and scan the area looking for any movement or for the threat to reappear. There is no movement and the patrol pushes on and enters the SHATT Patrol Base. I make my weapons systems safe and just sit back in the gunner's seat taking a small Condor moment. We have only been in Iraq for a few weeks, but already the deployment seems a lifetime ago.

1

NOVEMBER 2006

The Deployment (Travel from UK to Iraq)

Arnhem Company was an armoured infantry company with just over 120 officers and soldiers. We were one of five companies that made up a Battalion of around 600 people. We were a new Battalion called 'The 2nd Battalion the Duke of Lancaster's Regiment', made up of three great regiments, The King's Own Royal Border Regiment, The King's Regiment, and the Queen's Lancashire Regiment. We were based in Catterick North Yorkshire which is one of the UK's largest military garrisons and after 18 months of build-up training, we were ready for deployment on Operation Telic 9. Op Telic was the name the British Army gave for their operations in southern Iraq, and we were part of the ninth major deployment to Basra City. The tour was to last for seven months from November 2006 to June 2007.

On 7 November the second group of soldiers from Arnhem Company were due to deploy. A few days before Carl, our Company Quartermaster (CQMS), and two of his staff left to take over our stores and tents in Iraq. The second group was our command group made up of our Officer Commanding (OC), a Major in charge. Three young officers who commanded a platoon of around thirty soldiers. The sergeants their second in command. The Junior Non-Commissioned Officers (JNCOs) and some of our Warrior drivers.

They were all sat in the gym ready to go through the paperwork and check in their bags when the Commanding Officer (CO) of the

Battalion came in and asked for everyone's attention. He informed everyone that it was with great sadness that the Battalion had sustained its first fatality and that it was Kingsman Jamie Hancock of Chindit Company. Chindit Company had taken over the Old State Building (OSB) in Basra City a couple of weeks before. The OSB was one of the smallest bases in Basra, containing just a company's worth of soldiers and was the most attacked base in the city. Jamie had been on stag protecting the base in one of the sangers (watchtowers) when he was hit by a bullet (he had actually been killed the day before, but the CO rightly could not tell anyone until his family had been informed).

I could not believe it, we had not even got our full regiment in Iraq, and we had lost one already. I didn't know Jamie that well as he was in another company. I still felt sad, another young lad taken serving his country and the nightmare his family must of being going through. It was not the first time I had served with soldiers who had been killed in action. I remember as a young lad in Northern Ireland when five members of the King's Regiment got blown up on a checkpoint in Londonderry. I was a young soldier back then, no more than a boy myself, but I remember the older soldiers in command looking after and reassuring me as we deployed through the checkpoint on a cordon. This was now my job and I got around the lads due to deploy to reassure them and make sure they were all right before their flight. The Arnhem command group completed their check-in and boarded the coach to take them to Teesside Airport where they were due to fly out.

This left the Company 2IC, a captain, and me the Company Sergeant Major (CSM) with the soldiers who were made up of around seventy junior ranks. Over the next five days we checked all our equipment, did some more first aid training, and played some sport until the day came that we were due to fly out.

The British Army was in Iraq as part of the US-led coalition forces who had invaded the country in 2003 after it was confirmed that the dictator Saddam Hussein had weapons of mass destruction. The West said he had to be removed from power and a new Iraqi government established.

How did I feel about the British Army deployment to Iraq before we deployed? I knew the British public were not very fond of us being there and some saw us as just another Western force in somebody else's country. But I did see us as a force for good before we deployed. I knew Saddam was cruel and treated the people of Iraq very badly, often with torture and death centres. I had seen videos of the terrible 1988 Halabja Massacre on the Iraqi Kurdish people in a large-scale chemical attack which killed up to 5,000 men, women, and children. Surely this was proof of weapons of mass destruction. I also thought their way of life was poor compared to the UK and I was hoping we could improve that. I knew that a country like Iraq, if we did not help them find some structure, would become a breeding ground for terrorism against Western countries. I did think to myself would these feelings change by the end of the tour!! The fact of the above is, we were soldiers serving our Queen and Country and proud to do so. It was for the politicians to decide the strategic aim and long-term planning, so let's get on with the job I loved.

As Arnhem Company's CSM, I was the most senior soldier in the company. I had completed 18 years in the British Army and been on operations before, serving eight years over a number of different roles in Northern Ireland. Northern Ireland was a strange operation for the soldier who deployed there, as the 'rules to return fire' which was called the Yellow Card, was totally against the deployed force. I had been blown up, shot at with RPGs, machine guns and even had a coffee-jar bomb thrown at me. But due to the Yellow Card, I had never returned fire at the enemy who was the IRA. So, I was quite excited to be deploying to a new war zone, where my military skills hopefully could be tested to the full.

November 11th was the day the main body of Arnhem Company was due to start our trip to Iraq. I said goodbye to my son Daniel at home. My wife Lyn and my daughter Kirsty were dropping me off at camp. As we drove the short 10 minutes trip to camp the girls were nervous and I was putting a brave face on and trying not to make it any harder on them than it was. As we got to the company office I was about to get out of the car when Lyn grabbed hold of my arm and made me promise that I would not take any risks out there. I looked her in the eyes, and I promised (a promise I would break many times over the next seven months). We got out and I kissed and hugged them both as the tears rolled down their faces. They got into the car with Kirsty miming the words 'I love you daddy' with a tear running down her face as the car drove off. I didn't show it to my family, but I had mixed emotions. I was sad leaving them, knowing that I was about to put them through hell with seven months of worrying. On the other hand, I was excited to be going to Iraq and wanted to do a different type of soldiering.

I went to my office and checked over my kit. Being the CSM I always liked to get in first. I stood at my office window and watched as the company arrived. The lads were getting dropped off by their families and there were a lot of tears from them and the lads as they waved goodbye.

We moved to the gym with our bergens and black bags which were heavy and weighing us down. We were dressed in our new desert uniforms and all looking the part. Once we got there, I got the lads to drop off their bags and we moved to the armoury to collect the company's weapons. The weapons were all bundled up; this is where they are placed in padded green sleeves to protect them on the journey. Once back in the gym we got the paperwork checked for the weapons.

We then moved to a desk to get our paperwork checked. As I got to the desk a corporal out of the Adjutant General's Corps (AGC) checked my passport, med card, and dog tags (ID disc we wear around our neck in case we get blown up). They then gave me forms to check that my next of kin details were correct. Once I completed the form, we moved to a desk and got some American dollars as this was the money to be used in the camps within Iraq. This now left us with just our travelling day sacks that contain a small lightweight sleeping bag, wash, and shave kit, body armour, helmet, and a few personal things like an iPod and a book. We moved onto the coach, and I did a head count to make sure we had everyone. Once I was content, I informed the 2IC and we drove the five-hour trip to RAF Brize Norton.

At Brize Norton we were greeted by a JNCO from movements (who have the biggest wagon wheel badge you have ever seen on their arms) who welcomed us to Brize Norton and asked us to move into the waiting area. It was 0100hrs in the morning and we got told to make ourselves at home and that our flight was on time and due to leave at 0900hrs. There were bodies everywhere as the boys tried to get some rest before the flight. Some of the lads got out their sleeping bags, some got washed and shaved, while some just sat around talking. There was tea and coffee for everyone and also a TV with the normal midnight programs on. At 0600hrs we were called forward and given some breakfast which was a full fry-up. Our names were checked off again and we were told our transport was outside ready to take us to the terminal.

What a sight as we moved outside, there was an old red double-decker bus waiting to take us. We got on and everyone was laughing as Willo said, 'I can't believe we are going to fucking war in a double-decker bus'. The bus set off and after 15 minutes we were at the terminal building. We got off the bus and moved to the check-in point. Once we had checked in, we were in the waiting lounge when we were called forward to board the plane. The plane was a normal civilian charter flight. Once everyone was on, the air crew tried to make everyone feel at home, but you could feel the tension in the air, not surprising really as a lot of the boys had never been on operations before and were feeling pretty nervous. I was pretty relaxed and just wanted to chill for a few hours without having to be in charge.

The plane took off and a few hours later landed in Qatar. We got off and boarded a coach that took us past rows of American Air Force planes. It was dark and the place was lit up with massive flood lights. Even through it was night, the air was still a lot warmer than the UK. As we checked in, we were told that our flight to Basra was not for a few hours and to help ourselves to some food and drinks. This was great, as the base was supported by the US Air Force. Within minutes everyone was sitting there with butties, crisps, sweets, and cans of fizzy pop. The 2IC and I got some food and went to watch 'Match of the Day' on Sky to see how our teams had got on. John was a bluenose (Everton fan), and I was a kopite (Liverpool fan) so there was always a lot of banter. The company 2IC was the senior captain in the company, in his late 20s. He was an excellent officer who we were lucky to have. As well as being very good at his job, he was also a local Liverpool lad who the soldier could very easily relate to. John was slim, athletic, and really easy to get on with, you can say that everyone liked John, we classed him as one of us. As the company 2IC, John's job was to step up as the OCs when needed and help with the main planning of operations. John was a good friend and someone I would drive crazy over the next seven months.

After a few hours we got told our flight to Basra City was ready and for Chalk One to move forward (a chalk is what the military call a group of people who are waiting to board some transport). We all boarded the coach with our day sacks heavy from all the goodies we had taken from our American friends. We also had to take our helmets and body armour out of our day sacks for when we got in the Iraqi air space. We boarded our C-130 aircraft and sat cramped on the red net seats for the short 90 minutes trip to Basra City.

The engines started up and the plane began to shake. We were given little yellow ear defenders to try to block out the noise (which they never did). The journey was uncomfortable and if you needed a piss you had to use a shitty sink thing on the front wall of the plane which meant anyone sitting next to it got covered in piss. I had one near me but there was no way the lads were using it and covering me in piss. So, the lads on the other side of the plane were pretty irritated, as theirs got used twice as much.

After 60 minutes we got told to put our helmets and body armour on to protect us from any gunfire from the ground. The inside light switched from white to red with everyone adjusting their night vision. As I sat there, I looked around the plane. Most of the soldiers were awake and just staring into the space in front of them. I looked out of the window and could see, Basra City in the distance. For a major city it was not very bright and was in parts in complete darkness.

After a few minutes we heard the wheels opening on the bottom of the plane. The next thing we knew the plane dropped fast and our hearts sank within our bodies under the pressure. Within a couple of minutes, we had landed. It's what the RAF called an operational landing – dropping fast so you are not a target for any longer than you have to be. It was the early hours of the morning in Basra City and when we got off the plane the first thing you noticed was that the place was in complete darkness. This was to help and try to counter the indirect fire threat. Indirect fire is where the enemy attack you with weapons from a distance, which are not shot directly at you. The most common indirect fire is mortars and rockets which are filled with high explosives and fragmented metal, and designed to explode over an area causing injury and death.

With our helmets and body armour still on we were directed onto a waiting coach and moved to a room to get an arrivals brief. We had an arrival brief from some Lance Corporal who did not know how to talk and gave the complete brief at 100 decibels. Once he had finished, we filled in all the forms for new arrivals and then moved to a waiting room.

We were told our last part of the journey would be by helicopter to Shaiba Log Base (SLB). We waited for a few hours and then the call came for my chalk to move to the helicopter landing site (HLS). When we got there, we were told to wear our goggles due to the helicopter down force, as all the grit and sand flying around would damage our eyes. The helicopter was a Merlin and it landed and lowered its back ramp. We were given the green light by the Load Master (loady), and we ran forward and got on, moving past the General Purpose Machine Gun (GPMG) which was mounted on the rear ramp. We sat down and did up our safety belts. The engines roared and the Merlin took off and across the desert it went. As we were taking the short 10-minute journey the Merlin let of some counter-missile flares which popped and gave off a bright red glow in the air space behind us. Being so tired from our journey, we all shit ourselves thinking we were under attack to the great amusement of the pilots and the loady (wankers). We landed and we all moved away from the Merlin as it took off and went to get the next bunch of lads.

We moved to our coach and were dropped off at Bedouin Camp which was the transit camp in Shiba Log Base (SLB). As we got there the Regimental Admin Officer (RAO) was waiting for us. He gave us a brief and told us what tent we were in and that our first lesson was not till 1200 noon and to get some sleep. We moved to our tent which was surrounded by a three-breeze brick high wall to try and protect us from any indirect fire. We moved into the fifty-man tent where we grabbed a cot bed which was a green fold up bed. We got our sleeping bags out, got undressed and jumped in. I looked at my watch it was six in the morning, and we had been travelling for 36 hours and we were knackered.

We got woken up at 1140hrs and we got a quick wash and shave in an old stinking porta-cabin which consisted of six sinks and six showers. Once done I got the company together and marched them to the main briefing tent. The weather was still warm for this time of year, but you could still feel the cold wind and could tell those colder times were on their way. Before our welcome brief we got informed that four soldiers from the boat troop had been killed while conducting a boat patrol on the Shatt Al Arab waterway. Warrant Officer Lee Hopkins, Staff Sergeant Sharron Elliot, Corporal Ben

Nowak and Marine Jay Hylton had all been killed in an explosion that hit their patrol boat. Not the news you want to hear when you first arrive in Iraq.

We got our welcome brief, and they told us for the next three days we were going to complete our in-country training and that every soldier had to complete this before they were allowed to patrol the streets. After the welcome brief we got briefed up on all the creepy crawlies and diseases that we could catch and got told that if we did not wash our hands about twenty times a day, we would get D and V (diarrhoea and vomiting) which meant we would get isolated and be bedded down.

After this we moved to the cookhouse for our lunch. Outside of the cookhouse main door there were units of sinks. We had to wash our hands using a yellow anti-bacteria soap, dry them and then finish off using an alcohol-based gel which was a pain in the arse, but it was all worth it when we got to the food. There was everything from curry to steaks, salads, and pasta, to the lads' favourite, burgers and chips. We had our fill washed down with cold water which was situated everywhere in fridges around the tent. After lunch I went to the toilet, which was a portaloo. As I entered, I nearly saw my lunch again, as I had forgot the golden rule 'Don't look down.' The place was stinking and by God could these squaddies shit.

We moved to the briefing tent and were split down into groups of fifty and were given a timetable of lessons ranging from first aid to Card Alpha. We started with first aid and were getting briefed by a captain from the Medical Corps. He was telling us about gunshot wounds when we heard a whistling sound and then a muffled explosion. We all looked at each other and I said to one of the boys 'Did you hear that.' The captain was still teaching until we heard another whistle but this time it was much louder. I shouted 'GET DOWN' as a rocket exploded about 50m away. We all got on the floor and tried to get our body armour and helmets on as fast as we could. Once done we lay there on the wooden dusty floor, face down with our arms tucked under our bodies, as we heard another explosion. We lay there for 30 minutes not daring to move.

This is the first time I had been IDF by an enemy rocket. At first it felt surreal, as if it wasn't happening at all. But then you hear the muffled explosion and the shaking of the ground, that soon changes the way you feel, it feels very real. The worst part for me was when you heard the whistle of the rocket as it flew in. My whole body would tense up. The hairs on the back of my neck would react, not knowing where it was going to land and how much pain you were about to get caught up in as the fragmented metal flew through the air. So many different emotions darting through your body in just a short space of time. After the all clear was sounded we finished off the lesson as if nothing had happened.

After the first aid lesson we had a lesson on Card A which was a card with our rules of engagement on. It told us when we could fire our weapons and when we could not. If someone was committing an act likely to endanger life or our lives were in danger. Then we were legally allowed to fire our weapons. We were briefed on search operations and how the insurgents were attacking us and what were their favourite means of attack.

The insurgents in Basra City were part of the Jaysh Al Mahdi (JAM) and any thoughts we had about them being some stupid locals who were running about with an AK-47 without a clue were soon dashed. We were told that they were well organised, hard and determined fighters and because they were being backed by Iran, they were also well trained and equipped.

After a full afternoon of lessons, we had dinner which again was good. We then finished the day off with a couple more lessons. Before we finished, we were told that we had been attacked by three Chinese-designed Type 63 rockets that afternoon and that one person had been very lucky indeed. One of the rockets had hit a 4x4 with a soldier driving which passed through the back left window and straight out through the other window without exploding. His only injuries were a few cuts to his neck and face from the flying glass. Now that is what you call one lucky fucker. That night, still feeling fatigued after all the travelling, the company was in bed pretty early and we all had a good night of sleep.

The second day we had more lessons and went down an improvised explosive device (IED) lane which showed us how they were using piles of rubbish and mounds of dirt in the city to hide their bombs. It also showed us what to look for and how they were hiding their wires and what markers they were using. It was a great afternoon of training and one which would save many people's lives in the months to come. After the days training, we were given the night off and the lads watched a DVD and got a pizza from an improvised ISO container on camp. After the pizza, the lads got into bed and got some sleep. With the indirect fire threat being so high someone thought it would be a good idea for everyone to sleep in our body armour and helmets. So, the order came down to us and we tried to drop off to sleep with a couple of armoured plates sticking into our backs.

About 0300hrs we were woken up with three large explosions as three rockets hit the base. Everyone hit the floor and as we already had our body armour and helmets on, most of us just rolled of the bed hitting the floor. I tried this time not to overthink it, not an easy thing to do. It did make me feel helpless, listening to a couple of the boys panic, as there is just nothing you can do but reassure them and stay in your covered position. We stayed there for 30 minutes until the all clear was given. We then got back into bed and were woken at 0630hrs for the third day's training. It was funny to see some boys still on the floor that had not woken up when the all clear was given.

The third day was on the ranges, an area of land where we could safely fire our weapons. We all sorted out our weapons (rifles) so that the sights were all correct and legal to use. The sight is the optical part on a weapon used for aiming. We then moved onto different shoots. There was the top cover shoot where we fired from the top hatch of a moving Land Rover, and the snap shooting range where we fired double shots from different positions to sharpen our reflex shooting. We also did a grenade range and threw some white phosphorus grenades. We did some search team training and did our strike team drills which is where we attack a building.

At the end of the day, we all moved over to the hospital where Kingsman Jamie Hancock's body was. He was due to fly out of the SLB base by helicopter to the Coalition Operating Base (COB). We lined the route and his coffin draped in the Union flag was carried from the hospital to the waiting Merlin Helicopter. The back ramp closed, and the helicopter engine started up. It took off and flew away from us before turning around and flying low down the line of soldiers and off to the COB. We moved back to our tent with the third day coming to an end. We cleaned our weapons and got some sleep as the next day we were due to fly out to what would be our home for the next seven months, Basra Air Base (the COB).

The next day came and as we were about to leave, we were stopped and told that our flight had been delayed. So, we waited about for a few hours until we got the nod and moved to the HLS. Again, our flight was by Merlin but this time it was a daytime flight. We could see the outside of the camp for the first time. It was flat and sand for as long as the eye could see. The Merlin fired some flares to counter any SAM missile threat and after the short 10-minute journey we were in the COB. As we landed, we could see the old fancy terminal building with the 'Welcome to Basra Airport' sign still on the top of it. There was a large tower which was the control tower that stood out in the airport.

We moved to the terminal and a rep from our unit showed us which coach we were on. We moved to Camp C which was a transit camp and got some food which again was good. The 2IC and I moved to Camp D which was soon going to be known as Ladysmith Lines. Once there we met up with the OC and the Pl staff who briefed us up on the handover and what their patrols had been like. They had been going out with the unit we were taking over, who were the Prince of

Wales Royal Regiment (PWRR) and most of them had been in some sort of contact in the city. We were telling them our war stories of how we had been attacked by six Chinese rockets only to find out that they had been hit by ten in the last couple of days alone. We then went and met our CQMS who showed us around the camp. He showed us which tents were going to be for the soldiers and which tents were for officers and SNCOs. The tents were six-to-eight-person tents with a simple air conditioning unit to control the temperature. We noticed there were no bricks and no protection from indirect fire. You just had a cot bed and whatever the outgoing unit left you. I was lucky as I got a chair and set of hanging drawers.

I then met up with the outgoing CSM who told me how the handover was going to happen. The lads would take the BAR armour (anti-rocket armour) off their Warriors and place it on ours. They would then take off all the ECM which was a system to prevent the remote-control bombs from going off and fit it to our Warriors. Why all this was going on the Pl Sgt and myself would take over all the company ammo and get it sorted ready to give the soldiers. But all this would be placed on hold as their company were still on one and three hours noticed to move, and they could not handover until they had handed the commitment over to a different coy.

This was done at 0200hrs and both companies worked through the night to make sure that all the BAR armour was transferred to our Warriors as fast as we could. The lads then did the ECM which was a pain in the arse because our Warriors were meant to have been fitted with brackets in the UK before they were shipped out but for some reason they were not. The lads did the best they could and got all the stuff up and running. The Platoon Sergeants and I took over all the ammo. It ranged from 30mm high-explosive rounds to grenades and the normal 5.56mm and 7.62mm bullets.

When we were finished, it was well into the next day and the lads were tied, but it was not time to sleep yet. We thanked the company we took over and then moved them out of their tents before moving our soldiers in. We managed to give the lads a few hours' sleep before we had to move all the Warriors to the range to shoot the weapon systems. We moved to the tank park where our Warriors were kept and did our checks to ensure that they were working correctly. The Warrior was the British Army's tracked armoured personal carrier. It had a crew of three which consisted of the commander, gunner, driver and up to seven soldiers in the back. It had a turret which was armed with a 30mm cannon and a 7.62mm machine gun. Picture it like a small tank.

Our Warrior was call sign Zero Charlie, one of the command Warriors in Arnhem Company. We had a crew of three and four in the back all in support. The seven of us stood by the Warrior in the warm Iraqi sun. We were all dressed in desert combats with our body armour and weapons in the Warrior ready to put on. John was the commander and also being the senior captain was the company 2ic. John was about 5,11, dark hair, a local lad from Liverpool who had commissioned through the Royal Military Academy Sandhurst, which was some achievement. I was the gunner of the Warrior, but also a trained commander. I was also 5,11, but after 18 years in the Army my hair was more salt and pepper. Think George Clooney and you will get the picture. I had a pretty relaxed approach to leadership, where I would call all of my soldiers by their first names. This was a one-way thing and I was still sir to them. I believed to be a good commander I had to know the soldiers I was commanding and recognise their strengths but also their weaknesses. Don't get me wrong, as the CSM my personality also needed to have a bit of a bite for when the soldiers messed up. The last member of the crew was Chris the driver. Chris was a young lad from Manchester, dark brown hair, in his early 20s and a great Warrior driver, one of the best in the battalion.

In charge in the back was Sam a local lad from Wigan. Sam was also the Intelligence Sergeant for the company. Sam was about 5,11, with brown hair and a bit more serious than Wes and Marti who drove him up the wall. Wes was a corporal, fair haired local lad from Manchester. He was about 5 foot tall and a complete wind-up merchant. Marti, another Mancunian, was his brother in crime, 6 foot tall, blond hair blue eyes, bit of an Aryan race. The last person to mention in the back was Croz the company medic. A Liverpool lad, dark hair and about 5,10. Croz was a very good medic and it was nice to have someone so good covering our backs in case we got hurt.

The seven of us were friends and after 18 months of build-up training, we were ready. What we didn't realise is we were about to go through the most aggressive, violent, and deadly tour of Iraq the British Army had ever encountered. Over next seven months this group was going to form a bond which was going to last a lifetime.

Once the checks were done, we prepared our weapons for firing and last but not least we checked our communications as we never left camp without them working. With all this done we mounted up, the 2IC and I got into our Warrior. As the 2IC was in command of the range group, we led out with all our sixteen Warriors following on behind us. We got to the back gate which was just next to our camp and gave a radio check and booked out. The Warriors roared away as we moved out. This is the first time me and a lot of the lads had patrolled in Iraq. I could see the nervousness in their faces. I was pretty relaxed and more curious to what my new surrounding were like.

The range was a mile outside of camp, but the lads were moving the turrets from left to right watching for anything that looked out of place. When we got to the range, all it was was a stretch of road with a couple of old buses placed down 600 to 900m to the left. The lads got out the back of our Warrior and cleared the range and ensured that there were no bombs or booby traps waiting for us. Once this was completed, we lined up the Warriors and fired our 30mm cannons and then we fired our 7.62mm machine guns. We were now legally ready to deploy on patrol in Iraq. As we mounted up there were a few locals who turned up to see if there was any brass left that they could make some money from. They all had short dark hair with white Arabic clothing and flip flops on their feet. They turned up all four of them on one moped. We laughed as they ran around as fast as they could, looking under every stone. We moved back to camp covered from head to toe in sand and dust. Something we would get used to very quickly.

The first patrols were done by One Platoon and Two Platoon on 15 November. They went out doing night patrols in the local area outside of the city. Both doing four Warrior indirect fire patrols which went well apart from Two Platoon getting lost inside the base even before they got out of the camp. To be fair the COB was massive and took a bit of getting used to as most of the units were to find out. The lads in the company who were not on patrol still ended up being attacked with three Chinese rockets in the afternoon and with seven Chinese rockets in the evening. When they were on these patrols the OC was receiving orders on an operation called Op Octavia.

First Contact with the Enemy

In the early hours of the morning on 15 November the OC got the company (around 115 officers and soldiers) in the briefing tent. He informed us that we were tasked to take material to the Queen Royal Lancers who patrolled in the desert just south of Al Amara. The patrol would last 36 hours and consisted of over twenty-five vehicles. Ten Warriors and fifteen admin vehicles. We had a round route of over 300 miles to cover. We sorted out all the admin, placing boxes of water and rations into the back of the Warriors. We then put in our crash-out kit which consisted of our belt kit containing our ammo and FFD (first field dressing bandage), plus our day sacks containing a small sleeping bag, warm top, spare socks and bits and pieces like gloves and goggles. We put on our body armour, helmets and mounted our Warriors. We moved out of the tank park at 0900hrs on the morning of 16 November. We got to the front gate where we picked up our admin vehicles which ranged from lorries to Land Rovers.

We moved out and moved east down the MSR (main supply route) which was a three-lane wide motorway and full of normal Iraqi traffic. We had space between each vehicle of between 20 and 30m and the convoy stretched back about 1,000m. We had Two Platoon with its three Warriors at the front. All the admin vehicles were in the centre. The two command Warriors with the two support Warriors were in the centre of the admin convoy. This left Three Platoon's three Warriors bringing up the rear.

All the Iraqi cars avoided us like hell, even moving on to the other side of the road to get away from us. We later learnt that the American Army fired warning shots up north if they got too close due to suicide bombers. After an hour we headed north and started to move through the Iraqi southern oil field. We had been moving for about 50 miles when we had a breakdown with one of Three Platoon's Warriors. So, we had to go into all-round defence while our LAD fitter section tried to fix it. After an hour they could not get it going so the OC gave the order for it to go on the back of one of the lorries and the patrol continued heading north. One thing that stood out in the oil fields was the flares which were massive flames from the oil pipes that sometimes went 20 feet high. Another was the checkpoints with the Oil Field Police standing staring with their AK-47 assault rifles.

After a few painfully slow hours we reached the town of Al Medina. It was around 1500hrs as we moved into the town. Our weapons were placed at hand on top of the turret and our 9mm pistols were unclipped from their holsters as we entered the unknown. The streets were full of people and kids doing their normal day-to-day routine. They all started to wave and cheer as we went past so we started to wave back. It felt like we were heroes and even when we broke the low-hanging electric cables, they did not get angry.

Once we got through the town we headed north over the bridge and then turned east heading to Al Qurna, which had a reputation for being a hardliner town with plenty of enemy insurgents. After an hour we got to the outskirts of the town and again we got all our weapons ready just in case. The top cover was up which consisted of two lads in the back of the Warriors with their rifles ready and covering the Warrior's blind spots. The turrets of the Warriors were moving from left to right using their thermal sight to scan the surrounding area. Two Platoon moved forward and cleared the main junction we had to transit through. They stopped 50m short of the junction and four lads got out the back, two moving to the left and two to the right and then they started to patrol forward. They were looking for any IEDs and ensuring the area was clear. This was a dangerous time for the lads as they were out of the safety of the Warrior and the chances of small arms attacks against them were high. But nevertheless, they got out time and time again, doing their job to the highest standard. Once the junction was cleared Two Platoon secured the area and the rest of the patrol moved through and pushed north.

We went north for an hour before the OC moved the patrol into a holding area where we placed out our protection and all the commanders moved to the OC's Warrior. The OC confirmed what the next phase of the operation was. It also gave the lads a chance to get a brew on as it was getting cold. This gave the OC, a chance to use his sat phone and let our ops room know what was happening. It was nice to get out of the turret where you had to stand up with your body bent due to the heavy weight of the body armour. We had been travelling for over 12 hours and due to a couple of breakdowns it had been painfully slow. After 20 minutes we mounted back up and completed the last couple of hours of the journey to our rendezvous (RV) point.

When we got there, we were met by a CVRT (another little tank with just a crew) and followed them into the desert where we did the changeover of all the kit. After we were finished, we closed in to the OC, and he gave us orders for the next phase of the operation. It was now 0100hrs, we placed out our protection and the lads got their sleeping bags out and jumped on the desert floor for a couple of hours. It was cold in the desert night. The floor was hard, sandy and you could not help feeling you were about to get bit by a crawly at any moment.

At 0300hrs we got up still fucked and knackered as we sorted all the kit, ready to move by 0330hrs. The OC did one last check with the ops room on the sat phone and we moved out south away from Al Amara. After a short time, we hit the small town of Qal at Shlih and because we were going back a different route, we were to move through the town and cross over the bridge. As we moved near the town and the patrol closed up to help keep control and we headed into the town.

As we got to the bridge, we saw that it was broken and not crossable by our Warriors. We headed right and tried to look for a different way out of the town due to our vehicles blocking our entry route. This did not work, and we hit another dead end. At the same time one of the civilian vehicles got bogged in so we went into all-round defence to protect the recovery. We were trying to get into all-round defence when the OC's Warrior brought down the town electrics and all the live wires were bouncing and sparking all over the place. His gunner Frank had to shout at him to get down before he got fried. At the same time, I traversed the turret and got the 2IC's leg caught in the turret cage. Luckily for him and me his leg was not broken, just bruised. Not the best start to the return trip but hopefully things had to get better, or did they?

It was starting to get light, and we could see people starting to take an interest in us. A black car turned up with tinted windows and a local got out and got straight on his mobile. He was dicking us (gathering information) and passing the information onto the insurgents. Two Platoon and some of Three Platoon's Warriors were at the entrance to the town with Higgy's Warrior next to the fuel truck. The next thing they knew the sky lit up as they were contacted with about thirty tracer rounds from an AK-47, which flew through the air passing just over their heads. Everyone got down as the tracer bullets cracked down the road and the soldiers cocked their weapons as the shouts of

'CONTACT' flew over the radio. I jumped out of my turret and ran forward with Croz the medic just in case there were any casualties.

At the same time the OC was speeding up the recovery. Higgy and H were scanning their areas when the next thing they heard was a 'WHOOSH' as a rocket-propelled grenade (RPG) flew just over the fuel tanker and down the street which exploded behind them with a deafening noise. That was enough for Higgy, and he shouted at the driver of the fuel truck to follow him. He broke out of the town with the fuel truck and moved to a safe area until the rest of us could break out. He definitely saved the lives of his crew as the fuel tanker was the RPG man's main target and if it got hit, we would have had multiple casualties.

I got to the street corner and could see all of the lads in firing positions with their weapons in their shoulders covering down the road to my left. The Warrior turrets were moving left and right as the gunners and commanders scanned to their front.

'WHOOSH'

Another RPG flew down the road and bounced of H Warrior. It flew unexploded into the air, spinning into the distance. I saw Ryan one of the young lads in a fire position across the dirt sandy road. I shouted, 'Where's the firing point.' 'Fifty meters down the road, two insurgents. But they are firing from behind women and kids,' he replied.

'WHOOSH'

In slow motion I watched as another RPG warhead flew down the road. In disbelief I continued looking as it flew just past Ryan's head. The detail was unreal, I could see the rocket, the glow of the burning combustion pushing in along and the smoke trail it was leaving as it flew through the air, exploding on the waste ground behind us. You could smell the sulphur and smoke from the RPGs which just hung in the cold morning air. I shouted at Ryan 'MOVE BACK INTO MORE COVER' and smiled as he moved back behind his Warrior.

The OC told everyone to mount up as the bogged-in lorry was free. He told the 2IC to break out using call sign Zero Charlie, our Warrior. I ran back to the Warrior with Croz and we jumped back in. Our Warrior got to the front, but it was no good using the Warrior weapons as the streets were too tight together and there were too many side streets. 'Grab your rifles and man your positions.' The 2IC and I took up positions on top of the turret, with just our head and shoulders above the protection of the thick armour. Sam, Wes, Marti, and Croz did the same in the back through the back hatches.

We looked just over our sights. It was warm, but everyone could feel the cold breeze on our faces. Our hearts were pounding in our heads, but we were alert and ready to react. There were people everywhere, some just standing and looking and some hiding, shielding their kids from the firefight. We noticed a man in an army uniform come down the street and he had a good look around. When he saw everyone with their weapons ready, he ran back shaking his head. He was the lookout and he knew that if they were to fire at us now, we would return fire and there was a good chance they would be injured or killed. As we moved out, we could feel the cold sweat running off our heads and onto the small of our backs. But we were ready for them with our fingers waiting on our triggers. You could smell the sulphur and see the smoke which still hung in the cool morning air from the RPGs that had been fired. We broke out of the town with the Warriors roaring up the small street where we married up with Higgy's Warrior and the fuel truck just outside of the town.

We moved off to a safe area where we deployed our protection. The OC used his sat phone to inform the ops room of our contact. I went down the convoy to ensure there were no casualties and saw that one of the army lorries had been hit by an RPG warhead which had not exploded. The driver told me how he was sitting in his seat when it flew in the window and landed on the seat next to him. 'You lucky bastard, get your numbers on the lotto next week.' I stood in disbelief as he picked up the broken RPG warhead with all the explosive still in place: 'You want to see it?' We took it off him and placed it in a safe area.

I informed the OC that we were OK, and he gave the order for everyone to mount up and move off. The long trip went faster on the way back with no more Warriors breaking down. We went to Shiba Log Base (SLB) first and dropped off our admin vehicles. We then mounted up and moved back to the COB. We unloaded our weapons and moved back to the tank park. We closed our Warriors down and ensured they were ready to go again if needed and walked back into camp covered in dust, with our faces black from all the dirt apart from our eyes that were white due to the protection of our goggles. As we walked back into camp, I could see the boys getting greeted by the other lads who wanted to know about our first contact. Something that would become second nature as the tour went on and was already second nature for Chindit Company. We got cleaned up and I stood there in the shower with the warm water running down my tired dirty body thinking how the fuck did we get away with that one. We grabbed some food, feeling pretty good with ourselves for not losing anyone before jumping into our cot beds for some well-deserved sleep.

It was not my first contact under fire with the enemy in my career, having had a few from the IRA during my operational tours in Northern Ireland. This one felt different, though: the IRA would attack you and then extract themselves away from the contact. But the Iraqi insurgents were prepared to stand and fight, which was something new. Personally, it was pretty exciting and something we had trained for. I was concerned that no one had returned fire, but I knew that would be discussed. It was a strange feeling being put into a position where you might have to take another person's life. It was not something I had really overthought. I had belief in my own ability as a trained soldier and when the situation presented itself, I was confident as a solider and a human being that it would be for the right reason, to save a life and not to take one.

The next morning the fleet manager got the company down the tank park and working on the Warriors. One of our other Warrior companies who had been patrolling down the city the day before had a check done by Wolfie our ECM JNCO and a Royal Signals JNCO called Dicko, only to discover that their ECM was not fitted correctly. This also applied to our Warriors and the fleet was grounded until we were inspected and passed by an ECM expert. I was already pissed off as we had a crash-out drill that morning and the duty JNCO woke the lads but not me or the officers. So, everybody was getting a piece of my mind this morning.

The OC called for all the commanders from across the company. We sat in the briefing room going through the contact from the previous patrol. Talking about how we were going to improve and what mistakes needed to be addressed. One of the platoon commanders stated he was worried about the fact that none of the lads returned fire. I spoke up and explained about how the insurgents was using the women and kids as shields. I was confident that once one of the company had fired their weapon the confidence would grow. The OC also said he was happy with the call the lads had made, as killing a woman or child could destroy a man inside. Also, it was their call on the ground at the time. This is what made the OC and the 2IC stand out, as most of the company was chewing the fat, telling their war stories. They were looking at ways we could improve as a sub-unit. We all had to remember that once the tour was over, people still had to live with themselves and their actions. Over the next few days, the company worked flat out trying to get the fleet ready so we could deploy on operations.

It was now 19 November, and the company had another crash-out drill, to test our reaction. Me and the other CSMs were asleep in our tent. The next we knew the light went on and Willo, one of my JNCO, walked in the tent with nothing but his Union Flag underwear on, body armour, helmet with his visor down. Banging a riot shield with a truncheon, shouting 'CALL OUT, CALL OUT CALL OUT, MAN YOUR WARRIORS PRINCESSES.' He then walked out and woke the officers the same way. All the other CSMs sat up in their beds and just looked at me as Mogger said 'What the fuck Carl.' I just smiled as I got ready, thinking that took some balls by Willo, what a legend.

We got up knowing that at last our fleet was ready to go. One Platoon deployed on a Basra City patrol taking the Brigade Commander around the different city base locations. It was difficult at first for the commanders with navigation, and communication had been a complete pain in the arse. One Platoon commander was an incredibly good officer who had a quick, dry sense of humour. Always keen to be busy and out patrolling which was hard for his men to understand at times, but the right man with a good thinking brain in firefight situations. His patrol lost communication and took a wrong turn, which was easy to do in the city. But luckily for him the Brigade Commander he was escorting was understanding.

The rest of us were doing guards back at camp and being used as general dogsbodies. This is doing all the shit jobs around camp while the battalion was still finding its feet and trying to sort the camp out. We were working around the camp on a shitty job when we heard the alarm go off for an indirect fire attack. We all grabbed our body armour and helmets and jumped to the floor. We heard three explosions but luckily for us they were a few hundred metres away and no one was hurt.

One Platoon got back in from their patrol and the OC had a quiet word with the platoon commander and the others Pl commanders. We got warned off for a search operation that was going to be a fast ball for the following afternoon. We got told that C Coy 1 Yorks were going to be searching the main farm complex with Arnhem search team searching one on the outskirts of the farm away from the main complex. I was the company unit search adviser (USA) and had a team of eight search team members under my command.

We got up the next day and it was hot. We moved to the orders tent and got a brief on the search operation. We then conducted rehearsals before moving to the tank park at 1300hrs. At 1400hrs the patrol moved out. Me and six of my search team were all squashed in the back of one of Arnhem Company's Warriors sweating our bollocks off with all our kit on. It took 30 minutes to reach the area of the search that was just east of Basra City.

We got to the complex and jumped out. What we were greeted with was a couple of sheds and a well. The Recce Platoon cleared the area and deployed their snipers. With the area secure the lads set to work and searched all the buildings and surrounding area. They had a look down the well. It was a big well, 20ft wide and 30ft deep. It had a shelf about 20ft down and one of the lads asked could he move down and have a look. I looked at the rusty wall ladder leading to the shelf and made the call 'No way!' If he fell off the ladder, he would of just sunk and drowned with no way of being rescued. With the area searched we mounted up and moved back to the COB. What an anti-climax, but I still had to sit there for the next few hours having to write up the search report.

On 22 November we were in our tents when we got hit with a couple of rockets of indirect fire but again, they were not on target. The indirect fire was constant, and we had to be lucky every time, but the insurgents only had to be lucky once. On the morning of 25 November, we got up and noticed that Op Minimise was on. This is placed on when someone has been hurt or killed and they close down all the phones and internet so that family and friends do not find out from someone unofficial. We got briefed that Sergeant Jonathan Hollingsworth had been killed in a strike and search operation in the city. He sustained a gunshot wound and was evacuated to hospital where he later died from his injuries.

On the morning of 28 November, we were working in the tank park when we got hit by an indirect fire attack. We all jumped into the back of the Warriors that we were working on and closed the door. This time they were closer, and they hit us with six rockets which exploded all around us. On the evening of 29 November, we were in the briefing tent getting briefed up on an up-and-coming operation when we heard the whistle of a rocket fly in. We all jumped down and covered our faces. It hit and exploded just past our camp. It was loud, and you could feel the ground shake due to the explosion. They fired in five more rockets during that attack, which exploded just past our location, but again luck was on our side.

Over the next few days One Platoon and Two Platoon did a couple of night patrols trying to counter the indirect fire threat. The patrols went well with both platoons starting to get to grip with the drills needed for operations in Iraq. Three Platoon were tasked near the end of November. It was another patrol escorting the Brigade Commander around the city bases. Again, it did not go well and all communications with the patrol were lost with troops being tasked to check that they were OK.

Three Platoon's commander was a young new Platoon Commander who had joined the company just before Iraq. He was an ex-ranker who had earlier been in the Artillery Commandos. He was a likable gentlemen whose ability to relate to his men made him a pleasure to work with. He was a strong leader who had a lot of respect of his soldiers. He was also the one all the female clerks had an eye for because he was young and cute looking (their words not mine). Unlucky for him this patrol had earned him a chat with the CO who was hard on him and set an example. But the OC was waiting for him as he came out of the CO's office and picked him up ready to go again.

For the first few weeks in Iraq the weather had been good with the sun shining and the nights not so cold. But we woke up the next day and the place was flooded. It had been raining all night and the sand around camp had turned into a sticky thick mud. Most of the tents had water in them and many were flooded. The lads were out digging trenches around their tents to try and direct the water away from their bed spaces. Our tent was flooded badly, and we decided to get some wooden pallets and build our floor up to try and keep our bed spaces dry. We laid out the pallets and placed all our kit on top of them. It was not the best, but it was better than all your kit being soaked through all the time like some of the other tents. With the colder and wetter weather, it also drove the mice into our tents and the odd scream during the night was often heard. There was also another fashion trend around due to the wet muddy camp, WELLIES. They were everywhere and not just on the officers even the lads had them on. Not me: I was the Company Sergeant Major, and I made a stand that I would not be seen dead in wellies.

The Shatt Al Arab Hotel

On 30 November Two Platoon was commanded by a Captain who was in the Royal Marines and the only Royal Marine officer qualified on the Warrior fighting vehicles. He was a good officer, very robust, quick-thinking and always ready to do whatever his lads did. They were escorting the company's two command Warriors to the Shatt Al Arab Hotel for an O Group with the commanders there who were getting ready for a big up and coming operation call Operation Sinbad. The Shatt Hotel was an old hotel that banked onto the Shatt Al Arab Waterway. We moved out and joined the main MRS heading south.

We came to the first bridge (A POD Bridge) and moved across the main river. This was us entering the city and the first thing we came to was, an Iraqi Police checkpoint. They stood there on the checkpoint with their light blue shirts on, dark blue trousers and little peak caps, all of them looking like one of the Mario Brothers from the computer game. They were armed with pistols that they carried on their belt kit and AK-47 rifles. They all came out and looked but did not come across friendly or glad to see us.

As we moved through, we came to the first major junction called Green 19 and the lads got out and cleared the junction as it was often used for attacks by the insurgents. Once done, we moved through and came to two arches that were based on both side of the roads which we called Purple 1. Again, the lads got out and cleared the area as it was the area of recent attacks. Once done they mounted up and we pushed past the old Iraqi Naval base and then moved across the road and into the Shatt Hotel.

The Shatt was the home for the Staffordshire Regiment who were known for being a good armoured infantry unit. We got to the gates which were covered by a sanger (lookout tower). As we pushed through, we came to the tank park which is where the old gardens used to be. We parked up and the OC, 2IC and Pl commander went off to book in at the operations room and to meet the commanders of the Staffords. I moved to the QM's (Quartermaster) to meet my counterpart and to ask about where the lads were going to sleep when we came down here. As we started to move away from the tank park, we heard one of the guards on the sangers open fire at a target outside the base.

The first thing we came to in the camp was an outside tented area and we saw all the damage that had been caused by a mortar attack a few days earlier. The tents had been ripped apart, as the insurgents lobbed mortar after mortar of high explosives rounds into the base leaving several lads seriously injured. The lads were from the Staffords and 2 Rifles who also had lads based there.

All I can say is 'wow.' This was a reality check and it hit home hard just what would happen if a rocket hit one of our tents back in the COB. The 81mm mortars which hit these tents were smaller and still caused so much carnage. If a rocket which had more explosives scored a direct hit, we would not stand a chance. It was scary, to be fair, and totally outside of our control.

We pushed past the tents and came to the back of the hotel. It was a long building about three storeys high with what looked like an aircraft control tower on top that the unit used as a lookout tower. We walk up a few steps and entered a corridor that led to some stairs and the rooms of the ground floor. As we moved into the main hall there was a barbers located to the left with one of the locals who would cut your hair free of charge (let's be honest, you would not pay for that style of haircut). The main hall still had a big fancy chandelier hanging from the roof and at both ends you had all the plaques of the units that has been based there before (I found the old 1 Kings one from Op Telic 2). The hall had tables in there and was used as an overspill to the main cookhouse which was on the left.

We moved through and went past the front of the hotel were the quick reaction force (QRF) Warriors were. There were loads of portaloos and portacabins. I spotted an old disused swimming pool that backed onto the Al Shatt Arab Water Way. The QM's department was just around the corner, and I went in and introduced myself.

We got showed where the lads were going to get their heads down. Three Platoon were going to be placed in two small room in the cellar, while One Platoon and Two Platoon would be in the old gym just outside the main building. Coy Tac had a spare room on the first floor. While the fitter section and overspill had what I called Freddie Kruger's Den (believe me you had to see it to believe it, all that was missing was Freddie and an old burner). But we could not complain, it was all under hard cover and not in tents for which we were very thankful.

After the walk around, I handed over a nominal roll and I got a haircut with our CQMS, and we came out looking like a cross between one of the Beatles and one of the Goonies. The officers came out and after they finished laughing at mine and Carl's hair we mounted up and moved back to the COB. The one thing we noticed about the city was that there was rubbish everywhere. They must have just come out of their houses and lobbed it. The place was a complete mess, and the smell was nauseating but they just seem to walk around as if it was normal, which to them it must have been.

So how did I feel about the first month? Iraq was a lot different than I thought. It had a different feel to it, than other Middle East countries I had been to. It was a country in transition, but the Allied forces didn't seem to have a plan and end goal. The British Army had been there for over three years. Strangely it still seemed manic and unorganised. There did not seem to be an end plan in place, which was just madness. I was surprised by the amount of IDF we were getting and the pressure alone that imposes onto the deployed force. You had no respite. Even when you were off patrol back in your tent, we were under the threat of attack. I knew we had to improve as soldiers and a company or we would be in trouble. But I was enjoying it and had faith in the soldiers that they would deliver. We had been lucky, but I knew as we worked in the city more, that harder challenges would be coming thick and fast.

2

DECEMBER 2006

Deployment into Basra City

On the morning of 2 December, the company got up and had some breakfast. The food in Ladysmith Lines was not as good as most places we had been to in Basra. This was not the fault of our chefs as the kitchen they had was by far the worst in the COB. This always seemed to be the case in the Army, the units that went out and did the most dangerous jobs always seemed to get the worst camps and facilities. The ones who stayed in got the best camps, best cookhouses, and the best food. You can argue we got a break getting out of camp and they never, so the Army probably got it right.

After breakfast we moved to the briefing tent and got our orders for the short move to the Shatt Hotel. After the orders, the platoon sergeants got their platoons' admin sorted and we moved up to the tank park. The lads would be spending the best part of the week living out of the Shatt Hotel. Most of the soldiers were limited to just their fighting kit (weapon, body armour, belt kit) and crash-out day sacks due to the short amount of space in the back of the Warriors. Once in the tank park all the equipment was stored away, and the Warriors were checked over to ensure there were no faults. We mounted up and did a radio check before the OC booked us out. The company Warriors roared as we drove out of the tank towards the front gate, throwing up clouds of dust as we moved.

As we drove towards the front gate, we would go past all the different camps that contained all the units that were needed to sustain operations in Iraq. On the way we would pass the A1 village, which was the welfare area for all the troops. It had a few local shops selling everything from iPods to illegal copies of DVDs. It had a Pizza Hut, Curry House, and NAAFI, but we got told the best was a café called Effie where the milkshakes were the best drinks around. Not that we would know yet as most of the company had not been to the village due to the amount of time we had spent working. Now it is not what you are picturing, when I say Pizza Hut, it was a portacabin that sold pizza. Once past the A1 village we went past the command centres and moved through the first checkpoint which consisted of a sanger and a chicane.

These were manned by a company of a Territorial Army (TA) unit that had the responsibility of protecting the air base along with the RAF Regiment. We than drove for about a mile until we came to the camp's main checkpoint which was the airport's (COB) main entrance. It had another sanger and a few more walls to try and offer some protection. It was manned by the RAF. They also had the job of checking all the Locally Employed Civilians (LECs) who were mainly employed as general hands in different camps. As we got out of the camp there were always loads of locals and taxis who were waiting for people to come out of the airport. There were groups waiting around with the men in one group and the women sitting behind them. They had little stalls that made them their little cups of tea and strange-looking snacks.

We drove past the locals and went left along the main slip roads until we joined the main supply route (MSR) heading south. To make it harder for the insurgents we did not always drive on the same side of the road and would often cross over during a route to cause confusion and make our patrol routes unpredictable. This took a bit of getting used to driving into traffic, but the locals just got out of your way. The sight of a company-strength Warrior group patrolling was impressive, with the turrets scanning from left to right and the top cover up in the back looking out for any targets. The amount of dust must have been a nightmare for anyone following the patrol. Again, we moved over the A Pod Bridge and on through the Iraq Police checkpoint. We went on through Green 19 and Purple 1 and on into the Shatt Hotel a route that would become second nature over the next few months. We drove through the gate and went right and parked up before closing down our Warriors.

The OC and 2IC went and booked us in and I got the platoon sergeants together and briefed them up. The lads were to keep their helmets and body armour on due to the high threat of indirect fire and with the camp been smaller the threat was higher. We moved into the main building and got the platoons to wait in the main hall as the CQMS got the keys for all the rooms where the company were staying. The lads then moved into their rooms and got sorted ready to receive their orders. The faces on the fitter section and Coy HQ were worth seeing when they got showed 'Freddie's Den' but soon they would be glad to be there.

The OC, 2IC, and platoon commanders all came back from the O Group (what the army call a meeting) and told us that Company HQ, One Platoon and Two Platoon would be doing anti-indirect fire patrols at night and route protection during the day. Three Platoon were tasked as ICP (incident control point) protection and would be in the thick of it with the Staffords. The anti-indirect fire patrols would be four Warriors strong night patrols. This meant One Platoon had a problem as one of their Warriors had broken down. I informed the OC that I would assist One Platoon in call sign Zero Charlie Warrior and Frank said he was happy to be my gunner and that was that problem sorted. One Platoon was out at 2200hrs and Two Platoon was out at 2359hrs. We all grabbed some sleep before our briefs at 2000hrs. We got up and grabbed some scoff which was particularly good. We moved to the briefing room for our orders. We sat down as One Platoon sergeant checked that everyone was here and then he handed over to the Int Cell from the Staffords. He gave us a brief on the ground in the city we were going to be patrolling and then showed us the IDF firing points of the last few weeks. This was where the insurgent mortar teams had been firing at us from. He showed us where their patrols had been getting attacked and by what means of weapons. They had been getting attacked every day and blown up by IEDs, and shot at with RPGs and small arms fire (machine guns and rifles).

The units in the city never got a break and were really in the thick of it. In the city we patrolled using spot maps. This is where the British Army placed a coloured spot on a main feature like a junction or building to assist control of their units on the ground. There is one in the front of this book to help you build the route of the patrols. After he finished the platoon commander finished off with an outline of his plan. He asked if there was any questions and told everyone to be at their Warriors for 2100hrs for our final checks.

At 2100hrs we were at our Warriors and Frank who was the Coy Warrior sergeant major ensured the checks were done before informing the platoon commander that we were good to move. Our rifles had mounts inside of the turret for storing our weapons. In the city this took too long to grab your weapon. So most of us wedged in the rifles on top of our turrets behind the sights to our side secured down by the strap but easy to grab. With my rifle in place and pistol unclipped, we mounted up and did our radio checks before the Warriors roared away and left the front gate. As we left the front gate you had the boss's Warrior at the front with the second Warrior being commanded by the Warrior sergeant, the third by me (the CSM) and the last by a JNCO called Martin. We moved out the gates and went right down the road and past the old docks of the Iraqi Navy. There were a few old boats turning to rust at the port with one on its side.

We then pushed left into the city. This is where we got into the busy part of the town. There were cars and people everywhere and the lads were scanning with their weapons the best they could. It was busy for this time of night, but we got told that the locals came out more at night when it was cooler. The people in the city were not friendly and did not want us to be there. They all came out and stared at us with their dark brown eyes and thick moustaches. You could feel the cold of the night on your skin as the sweat ran down your face and stung your eyes. The patrol stopped and did a vehicle checkpoint (VCP), and the lads got out and checked a few cars. The place had rubbish everywhere and you could smell the rotten rubbish which had just been lobbed onto the streets. The lads were scanning the rooftops and alleyways looking for any firing points the insurgents might try and use.

With the VCP done the patrol mounted back up and moved off to check another area. I moved to the back and let Martin's Warrior move past me. We had been patrolling for about 90 minutes and were moving past the junction at Yellow 9 when for some reason I looked over my right shoulder. I saw a flash behind us about 50mm away. Being on top of my turret I grabbed my rifle and swung around as the RPG warhead went 'WHOOSH' just past my Warrior and the Warriors in front before exploding just in front of the patrol. I cocked my weapon, placing a round in the chamber, and got my weapon into the aim and pointed it at the dark figure behind us that had just fired at us with an RPG. This was it: I had been in the army for 18 years and had so far never fired my weapon in anger. I steadied my breathing for what seemed like a lifetime. I squeezed the trigger. 'BANG.' The rifle rocked as it fired. The 5.56mm round screamed towards my target. I fired again trying to prevent the insurgent from getting off a second shot and again the round screamed off. I was giving it my all and went to fire my sixth round only to hear a dead man's click. I looked down to my weapon and tried to clear the stoppage, but it was no good, I had rounds blocked everywhere. By the time I got the weapon sorted we were 100m down the road and the insurgent was long gone.

The boss reported the contact and also that I had returned fire. Frank was laughing as he pointed out that I had grabbed my rifle instead of telling him where the insurgent was so he could get the main weapons of the Warrior onto the target. I gave him my apologies as the patrol headed back to the Shatt Hotel. When we were back in, I checked my weapon to see why it had jammed and noticed that I had a dent in the magazine. I promised myself that it was never going to happen again while I was in a contact. When we were back in the building, I had to see the duty officer. He asked me if I had hit the insurgent which I replied 'no.' I then had to write a statement that went to the CO to ensure that all procedures where correct and within the law (which of course they were). After this I grabbed some sleep as we were out in a few hours again. Two Platoon deployed after us with their patrol going well with no incidents. We were happy with the night patrols, but we still never managed to stop the insurgents who still hit the Shatt Hotel with six mortar rounds which exploded in the base.

I had mixed feelings about my first rounds fired in anger at the enemy. The first was that of excitement. This is what I had trained to do, and it felt good doing my job to the full. I also felt disappointed. Surely after 18 years this was not it, five rounds and a stoppage. I suppose time and fate would decide that for me, but from a combat soldier's point of view, I wanted more. I was also aware that sometimes you have to be careful what you wish for.

At breakfast we were briefing up the OC and 2IC on the following night patrols and they were both glad that we had returned fire and that no one had got hurt. They were glad because the company had to meet the insurgents head-to-head otherwise we were going to lose a lot of them to enemy fire. Believe me when I say the JAM insurgents in Basra were good, brave, and always willing to take the attack to the British Army. So, we had to be just as willing to fight as they were, or we would come off worse than them with many of our soldiers in body bags.

The company had to be in position by 0700hrs so that the Staffords Battle Group could move through and onto the area they were working. They were on an operation called Operation Sinbad. This was an operation where the Army moved into an area to improve things like schools, water pipes and kids' playing areas. The Staffords were the close protection group for the engineers that were conducting the work.

We got to the tank park at 0615hrs and sorted out all the Warriors and mounted up. One final radio check and the OC gave the command to move out. We pushed out and headed left towards the city. We moved past the docks leaving One Platoon in place at Purple 3 and the rest of us pushed up to the roundabout at Yellow 7. Coy TAC stayed in place just past the roundabout with Two Platoon pushing north a few hundred metres to the junction at Yellow 5 to secure that area. There was a lot of traffic on the road and the OC was going mad with one of the Two Platoon Warriors for driving over the yellow and white kerb stones and crushing them (it drove the locals mad). The Iraqi Police turned up and started to control the traffic as we were causing a few problems with the size of our Warriors. There were a lot of kids around the area, and they were all around Coy TAC and Two Platoon's locations (which we did not mind as they made the insurgents think twice about opening fire). One Platoon's location was pretty quiet with their Warriors spread over a stretch of road of around 400m. Call sign 12 was at Purple 3 and had One Platoon's Warrior sergeant in command. He was situated on the left-hand side and was facing left coving the west side of the road to the roundabout. They were in their Warrior when a local man on a bike passed their Warrior heading west.

'BANG'

There was a massive explosion and a blinding flash of light that quickly turned into smoke. The local man on the bike went flying across the road as he got caught up in the explosion. We were sat in Zero Bravo and Zero Charlie Warriors when we heard the explosion and the few seconds that it take the nearest call sign to answer up seem to last a lifetime as you sit there not knowing if your lads are dead or alive. One Platoon's Warrior sergeant got on the radio and sent the contact report. He told us that there were no casualties on our side but told everyone about the local man who drove into the infra-red beam, breaking the circuit and causing the IED to explode. The company had been lucky as nine of their Warriors had drove past the device. Luckily for us it must not have been armed at the time and might have been aimed and set up for our dismounts.

We were about to go into a cordon operation when we were informed by call sign 12 that the Iraqi Police had turned up. They were there straight away and threw the local man's body into the back of one of their 4 x 4s. They started the process of cleaning up. It was a bit suspicious how they turned up so fast and cleared the IED away. We were starting to get suspicious of the Iraqi Police Force as they always seemed to be about when we got attacked. The driver of call sign 12 was made up that the Iraqi Police were cleaning up as the thought of going into a cordon operation spending hours on the ground and missing his scoff was not worth thinking about.

The OC informed the operations room that the area was secured. The Staffords' Warriors moved through our locations and onto their area. They were working in the Al Hyyaniyah area of the city, what we called the Shia Flats which was by far the most hard-line area for the insurgents. Once they had moved through our positions, Two Platoon left their positions and moved south through our position at Yellow 7 and then we all left and moved back to the Shatt Hotel. Once back in camp, we were on three hours' notice to move in case we were needed on the ground. This did not last long as we were moved up to one hour's notice to move due to the Staffords been in contact the minute they entered the Shia Flats.

Three Platoon were located in the middle of the Shia Flats protecting the command group. On the route in, the main Warriors of the Staffords and Three Platoon came under small arms fire but with the Warriors being bulletproof they pushed on until they got to their positions. Three Platoon got to the location and the lads got out and cleared the area so the Warriors could move in and set up the command area. The engineers got to work on the school they were repairing and water pipes they were fixing. The Staffords who were their protection group had already been in contact for most of the morning. They had fired loads of rounds including their main armament, the 30mm cannon. Back with Three Platoon, one of the NCOs was moving around the area checking that all his men were in good fire position and covering the ground correctly. 'CRACK'. He hit the ground as a bullet smacked into the wall by his head, covering his face in dust. He reported to the platoon commander that there was an enemy sharpshooter on the ground and that he had just missed him firing a single round. The word got passed around and everyone made sure their fire positions were good.

The operation had been ongoing for three hours and the engineers' work was now ending which was just as well because the locals were starting to turn up in numbers and the lads working were starting to get some minor aggro. At the command position there was a group of about twenty youths building up. The boss got the word to mount up and the lads moved to their Warrior and got in. The locals spotted this and started to brick the soldiers. The commanders and the top cover got the worst of it with bricks and stones hitting and falling all around them. They started to move out with the boss's Warrior leading, pushing through the crowd. 'SMASH, WOOFF' the second Warrior was alight with flames licking all around the back of the turret as the first petrol bomb exploded. The Warriors kept on going. 'SMASH, WOOFF' again as two more petrol bombs hit the Warrior causing two shields to fall off to the delight of the local crowd. 'LEAVE THEM' shouted the boss over the radio as the Warriors pushed through and moved out of the Shia Flats.

The Staffords had to fight their way out of some of their positions with one mad insurgent trying to block a Warrior's route with his car as the others ran around the other side with their petrol bombs. Seeing the danger, the commander ordered his driver to push on before someone got hurt or killed. The Warrior roared as it smashed into the car and the Warrior rocked back and forward as it smashed over the car and away from the locals advancing with their deadly petrol bombs. The patrol got back with no problems and the lads got some scoff and a bit of sleep before it all started again tomorrow for the second day of the operation.

Not Arnhem Company as we were on night patrols again trying to stop the mortars and rockets being fired into the camp. I was with One Platoon at the tank park and had just checked my Warrior and was moving back to the main building with our company medic Croz. We were 10m from the door when we heard the shout of 'INCOMING'. We both hit the floor as the whistle of the first mortar round screamed in. There was a large explosion as the mortar round exploded about 50m away. We crawled to the door and just got into the doorway as the second and third mortar screamed in. There were two more explosions again about 30m away. I said to the medic that the explosion would be pretty close to the tank park and that most of One and Three Platoons were still there working on their Warriors.

One minute had passed since the last mortar rained in and I turned to the medic Croz, and said, 'Fuck the soak time we need to check the boys are OK follow me.' As we both got up and moved out of the protection of the doorway. We were 10m from the building when we heard the scream of the next two mortars falling in. 'BOOM, BOOM.' They were so close this time we could see the flashes of the explosion. We hit the ground as we got covered in the dirt and sand again. We turned around and crawled the 10m back into hard cover. As we lay there Croz turned to me and said, 'Fuck me sir if you do that again I will tell your wife'. We sat there smiling more from relief than anything as we waited to see if any more mortar rounds were incoming.

I waited five minutes and said to the medic, 'Sorry Croz, we need to check the boys.' Again, he got up with me and we headed out of the door and started to move to the tank park. At the tank park we found

One and Three Platoons safe, taking cover in any bit of protection they had found. There were lads under the Warriors, in ISO containers and even one in a portaloo (he said he was shitting himself). I told them all to follow me and we moved quickly back to the protection of the building. Luckily for us there were no casualties, and no more mortar rounds that night. The only thing from this mortar attack we did have to deal with was the despair of Three Platoon when they saw that one of the mortars had hit the Pizza Hut which was blown apart. I do not think they ever did recover.

Two Platoon were out first on the second night. They got down the tank park at 2100hrs and sorted out their Warriors. With everything done, at 2200hrs the Warriors pulled off with one of the platoon's corporals Shane leading. The platoon commander's Warrior was second, the Warrior sergeant's Warrior third and bringing up the rear was the platoon sergeant's Warrior. They headed east out the main gate and down the runway towards Purple 3. At Yellow 7 they headed south-east towards Red 20 and conducted a VCP. After 10 minutes they mounted up and headed south before heading west at Yellow 4 towards Yellow 9 the location of One Platoon's RPG attack the previous night. At Yellow 9 they stopped and scanned the area to see if there was anything happening.

After a couple of minutes, they push on west along the road. 'BOOM'. There was a blinding flash and smoke as call sign 21 drove into the explosion with the commander shouting 'Contact', over the radio, 'and no casualties' straight away. After the smoke had cleared the gunner shouted, 'TO OUR FRONT 50 METRES, TWO UKMS [unknown males] BEHIND RED CHARLIE [car], 1 LONG [rifle] AND 1 RPG FIRING TOWARDS US'. 'WHOOSH'. The RPG missed the turret by inches but the rounds from the AK-47 were pinging all over the outside of the turret. The commander shouted, 'WHAT ARE YOU WAITING FOR A FUCKING INVITATION.' The gunner grabbed the safety switch and selected the chain gun. He steadied the sight on the two UKMs before stamping on the firing pedal. The chain gun kicked into action firing its deadly 7.62mm rounds toward its target. The surrounding area lit up as the one in one tracer flew towards the car, cutting the vehicle and area to bits. After fifty rounds the commander shouted 'STOP', the gunner deselected and applied the safety catch. Seeing what was happening at the front the platoon's Warrior sergeant had also spotted the UKMs and had grabbed his rifle and fired ten rounds from the top of the turret but by the time he fired the lead Warrior had already removed the threat.

The patrol pushed on with the platoon commander sending the full report including how many rounds were fired and how many claims (unconfirmed dead insurgents) the gunner was claiming. They pushed west and checked the area around the L-shaped flats before they headed back into camp. Once in, the commander and gunner of the lead Warrior saw the duty officer and did the statements for their contact. Once Two Platoon was back in the camp, One Platoon left for their patrol. Luckily, it passed with no incidents and all the Coy Warriors were back in base at 0230hrs for a short kip as they were needed again for route protection on day two.

The next morning the commanders of Arnhem Company again met up at breakfast and the OC was briefed up on the night patrols. I did not know why as he always sat in the ops room with the coy 2IC to ensure his men were all right on the ground. After the back brief we confirmed his orders from the previous night and headed out to the tank park to prepare our Warriors. We mounted up and moved to the area we had to cover which was from the L-shaped flats to just west of the junction at Blue 17. Once in position the OC informed their ops room that they could release the Staffords Warriors.

The position we were in was a shithole with the mixture of the local waste and the smell of stagnant water forcing some of the lads to gag. Luckily for us the Staffords were quick off the mark and had passed through us in quick time letting us withdraw back to the Shatt for some sleep before we started again that night. The Staffords and Three Platoon had a quieter day with only a few small arms attacks against their position. The work they had been tasked to do was completed in a few hours by the engineers. They all moved back to the Shatt and then it was over to Arnhem again to conduct the night patrol and try and counter the mortar threat.

The commanders decided that night it would be better for the patrols to stick to the south-east of the city and try and confuse the insurgents as to our whereabouts. One Platoon was out first patrolling the area from Camp Warehouse to the south of Yellow 1. On the way back in we had to drop an interpreter off with Blenheim Company who were the quick reaction force (QRF). We entered the main gate that was protected by the local Iraqi Army and pushed past about twenty big old warehouses and found their company in the bottom right-hand corner. I jumped out and took the interpreter to my old mate, who was the CSM of Blenheim Company. Lee was in the next bed space in my tent and was as good a soldier as the Army could get. He was sleeping on the floor next to his Warrior and jumped out of his skin when I woke him. His uniform was always immaculate and even after jumping out of his doss bag his kit still seemed to be ironed (the twat). Once the interpreter was handed over, we continued with the patrol and headed back to the Shatt.

Two Platoon again took over from us, leaving the Shatt as we entered the base. They were working just north-west of Green 19, but they had to clear it first before moving through it. The lads dismounted from the first Warrior and two lads moved each side and started to move forward. They were 20m past the junction when a loud crack broke the nightly silence. A small dust cloud puffed up as the bullet hit the ground just to the side of the team commander. The lone gunman was not located, and the platoon commander shouted it's clear enough get back in. The lads did not need telling twice and mounted back up.

The patrol moved on and about 100m past Green 19 they stopped as one of their call signs spotted a bunch of men with weapons on the ground just to their right. The platoon commander radioed into the ops room to ensure there were no friendly call signs on the ground which they replied that the area was clear. The platoon commander sent the two sergeants' Warriors to the right as the fire support cover group and also to fire up some light on his call. Once they were in position, he started to move towards the UKMs with his other Warrior just to the right. They were 100m short of the UKMs with their gunners' sights rigidly fixed onto their targets. The order was given to put up some light and the platoon sergeant fired his light rockets into the air so they would open in the air above the UKMs. He fired three rockets turning the night into day and the platoon commander shouted straight away over the radio for everyone to hold their fire because he had spotted that they were friendly troops. He informed the ops room who phoned the COB to find out why troops were on the ground without them knowing.

It turned out they were surveillance troops who had not submitted their patrol trace through the chain of command. Someone would have their bollocks on the line for that. But it shows how close our troops can come to having blue on blue (what we call firefights between friendly forces). Two Platoon pulled away and continued with their patrol before returning to the Shatt for some rest. The company had just got into bed when we heard the alarm go off for a mortar attack. Being so knackered most of the company just rolled of their cot beds and pulled on our body armour and helmets as the base was hit with another six mortar rounds of indirect fire.

Again, the company got up and the commanders met in the cookhouse over breakfast. The OC came in with the good news that the operation was completed and that after lunch the company would be released back to the COB under our own Battalion. I informed the OC that we had a bit of a problem as some of the company had been going down with D and V (diarrhoea and vomiting).

I explained that where One Platoon and Two Platoon had been sleeping. The area had twenty portaloos outside and that the flies had been doing their job spreading the shit. We had five lads bedded down in the medical centre and the OC told me to see the medical officer

(MO) to see if we could take them with us. I walked in the medical centre and spoke to the MO who said that four of them would be fine, but they would have to fly the other one out in a few days when he was better. As me and the CQMS left the med centre we had just got into the protection of the main building when we heard the first of eight explosions as the insurgents hit the base again with yet another indirect fire attack. With the Shatt base being so small and tight every time they got attacked the lads based there had a real hard time. Once the all clear was given we thanked our kind hosts (the Staffords) who had made us feel so welcomed in their base and mounted up at the tank park.

We pulled out of the camp and completed the short 20-minute trip back to the COB. As we parked up in the tank park, One Platoon sergeant said he had a problem and informed me that two of his lads had shit themselves on the route back and it looked like they had D and V. I got the two lads who both looked like death warmed up and dropped them off at our med centre knowing that we would not see them for the next few days.

I was sitting talking to the OC who was saying how well the Staffords had performed on Operation Sinbad. He looked at me and asked, ‘Do you think our lads can perform so highly?’ I reminded him that the Staffords had only been in Iraq a few months ago on a different Op Telic and if he looked at what the company had done in the last four days it was obvious that we were improving fast. So, my answer was ‘Yes.’ But the OC being the man he was, he was always looking at ways to improve the company and improve our performances. After the O Group I got some scoff and managed to get some sleep as the company was knackered after the last four days, and the kind insurgents even gave us a night off by not attacking us with any rockets.

A Couple of Broken Souls

After being in Iraq for just under a month, it soon came to light that such heavy combat fighting was not meant for everyone and those who deployed would have different levels that was acceptable for them. There is nothing wrong with this and by no means is it classed as cowardice or a weakness in the modern army and warfare. It is a mental state that some can go through and some cannot. It was the commanders and leaders in Arnhem Company's job to decide who and how to help people deal with the fear.

After a heavy night of fighting, where the company was ambushed with a couple of bombs, loads of RPGs and a shitload of firepower by the Basra insurgents, We got back to the tank park and a couple of lads from different platoons were struggling. One, who was a driver, threw his helmet and was adamant that there was no way he was going out there ever again. No one could calm him down. Myself and Ste Tabbs got the lads to leave and sat down with the lad, made him a brew, and tried to console him. I looked the lad in the eyes and knew that it was not for him to be put in these situations and if we forced the issue, he could very easily lose it, causing harm to himself or resulting in someone else being hurt. Ste was an old hand and very experienced. He called me outside and said, 'I could do with someone to help me maintain the fleet in the tank park'. This gave Ste more flexibility to get on the ground, but also offered us a route to keep a solider here in Iraq, which is something he could be proud of. I spoke with the OC, and he was happy with our plan, and we moved him in with Ste. He was still under indirect fire for six months, with rockets and mortars exploding in camp every day, but it took away the direct fire threat.

The other lad was a bit younger, and his platoon Sgt found him by the side of a Warrior with his head in his hands crying. I was called over and took the soldier for a brew. Again, I looked the soldier in the eye but knew he had it and just needed to grow into the role. I placed him in the stores with Carl for a couple of weeks, just to give him some respite. Sometimes a little break from the fighting is just what a soldier needs. Two week later the company were due to go on a patrol in an area where we knew the insurgents would take us on. I briefed up the 2IC and he agreed for Ste to take my place as the gunner in the

Warrior and let me go in the back, on top cover with Wes and Marty. Everyone was briefed up on the plan and I went and informed the young lad that he would be on patrol that night with me in the back of the 2IC Warrior.

The patrol set off and the four of us got up to protect the Warriors' blind spots. As expected, we were soon under heavy gunfire with tracer rounds flying all over our position. The young lad as expected dropped and curled up in a ball in the back of the Warrior. I went down and looked at the lad and reassured him that he was fine. I told him to take my lead and follow my actions. We stood up and both placed our weapons in our shoulders. We both cocked our weapons, and I told him that I was going to fire at the left flash, and he was going to fire at the right. He nodded and we started firing. Soon we were moving through the city, and he was meeting every contact head on and holding his own.

Once out of the city, the top cover got down and Wes and Marty made a big fuss on him about how well he had done. Back in the tank park, the lad walked away feeling six feet tall and completed the rest of the tour without any issues at all. It is amazing what you can pick up from *Band of Brothers*. Both soldiers completed the remainder of the seven-month tour and walked away proud of what they had achieved, something that would have not happened if they were both medically removed from Iraq.

On 6 December we got up and the OC informed everyone that there was an operation coming up the next day and to get all the kit sorted out, so the company was ready to go. The platoon sergeants got told to get the lads down the tank park and to get on with the admin. The platoon commanders went with the OC and 2IC to the briefing tent to conduct the planning of the operation with the CO. So, I went for a brew with Carl before I started the paperwork. Carl was a good lad and my 2IC in the company. He was married and a massive Blackburn Rovers fan. I got on well with Carl, as he wasn't afraid to speak his mind which I liked.

With the day taken up with all the admin, we had the company O Group at 1800hrs as usual, and the OC informed everyone that we were to be in the briefing tent at 2100hrs for orders on a strike and search operation that was taking place the following night. We were informed that Cpl Brown of Chindit Company had been shot in the face earlier that day on a patrol in the city. He was still alive and was going to be moved back to the UK to continue his recovery. He was lucky and if it were not for the bravery of his mate who was part of his recovery Warrior jumping up under fire and extracting him out of the area, he could well have been killed. His mate later got awarded the Military Cross for his bravery.

We had our evening meals and got our command kit (notebooks, maps and folders) and moved to the briefing tent. Inside there were seats laid out in the shape of a horseshoe. In the centre there was models of the targets area and maps and photos all over the wall. We sat down and the ops officer checked that everyone was here. Then he handed over to another officer who briefed us on the ground and the targets in detail we were striking. He then handed over to the Intelligence officer who briefed us on the threat and types of attacks that have happened in the area.

The CO took over and was going through his plan when we heard the whistle of an incoming rocket. We all dived onto the ground and covered our faces as the rocket exploded about 100m away. We stayed on the ground as we heard the explosion of the second rocket, but this one was further away. After five minutes the CO said, 'Let's get on with it' and we got up and sat on the seats with our body armour and helmets still on as he finished off his plan.

The Battle Group were going to be striking two Alphas (target houses) with C Company, 1 Yorks striking the first Alpha with Arnhem company as close protection and our Recce Platoon striking the second building providing their own protection. Blenheim Company were providing the outer protection and Egypt Squadron the route protection in their tanks. So, with that amount of firepower, it was going to be a big operation. They finished off the brief by telling us what medical support we had, and which fitter section was providing cover for which group if their Warriors broke down. With the orders completed, the OCs stayed with the CO for rock drill (this is where they go through the plan and can ask any questions on a one-to-one with the CO). Everyone who was not needed left and went back to their tents.

There were six people in my tent: I was in the bottom right-hand corner. Lee was next to me; he was the Blenheim Company CSM. Lee was one of my closest friends. He was married with two kids and an outstanding soldier. The only issue with Lee was that he didn't like football, but he was Scottish. Next to Lee was Mark who was the Egypt Tank Squadron CSM, I didn't know him that well, but we soon became good friends. Across from me in the bottom left corner was Mogger who was Blenheim Warrior CSM. Another very good lad, who everyone liked, he was from Middlesbrough but for some reason thought he was Scottish. Next to him was Frank who was Arnhem Warrior CSM and in the Small Arms School Core. All the lads were married with kids.

The last one to mention was Paul. Paul was not just one of my best mate, even our families went on holiday together and our wives grew up together in Northern Ireland. Paul was another very good soldier and an outstanding marksman with the rifle. There were two issues with Paul, one he was a Man Utd fan and the other he was ginger and smelt like a bus stop. We had a great tent with people who all got on. We were all the same rank, and it was the only place that we could relax properly in camp. We had a TV and DVD player between me and Mogger and when we did get a night off it was nice to chill out with mates and relax.

We got up the next day and spent the morning doing the final checks on our Warriors. We then moved them into position, so they were in company-strength lines. After lunch we did our rehearsals before grabbing a couple of hours' sleep before the operation began.

At 2200hrs we moved to our Warriors and sorted everything out. We were all mounted up and got in the correct order as we moved to just short of the front gate. At 2330hrs the first group moved out which was Blenheim Coy in their Warriors and Egypt Squadron in their main battle tanks. After 30 minutes they were in position and the strike groups set off.

Strike Group 1 was made up of ten Warriors of Arnhem Coy and six Snatch Land Rovers from C Coy 1 Yorks. The second strike group was made up of six recce Warriors and four from the Battle Group HQ. We moved out and moved over the bridge and down to Green 19. At Green 19 we headed left until we moved under some big arches that we called Green 20. As we were moving, we moved past Egypt Squadron tanks and Blenheim Company's Warriors who were doing route protection until we got to Qarmat Ali Bridge.

At the bridge we speeded up with the engines roaring and Warriors shaking as we moved towards our targets at speed with Two Platoon leading the way. We moved over the bridge and headed right, then left into the street where our target Alpha (house) was. Two Platoon left two Warriors at the bottom of the street and the other two pushed up pushing past the target Alpha. The command Warriors stopped at the Alpha and the Snatch Land Rovers pulled up and the lads jumped out and got into position ready to strike the building. The OC gave the word of command 'go' and they kicked the front gate in as they ran towards the front door. At the front door they used the bumper and knocked the door down and made entry to the building.

Outside all Arnhem Coy Warriors repositioned themselves to try and offer as much protection to the strike teams as possible. I moved call sign Zero Charlie down 20m and covered down a dark alleyway. The word came over the radio that they had found the Bravo (male) and had found a lot of munitions. The OC jumped out with Carl and Smudge as his protection men and went forward to have a look so he could send back the details to the CO. It was a warm night with a cool breeze passing down the street. There was no sign of life anywhere with just a few badly positioned streetlights giving off a dim glow.

The OC, Carl and Smudge made the quick dash from the Warrior and entered the building. At the same time, the 2IC jumped from my wagon and got into the OC's Warrior, as they had better comms with the ops room. Back at the building the OC's group had seen all the munitions and was talking to the search team commander to see how much longer he needed on the target before he was happy to lift. Frank who was in with the 2IC in call sign Zero Bravo had been dying for a piss since we left camp and told the 2IC to keep watch as he jumped on the back deck and relieved himself.

The OC had just left the target building and was moving back to his Warrior when the sky lit up with tracer bullets flying down the street just passing over the Warriors. The OC hit the deck that fast that Carl and Smudge thought he had been hit until they saw him getting into a fire position. Back with call sign Zero Bravo, Frank was halfway through his piss when the bullets started to fly. He just jumped into his turret with piss still flying everywhere and a nice wet patch on his combat trousers. We all scanned with our sights, but the gunman was nowhere to be seen.

Again, the sky lit up as another burst of tracer from the heavy machine gun let rip. Still the fire positions was not seen. We fired up some light to try and help identify the position but still we could not see where it had come from. With the search completed we got the order to withdraw. We mounted up, with the male from the target building being bagged and tagged under arrest. We also place all the munitions into our Snatches and got into the correct order of march ready to move on the OC's word.

Three Platoon were attached to the tanks and had a position secured at the mouth of the bridge. The dismount of call sign three one were called back to their Warrior and told to mount up ready for the withdrawal. The four of them were at the back of the Warrior when in slow motion one of the lads saw something fly over a nearby wall and land just to the left of where they were standing. It hit the floor with a chunk and the lad who saw it spotted it was a grenade.

'GRENADE'

he shouted as loud as he could as he dived to the right of the Warrior. The lads had trained for this and the remaining three just followed to where the first one had dived. They all landed in a heap by the right-hand side of the Warrior. They covered up the best they could as the loud explosion ripped through the night, covering them in sand and dust. They got up and checked each other for any injuries but they had been lucky tonight. They jumped back into the safety of the Warrior and shut the door ready to move. But the Warrior turned out to be not the safest of places as the commander gave the command to move forward the driver misheard, and the Warrior reversed into the river. But the company was in luck, as our recovery Warrior was next to him and just hooked him up and pulled him out.

The OC gave the word of command to move, and we pushed out of the target street. We turned right. Being the first Warrior I spotted something to our front and fired some light down the street only to see it drop short and fall in a garden 100m to our front. We pushed on and moved out of the estate and all formed up ready to cross the bridge. The call came over the radio that one of the recce Warriors was bogged in, so they asked for our support Warrior to help them out. They went to assist the recce Warrior and Arnhem Coy moved out and crossed the bridge into a holding area.

Call sign 24 Alpha was our recovery Warrior and as he approached, he could see that the Recce Platoon were in a firefight with tracer flying from both sides. As they got to the bogged-in Warrior they jumped out and started to hook the Warrior up so they could drag it out. They had been working on the recovery for five minutes and it was going well. The commander was in between the two Warriors with the driver in his hatch waiting for the command to start moving back. The third lad was by the side of the Warrior with his rifle trying to give them a bit of protection.

The houses around them were one to two storeys high. They had flat roofs, with a lot of alleyways and low wires located in between them. In a flash a man appeared in the middle of one of the alleyways about 50m away. He had an RPG in his right shoulder. 'BANG WHOOSH'. The RPG went just over the Warrior and flew down the street leaving a trail of smoke from the man. He dropped the RPG and started to fire his AK-47 rifle. A shower of tracer bullets flew through the air and bounced off the Warrior.

The protection man saw the flash of the weapon firing and dropped onto one knee. He brought his weapon up to his shoulder and steadied his sight onto the target. 'BANG' he fired and kept on firing until the target had dropped and there was no more threat. With that situation over they continued to recover the bogged-in Warrior and within 10 minutes the bogged-in Warrior was free and the patrol moved off with two UKMs detained, and a small amount of munitions recovered. We all moved back to the COB where we dropped of the detainees and the munitions at the detainee centre. We got mortars, ammo, an IED ready to be used along with a few rifles, a heavy machine gun and an RPG warhead.

Once we had closed down, I moved a few soldiers to the company office and did statements for the ones that were claiming the hits during the contact. Once they were all done, I got them all together and dropped them off with the duty officer. I informed him how many bullets the company had fired and told him we had not lost anything. On finishing the paperwork, I bumped into Lee who was the CSM of Blenheim Company. He told me how one of his lads had broken his leg when he had got it caught in the turret. Himself and the medic needing to extract him of the ground to the field hospital. I moved back to the tent where I got a shower, something to eat and got into my bag. I lay there in my doss bag thinking God, it was only 8 December and we had been in contact every day so far this month.

Things had to slow down soon; it was just manic. With all the post admin completed I dropped knackered into a sound sleep.

We got up at about 1500hrs and I briefed the platoon sergeants to conduct a 100 per cent kit check and told them this was going to be the routine from now on. We had our company brief and the OC told us that we were not out that night and to try and catch up on some sleep.

After the evening meal I phoned home and had a walk around the lads' tents to ensure that they were all in good form. There were a few of them now who had been in some pretty scary firefights, so it is always made sense just to check on them. With all the lads being in good form, I went and briefed the OC and 2IC before moving back to my tent to chill out a bit. I got in the tent and got a quick shower. The lads in my tent were waiting for me as one of them had lent a DVD to watch. We sat down and turned on the TV and pressed play. As the DVD started, we heard the now-familiar sound of a rocket whistling in. We hit the ground as it exploded about 100m away. We were hit with six rockets but the first was the closest they got to our camp and the others were about 200 to 300m away around the area of the A1 welfare village. We just lay on the floor with our body armour and helmets on still watching the film until we received the all clear.

The drills at nighttime were for the guard to clear the main walkways to ensure there were no blinds (rockets that had not exploded) and for everyone to stay in their tents where possible. We got into our beds about midnight only to be woken up at 0200hrs with one rocket of indirect fire. Again, it was not near our camp and after 30 minutes we just went back to sleep. In the morning after a night where we had been attacked, they always called an Op Wide-Awake. This is where the whole camp has to be searched to ensure there are no blinds.

The camp was split up into quarters with each company being given an area. Once all the areas were done, we reported to the guard room who then let the COB ops room know that our camp was clear. After

Op Wide-Awake the lads moved onto the range. Where everyone checked their sights were zeroed and weapons were firing correctly.

After this I moved to the company office that we shared with Blenheim Coy HQ. The OC asked me to call for the platoon commanders and when they arrived, we all moved into the OC's office. The OC said that we had a job come in to escort the Brigadier around the city bases again and who wanted it. I was surprised to see each of the platoon commanders wanted it. The OC gave it to One Platoon and told him he had less than 24 hours and to get his orders sorted out. The rest of the day was spent getting One Platoon ready and Two Platoon who were stepping up to one hours' notice to move with Three Platoon in reserve.

The day passed quickly, and we had our company O Group at the end of the day before having our evening meal. We moved into the cookhouse and grabbed our plastic plates and knife, fork, and spoon. We grabbed our food; I had steak with all the trimmings and sat down to enjoy my meal. I had taken two bites of my meal when the alarm went off for an indirect fire attack. We hit the floor as we were hit with three rockets of indirect fire landing about 150m away. We just lay there on the floor eating our dinners like dogs. After 20 minutes the all clear sounded with some big Yank voice calling 'ALL CLEAR' three times. The rest of the night there was no more indirect fire attacks, and the night was quiet.

The next day One Platoon got up, grabbed some breakfast and moved to the tank park. After they had sorted out all their kit, the platoon commander booked out through the ops room and moved to Brigade HQ, which was just past the A1 welfare village, to pick up the Brigadier. They were 20m short of Brigade HQ when the first Warrior was caught by a blast on the left-hand side of the road. The flames licked over the left side of the Warrior causing the Warrior to rock to the right. The platoon commander, who luckily for him was down at the time, sent the contact report over the radio and stated that they had been hit by a roadside IED in camp.

The platoon sergeant who was commanding the last Warrior saw the Warrior take the blast but also saw two other explosions 50 and 100m away and quickly corrected him that they had just been missed by a rocket and that the camp was in the middle of an indirect fire attack. Within seconds the alarm was going off and the Warriors pulled up at Brigade HQ. The lads stayed in their Warriors, closing down the hatches to give that little bit more protection. After a while, the call was announced for the all clear and the Brigade commander joined the patrol and they set off towards the city. They went to the Shatt Hotel, Basra Palace, and the Old State Building before returning to the COB. The patrol this time went well with the Brigade commander phoning the CO on his return to say how well One Platoon had performed.

On 11 December, the company Warriors moved to the ranges again and fired their 30mm cannons and 7.62mm chain guns to ensure the sight were set correctly before returning to camp. Once back, One Platoon and Two Platoon were warned off for a patrol in the city in a couple of days' time. They would be deploying to Basra Palace for a few days to support the units there. With it being a bit of a slack afternoon, me, the 2IC and Carl headed off to the welfare village for the first time to see what it was like. We jumped in a Land Rover and drove the short five-minute trip and parked up.

We got out and walked through a gap in the blast wall and was greeted by hut which sold pizza, which had a number of plastic tables and chairs outside it. Next, we went past the curry house before walking into one of the local's shops. It was clean inside and was selling loads of illegal DVDs, a number of iPods, MP3 players and cameras. I got a couple of DVD films that were not even in the cinema at home for the kids which cost $8 for them both. They were meant to be $10 dollars, but you always got them down. The next shop was not as clean but was selling all the brands of cigarettes cheaply at $8 for 200. They were not the good brands, but I got 200 for the mother-in-law as she would smoke rolled-up shit if she could.

We then moved to the NAAFI where they had the genuine cigarettes which were a bit more money at $19 dollars for 200. So, I grabbed 400 to send my wife as they were still twice as cheap as the UK. We then got a milkshake at the Effie and the lads were right, they were good. You could also get food that made a nice change from the food in our camp.

The next day passed quickly for the company, but it was a long day for me as I had to go to Brigade for briefs on IEDs. We had a morning of briefs and then went for our lunch. We walked into the cookhouse and stood their staring. It was like a hotel. They had the main meals bar, salad bars, burger bars and omelettes. The cheeky twats even had a Mr Whippy ice cream machine. We had our food and continued with the briefs, updating us all on the latest trends and devices.

The next day was spent with One Platoon and Two Platoon sorting out all their kit as they were deploying to Basra Palace later in the day as part of an up-and-coming operation. With all their kit sorted they got to the tank park and were getting their final brief of their platoon commanders when the alarm went off for an indirect fire attack. The platoon all hit the ground as they heard the first of two explosions fall in about 70m away. When the all clear sounded, they mounted up and moved to the front gate as one group. They set off and after an hour patrolling through the city they arrived at Basra Palace.

Arnhem's Company First Injury

Basra Palace was one of Saddam's old palaces that he had situated around Iraq. There were about four palaces that belonged to the old leader as well as his sons in the complex. The British Army took over it during the war and had a large force based there. There were also a few Americans and Romanians there, but the main force was British. One Platoon and Two Platoon got shown where they were going to sleep. The commanders went off to get briefed on the operation that was starting the next morning. The operation was another Operation Sinbad, and they were working near the Old State Building (OSB), laying some new pipes for fresh water supplies. Once briefed, they returned and briefed the lads before getting a short rest before the early start the next day.

The next day started with Basra Palace getting hit with four mortar rounds of indirect fire in the morning with the rounds exploding close to the main building. Once the all clear was given One Platoon moved out first and moved up the Pinks and secured from the junction at Blue 1 to junction at Red 9 just north of the OSB. Two Platoon, who were also out on patrol, were escorting a water bowser from the Palace to the OSB. They moved out with their four Warriors and two admin vehicles up the Pinks and past One Platoon's Warriors approaching the OSB from the east. Just before they got to the OSB they informed the base that they were coming in the east gate with their convoy.

This caused a problem for the OSB as they had just had fresh concrete laid on the east gate. So, they told them to move to the west gate and enter there. The patrol moved around, and it soon became clear there was no way the admin vehicles were getting into the base at this gate. At this point, the patrol started to receive small arms fire that was hitting just to their right. Two of the gunners spotted the firing position of two of the insurgents and steadied their sights before stamping on the firing pedal and forcing the insurgents to go to ground. The platoon commander, seeing the danger, headed into the base and went to the ops room to point out that if they did not open the east gate someone was going to be killed.

The platoon sergeant, who now had the command on the ground with the boss being inside, started to receive gunfire on his position but this time the bullets were bouncing off his Warrior. Again, the gunners spotted the firing position and returned fire with their chain guns. The insurgents responded with two RPG rockets that flew through the air and exploded just to the right of their Warrior. The explosions were loud and covered the area in a dust cloud. The platoon sergeant decided he had seen enough and moved the patrol away from the western gate and met up with a Chindit Coy Patrol on the east side. They decided to fuck the concrete and led the patrol into the safety of the base making nice patterns on the floor of the east gate floor. One Platoon moved back to Basra Palace after the day work while Two Platoon stayed in the OSB working from there on the second day.

December 14th was the second and last day of Operation Sinbad and One Platoon had the task of a city patrol in the morning. They set off at 0830hrs and had patrolled from Basra Palace to the bridge at Red 9. The patrol moved down the back street and entered the east gate of the OSB. After a 10-minute break the patrol left through the west gate and moved towards Blue 4. When they got in the area of Blue 4 the second Warrior was hit with a massive explosion. 'BOOOM.' The Warrior took the full force but continued going for 100m until coming to a stop due to damage to its running gear.

The commander who was chest high in the turret got hit by the blast, knocking him out and causing his body to hang over the right-hand side of the turret. Only being grabbed by his gunner at the last minute preventing him from falling out and dropping onto the road. The locals around the street started to cheer thinking that the commander was dead, but he came around after a couple of minutes and only suffered concussion.

The driver in the second Warrior was not as luck as he drove into the blast behind the second Warrior. Although he had protection in the form of patrol goggles on, he still received some of the blast to his face. Being dazed, he felt the warm blood from a cut above the right eye running down his face and into his right eye making it impossible to see out of. His left eye had been hit with a bit of shrapnel also blinding him in that eye. So there he was blind, unable to see, knowing that the insurgents often covered their IEDs by gunfire. Being a young lad not even 20 years old he calmly told his commander (the platoon's Warrior sergeant) that he could not see and to guide him back. Working together they got the last two Warriors of the platoon out of the contact point, where they were able to get the medic in the back to have a look at the driver's face.

The medic told the commander that the casualty needed to get off the ground straight away and that we needed to get him casevac'd to the hospital at SLB. The sergeant jumped out of the turret and got into the driver's seat. The platoon commander had already been in touch with the OSB ops room and asked for some support. The QRF were with One Platoon in minutes and escorted the patrol back into the OSB. Once in the base they moved the injured driver to the med centre where he was given a morphine injection. They then got a patrol who took him to Basra Palace. On the way the injured lad was high-fiving everyone as the morphine kicked in, making him as high as a kite. Once in Basra Palace the IRT (immediate response team) who get crashed out every time someone is injured or killed, had already landed, and were waiting to take him straight to the military field hospital at SLB. He was rushed straight into theatre where they operated on his left eye to try and save his sight.

Back in the COB in Ladysmith Lines we heard the call for the IRT to move to the HLS come over the camps Tannoy system. I was in the CQMS tent when we heard this, and I said to Carl I need to make sure everything is all right, the boys are on the ground at the moment. I walked up to the ops room where the OC grabbed me and pulled me to one side. He told me that One Platoon had been hit by an IED and someone was hurt. I felt sick and lost as my lads were on the ground in trouble and there was not a thing I could do but to sit and wait for information.

The OC, 2IC and myself sat in the ops room until the news came through who was injured and what it was. We got told it was not life threatening and they were operating on him now. We had to keep all this information to ourselves as Op Minimise was now in place until his next of kin had been informed. Within a couple of hours One Platoon and Two Platoon were back and we were waiting to meet them in the tank park to ensure the lads were OK.

A few of them had been covered in blood and I told the platoon sergeant to get the kit off them straight away and get it bagged and handed into the CQMS who would swap it for new kit. We got the boys straight into the cookhouse dirty. They got some scoff in them and back in their tent for some sleep as quickly as we could. The boys were getting some well-earned sleep that night.

The next day I got a patrol together and we headed out of the COB and completed the short trip to SLB where we moved to the Field Hospital and parked up just outside the main gate. I left some lads with the Warriors and myself and a few of his mates moved into the hospital and moved to the ward where the injured driver was bedded down. As we entered the ward, we were stopped by one of the nurses who asked who we were here to see. I told her and she told us that he was allowed four at a time around his bed and to wash and use the gel before we entered.

We moved down the ward that was full of lads that had some terrible injuries where the insurgents' bombs, mortars and bullets had ripped their flesh apart. I could not help thinking to myself that the British public would be shocked to see just how many of their forces were getting hurt each day. They always hear about the deaths but never about the injuries. I suppose it would not be good for votes for the MPs. After 10 minutes I left and told him to look after himself and not to rush back as he was due to fly out to the UK to complete his recovery. After 30 minutes the lads came back and we mounted up and completed the short trip back to the COB.

Back at Ladysmith Lines I briefed the OC and found myself a quiet office with a phone in that I could use. I got the details for the injured lad's parents and dialled the number and waited for the ring. His mum answered and I explained who I was and that I had just come from the hospital where I was speaking to her son. His mum started to cry as I told her he was going to be fine and was due to fly to a hospital in Birmingham the next day. I gave her some details and told her that all the company were thinking of her, her son and family at this time. She thanked me and said that she appreciated the phone call and me taking the time to let her know that her son was OK. All this information had already been passed on to her from an officer back in the UK. But it was more personal and respectful to hear from someone on the ground that had seen him.

I briefed the OC what I had done who thanked me. I lay in bed that night thinking we have only been in Iraq for just over a month and how luckily the company had been not to have had anyone killed and only one injured. I hoped he would be our last injury and that our luck continued.

The next day the fleet manager got the broken Warrior back and with our fitter section and they set about to try and fix the damage. It was in a mess and was going to be off the road for long time if not permanent. There was also a lot of blood in the driver's compartment that also needed to be cleaned. Steve our fleet manager stepped up and set about cleaning the driver's compartment the best he could. The rest of the day was spent sorting all the kit out and after the shock of the day before we got some first aid training done just to keep everyone on their toes. We had our company meeting and spent the evening chilling out and I even got some time in at the gym.

The next day was 16 December, and I got the message that the injured lad would be flying home and would be calling in at the camp first to get a bag and a few things together. I met him and took him to see the OC first who had a quick chat with him. After this I took him to his tent, and we got his bag sorted. I told him not to worry about the rest of his kit as we would box it up and send it back to the UK. Once done, I made sure we had all his operational kit and took him to the front gate of our camp where he was picked back up by an ambulance and taken to the air terminal. We did not see him again until we got back from Iraq as his injury had not healed in time and kept him from returning.

That evening Three Platoon were on patrol on the outskirts of the city and moved out and patrolled down the river moving back to the area of Camp Warehouse, before returning to camp with the patrol going well. It was 0200hrs when the alarm went off for an indirect fire attack. As usual we rolled off our cot beds and landed on the floor where we grabbed our helmets and covered ourselves with our body armour. The first one whistled in and exploded about 100m away, the second one we just heard the explosion about 150m away. We were getting used to these attacks and now we were getting fed up with waiting 30 minutes for the all clear to sound. So, a few minutes after the mortars stopped falling, we would jump back in bed with our helmets and body armour still on until the all clear was sounded.

The next day we got warned off for a double strike and search operation in the Al Amnal area of the city. The Recce Platoon and Arnhem search team under the command of our OC were to strike and search the first while C Company would do the second. We had our orders and we got told that the strike and search teams would not be in our Warriors but in Snatch Land Rovers to help with the tight streets and alleyways. This was not good news as the Snatch had hardly any protection compared with the Warrior. The Warriors could take an IED blast (well most times anyway) but in a Snatch you get hit once and that is it – you are dead. We did our rehearsal and went over the orders again to ensure everyone was happy.

Prime Minister Tony Blair's Visit

In the evening, we put on our best combats and moved down to the air head. They had the tanks laid out as well as a helicopter and there were troops there from all the units that were based in the COB. We were there for the visit of the Prime Minister Tony Blair who had come over to see the troops to wish them all the best for Christmas. We lined up as he arrived and then he walked down the line talking to all the troops. I was standing next to Paul, and he stopped to talk to us and asked what the patrols were like. We told him the truth and he listened before he moved on shaking our hands and wishing us the best. He spent a good hour going around the lads trying to talk to as many as he could before he was moved onto a meeting with the Brigade Commander.

As soldiers we tried not to make things too personal and political. We had our opinion and did discuss stuff between ourselves, but very rarely expressed them outside of our military group. What I will say is in my time in the military, I never ever classed myself as working for the government. I was there as a soldier to represent the people of the UK and serve the Crown. I was a passionate royalist and loved the Queen and our Royal Family. We moved back to camp and had our evening meal. A few weeks later Gordon Brown visited but most of us were on patrol. The next day we did some more rehearsals before checking that all the kit was in good order and we positioned our vehicle in the right order of march ready to go.

Arnhem Search Team Go In

At 2100hrs we moved to our Snatches and drove to the front gate. The whole place was covered in a thick fog. We all set off moving to SLB where we would be staying for a few hours before the strike went in. Due to the fog, we were moving about 3mph. It was taking forever to complete the short trip to SLB. A couple of Warriors ran into each other. So, the CO made the call that the operation should be delayed for 24 hours as moving into the target area in these conditions would have been dangerous. So, we made the painfully slow trip back to the COB where we closed down and got some sleep.

The next day we did some more rehearsals before moving to the tank park at 2000hrs. There was still a bit of fog about, but it was not as bad as the previous night. We completed the short trip to SLB where we got a brew and managed to grab a couple of hours' sleep in our seats before moving out. Blenheim Company was moving first and moved out to secure the route around the estate we were going to be working in. Ten minutes later we left in our convoy of Snatches.

We moved out of SLB and turned right and headed towards the city. After half an hour we reached the bridge at Red One. The outer cordon got told to move to their positions and within 30 seconds we got,

'GO, GO, GO.'

The Snatches speeded up and got onto the main road, turned left, and went over the bridge at speed. Once over we went through another police checkpoint before turning left a mile down the road, we were flying. We entered the housing estate, and the roads were very tight with car parked on both sides. There were low wires hanging everywhere and the road had big potholes all over it. The place stunk and there was not much room to move the vehicles. We entered the target street, and the Snatches were making best speed to try and keep the upper hand with the surprise.

We got to the target house and there was a small light on downstairs. The recce lads got out and got ready to strike the house. The search team lined up behind them with the search team commander at the front of our line. We all put on our rubber gloves to help keep the evidence from being cross contaminated. Then we noticed that two of the recce lads had gone to the wrong house on dismounting and the commander was not messing about and got them back sharply. He told the first two to go whose job it was to break in. They ran towards the gates and started to kick in the gate which turned out to be a tough job until an old man inside the building opened the gates with the handle, not the best start. But it was good for us at the back pissing ourselves laughing.

The lads did not mess about and were soon in the building and securing the place and the people in it. Once they had it secured, they moved all the females and kids in one room and all the men in another. The strike team commander gave me the thumbs up, and I entered with the search team ready to search the building. We moved into one room and the search team commander numbered off the rooms so the search pairs could search rooms in the order he wanted them to. We placed the female searcher in the room with the women and kids and got one of the recce boys to keep an eye on her. The house had one living room, one kitchen, one toilet and three bedrooms on the bottom floor.

The second floor had four small room on the roof that was being used for storage. The search pairs set about searching the rooms with the search 2IC doing all the paperwork. We were striking the house due to information that the owner was working as a border policeman and was helping to smuggle weapons over the Iranian border. The policeman got moved away from everyone else in the house and moved to the kitchen where his hands were secured with plastic cuffs and then he started to get questioned by an Army Tactical Questioner. Now, the TQ was one of the calmest, nicest people I know, but shit he was like a man possessed in this role. I just walked in as he was in full flow playing bad cop, thinking who the fuck is this man?

The place was a madhouse. In the kitchen there was a load of shouting going on as the man got questioned. In the room full of females and kids they were screaming and crying due to everything which was happening. But we had to push on and do our job as fast as we could. One of the search pairs got told to search the room where the females and kids where and I went with them to ensure they respected them the best they could while doing their job.

There were about four adult women and six kids. They were all sat in the middle of the room on a load of cousins. The wife of the policeman came up to me and started to speak Arabic. She had deep dark eyes which were full of tears and was wearing long black Arabic clothes. You could not help but to feel sorry for them. But we had a job to do and hopefully all this would be worth it in the end if Iraq turned out to be a better place for the people who lived there. I got her to calm down using hand signs when one of the boys called me over. He had found some ammunition and pistol magazines in a bag in the drawers. I told him 'Well done' and to take all the kit to the search 2IC for documentation.

In another room we found a number of mobile phones and computers that we were taking back. The OC got briefed that we would be finished on task in 10 minutes and what we had found on the search so far. One of the lads went into the toilet to give it a quick search. I followed him in, and we were greeted by a small room with a bottle of water in it and a lone hole on the floor with two footprints ether side. Now think back to the toilet in the film *Trainspotting* and it gives you an idea what we were looking at. The lad looked at me, turning white, and asked, 'Do you want me to check inside the hole sir or what?' I looked at him and started smiling and replied 'Fuck it, let's get out of here', much to the young lad's relief.

The OC came back and said we were lifting in one minute and we were going to detain the policeman. One of the recce boys arrested the man and we moved him outside and into the back of one of the Snatches. I counted the lads out to ensure that we had everyone and that we were leaving no one behind. As we were leaving the house went mental as everyone realised that we were lifting their man. I shut the door so we could control the situation and we all mounted up and moved out of the estate.

On the route back we went back over the bridge and then went the long way back moving past SLB before arriving at the COB 90 minutes later. We moved straight to the detainee centre and handed over our prisoner and then took all the kit in we had found and handed it over to the RMP. We then moved back to Ladysmith Lines where daylight was breaking and after a shower and some breakfast we crawled into our pits for some sleep.

The Shia Flats

On 20 December we handed over guards and went back onto one and three hours' notice to move. The next day, we got warned off for a strike and search operation in the Shia Flats area of the city, which was going to be taking place the following night. I went over to the tank park to brief some of the commanders up when we heard the whistle of a rocket falling in. We hit the ground fast and hoped for the best. The explosion was deafening as it landed just outside the tank park. There were another three rockets during that attack, but they landed to the left of the tank park in the area of Camp C.

After the all clear was sounded we started to sort out all the equipment, getting it prepared for the operation that was taking place the following day. That night we had our Coy O Group, and the OC told us that the orders for the Battle Group operation would be at 2100hrs and that all commanders had to attend. We grabbed some scoff, and I got a brew for the orders as I had a feeling it was going to be a long one. They told us that the operation was going to take place in the Al Hyyaniyah (what we called the Shia Flats) and that it was a strike and search operation.

We got told that the route would be secured by the tanks. Blenheim Company would provide the outer cordon with Arnhem Company and C Company going in to do the inner cordon and the strike. One Platoon and the Recce Platoon would be the first in, out of our group with Company Tac next before the Snatches of C Company followed up by Two Platoon and Three Platoon. They went through all the orders and after a couple of hours we had finished and left all the OCs to conduct their rock drills with the CO. (Rock drills are a more informal part of the orders where the commanders can ask question to the CO on a one-to-one basis to ensure they understand his plan.)

Back in our tent we were chatting about the operation. I remembered the CSM of the outgoing unit answer when I asked him what not to do over here. He replied, 'Don't go into the Shia Flats area!' I said, 'What, at night?' and he replied 'No, not at all.' Well, we were soon to find out why. We woke up the next day, went into rehearsals, and finished with the OC going over the plan one last time with all the commanders from the company. We had an early dinner and got a couple of hours' sleep before we were due down the tank park at 2300hrs.

At 2200hrs we got up and got a brew before we moved to the tank park. At the tank park we did all the checks with me going around doing spot checks on the lads for different things like dog tags and med kit. We mounted up and moved to the front gate in the correct order of march with the tanks at the front, then Blenheim Company and last Arnhem Company, the Recce Platoon and C Company.

At midnight, Egypt Squadron and Blenheim Coy rolled out and 20 minutes later we started to move. We could tell we were in for a busy time because even before we had left the front gate Blenheim Company had been contacted with three RPGs already. We moved out of the COB and instead of going left or right onto the main MSR we continued over to the bridge and into the city rubbish tip. The Army put codes words on everything and the code word for the rubbish tip was Old Trafford. Being a big Liverpool fan, I was made up. The place stunk and made your eyes water as the locals often set fire to it to try and break it down. It took about 10 minutes to get through and then we had to cross a road with a bridge near it that we called Yellow 1.

After this we had a dusty stretch of road for a few miles that they called Route Anfield that led to the bridge at Red 1. But we were not going that far and turned left and went over a bridge we called Yellow 1. We moved up to the checkpoint and got held there while we waited for Blenheim Company to get all their Warriors into place. All we could hear over the radio was contact as they had to fight their way in just to secure the outer area of the flats. Once they were in position, we got the order to move and One Platoon with the Recce Platoon started to move forward. We left a gap of 100m before we moved off with the main body with our Warrior call sign Zero Charlie leading. When One Platoon and the Recce Platoon got just short of the main junction at Yellow 3, they got ambushed by RPGs and small arms fire from the right. One Platoon did not stop and continued pushing forward.

The Recce Platoon, always ready for a fight, stopped and returned fire with each of their gunners firing the 7.62mm chain guns. This is not what the OC wanted as he had to keep the armoured column moving.

I was shoulder high in the turret with the 2IC next to me and we were watching the firework show in front of us with tracer flying all over the place and RPG warheads exploding left, right and centre. It was pretty impressive and all of a sudden, the 2IC dropped down and started to scream 'GET DOWN!' I continued to watch and told him to calm down as the bullets were miles away. The lads in the back were laughing as he shouted again 'CONTACT GET DOWN YOU DICKHEAD' I turned and said, 'I know there's a contact, I am watching it and who the fuck are you calling a dickhead.' He shouted 'NO, CONTACT RIGHT, GET THE FUCK DOWN'. I looked over to my right just as a volley of tracer flew over my head. Humbly, I dropped into my seat and traversed the turret to the right and tried to spot the firing point. The 2IC saw it first and gave me a sighting report so I could see the firing point. I saw the flashes of the insurgents' weapons as they kept on firing. I steadied my sights onto the target as did the gunner of Two Platoon sergeant's Warrior who had also spotted the firing point. The insurgents upped the ante by lobbing a couple of RPGs at us. I stamped down on the firing pedal at the same time as the other gunner did in call sign 22 and we both fired fifty rounds of 7.62mm from our chain guns until the insurgents stopped firing. I made sure both weapons were good to go as we got nearer to the Shia Flats.

One Platoon had pushed past the friendly Warriors doing the outer cordon and at the junction of Green 38 they turned right and entered the Shia Flats. Because the other Warriors had stopped, they were on their own. They started to get contacted by small arms and RPGs straight away and they stood their ground with their gunners firing their chain guns whenever a target was spotted. The Warrior leading us into the Shia Flats got a bit mixed up with all the firefights and the OC gave the 2IC the nod to get in front and to lead in.

The company caught up and as we approached One Platoon they were getting whacked by a number of RPGs and small arms. The front Warrior, call sign 11, which was commanded by Martin had six dismounts in the back as well as three crew. They moved forward with the platoon commander and as they turned right their Warrior was hit with a massive explosion rocking it to the left. Martin asked all the lads if they were OK and one of the lads in the back said they were fine, but fuel was leaking out of the fuel tank and filling up the back. They got the boys transferred over to different Warriors and the crew cracked on with the broken Warrior the best they could. They had been hit by the new RPG 29 that was faster and more penetrating than the old one we were used to. The Warrior had not been fully penetrated but it did cause something inside to splinter off and pieces of it broke the fuel tank. The lads had been lucky.

The OC was getting pushed on from the CO to keep the patrol moving. He got our Warrior to lead and was pushing the 2IC hard to get things moving. Me and the 2IC where head high in the turret and had just moved past a junction when on the 2IC's side there was a couple of explosions that slammed into the turret, forcing us both off our feet. The OC who Warrior was behind us got on the radio and told us to keep moving. The 2IC, with his face blackened from the explosions and me pissing myself laughing at him, calmly came on the radio and told the OC that we had just been hit with two RPG warheads and to give him a few seconds to sort himself out. The OC replied with a 'Roger out'. We pushed on and entered the target street where One Platoon had pushed all the way to the bottom to secure that area. Two Platoon and Three Platoon stayed at the other end. This left the Recce Platoon and us in the centre with the strike teams.

We positioned all of the Warriors to give the strike teams protection and got the top cover up to maximise our protection. There was a chill in the air that night, but we were all soaked wet through with sweat. The street where the target house was on was tight with cars on both sides of the streets. The road was in a bad state and the houses were all jammed together with little room or space. There was a lot of wires hung across the road and we had to grab our antennas when we moved under them to stop them from being dragged down. The place had a lot of rubbish on the street as well as sewage, which made your nose tingle with the stench of the place.

As we moved down there was an old donkey by the side of the road that would not move out of our way. I told the driver to keep going as I knew the donkey would move as we got closer. We moved up and then got ourselves back into position to offer protection. The OC jumped down without telling the CQMS who was his cover man and went into the target house. When he got back in Carl told him not to do that again. The OC never argued and replied with a tame 'OK, OK'.

After a few minutes, the night exploded with noise, the place was mad. There were insurgents running everywhere on the rooftops, with tracer bullets and RPGs flying all over the place. A few explosions were seen on the side of the Warriors, and you could hear the gunfire and pinging of the bullets as it hit the metal. As the streets were so tight, I could not use the Warriors' weapons and I had my rifle in my shoulder in the top of the turret.

I was scanning the area to our front when I saw a man appear about 30m away. He was dressed in white from head to toe in Arabic clothing and he had an AK-47 and was firing at three forward call signs from the hip. I steadied the sight of my rifle onto the centre of his chest. I had no time to steady my breathing. I pulled the trigger and saw his white chest turn to red through my site. I continued firing until the man had dropped and there was no chance of him getting up and endangering the lives of the forward call signs. After a few seconds I was out of ammo and chained my magazine as the 2IC reported what had happened over the radio. The 2IC was covered in my empty cases and just looked at me and said, 'A bit of a warning that you were going to fire would have been nice.' I smiled as I continued to scan the area.

Five minutes had passed since I had opened fired and me and the 2IC were scanning the area to our front. The next we knew we had bullets cracking past us and pinging off the turret. We both spun around with our rifles and could see the flashes of the insurgent's AK-47 rifle as he emptied his whole magazine in full automatic all over our position. As we tried to bring our weapons up into the aim, we heard one of the top cover Marti in the back call out, 'I have got him,' as he opened fired with his rifle at the insurgent on the roof 20m behind us. The man dropped as Marti's accurate shooting met its target. Marti kept an eye on the area as the 2IC and I, said thanks and that the brews were on us back at camp. We knew we had been lucky, and God only knows how me and John had not been hit as the bullets where bouncing of the metal all around us. But we still had to hear Marti going on for the next few months about how he saved our lives.

The strike teams had almost finished, and the OC told the CO that they would be lifting from the target house in five minutes and that we had a small amount of munitions we were bringing back. They were also detaining three men and bringing them back for questioning.

We got all the Warriors sorted out facing the way we would be leaving and waited for the call from the CO to lift. It came a couple of minutes later and we moved off, back out the way we came. The insurgents were waiting for us and as the Snatches drove past, they opened fired with RPGs and small arms fire. It was their mistake as C Company's soldiers on top cover in their Snatches were ready. They all opened up, firing with their rifles, light machine guns and under slung grenade launches. It was a good return of fire and the insurgents moved away from their positions pretty fast.

One of Three Platoon's Warriors was moving past a building when the commander spotted a man on the roof with a AK-47. He never had time to grab his rifle that was in his turret and the gunner would not be able to get the Warrior's weapons onto the target quick enough to stop him firing. So, the commander, a Corporal called Mac, grabbed his 9mm pistol and fired at the man with nine bullets, hitting him and forcing him to drop onto the roof out of sight. As we were leaving the Shia Flats, we came to the end of the estate when John shouted.

'CONTACT RIGHT, TRACER GUNFIRE'

I looked right and the top covers moved over ready to engage with their rifles. We all started laughing as we saw an HGV truck with a trailer which had orange lights along it side moving towards us. It had been one of them nights and we moved out with the odd tracer round still chasing us as we moved over the bridge just past the yellows.

We turned right into rubbish tip and the 2IC and me looked at each other. I said to him how the hell did we get out of that without losing anyone. He shrugged his shoulders as he told everyone well done and to remember that their weapons were still made ready and to be careful. We moved into the front gates of the COB and pulled over on the right-hand side to unload all the weapons. Once done we moved on and fuelled up and headed off to the tank park. I got all the lads together and did all the post-patrol paperwork like statements and so on. There was a few lads who had fired but not as many as I thought for such a heavy night of contacts. The lads in the company were good at what they did, and never once so far had I thought someone had fired their weapon when I thought they should not have.

I informed the OC that everything was done and gave him an account of what was fired. He told me to tell the lads to get their heads down as one of the platoons were out tonight and that we had just been warned off for another big operation in 24 hours. I turned and looked at him and said what Christmas Day. He laughed and just said 'Happy Christmas Sergeant Major'. Again, we grabbed some food and got a quick shower. We got into bed and the minute we closed our eyes we heard a rocket whistle in, the explosion was pretty close as we jumped of our bed and tried to get into some protection on the floor. We stayed there as another one whistled in quickly followed by another close explosion. As we were laying there, we all started to laugh as Mogger turn around and said, 'I guess we pissed them off tonight then.' After the all clear was sounded we fall into a heavy sleep.

A Basra City Christmas

A few hours later we got up and started to get everything sorted out for the next operation. The OCs and the CO had already started planning this and the admin was well under way. Three Platoon were told that they would be out that night with a platoon of Snatches from C Company, so they were busy getting ready for that. Everyone else was to be in the briefing tent for the Battle Group orders. The operation was going to be a strike, search and destroy mission and because it was spanning out over Christmas Eve and Christmas Day some joker called it Operation Thyme.

We got told that this was going to be a brigade operation to close down the Basra SCU (Special Crimes Unit) section of the Basra Police. They were a section of their police force that operated on their own countering organised crime. But British Army surveillance showed that they were responsible for a lot of the attacks in the city on us and also their own people, with a lot of kidnapping and torturing being carried out at the location. The SCU building was also being used as a prison and the prisoners were to be moved to a different prison. The tanks and our other company, along with troops from the Rifles, were going to be the protection on route and around the SCU building. The Staffords were going to be the main force striking the building because this was a joint operation between the British Army and the Iraq Army. Once everything was secure Arnhem Company (us) and an Iraqi company would move into the SCU Building and transfer the prisoners to their new home. That was the basic plan, but the orders went into a lot of detail lasting for a few hours. That consumed what was left of the day, and we did as much as we could to try and give ourselves maximum time the following day, Christmas Eve.

Three Platoon and a platoon of Snatches were out that night on a city patrol to try and counter the indirect fire threat. They mounted up and once the platoon commander was happy, they moved to the front gate to meet up with their Snatches. They were going to be working in two groups with Three Platoon Warriors as one group and the Snatches as the other.

They moved out with the Warriors leading and got onto the MSR heading south. They moved past the bridge and police checkpoint and moved to Green 19 where Three Platoon started to conduct a VP (vulnerable point) check. Once it was clear the Snatches pushed right and started to receive small arms and RPG fire. Three Platoon were soon there to help them out and as they pulled up the platoon commander felt the wind rushed past his face as an RPG missed him by inches. One of his boys in the back spotted the RPG gunner and steadied his sights onto the main mass of his body. Trying hard to control his breathing, he pulled the trigger and the weapon bolted into action as he fired five rounds at his target, putting an end to the threat the insurgent was posing.

Three Platoon now had the area secured and stayed in place while the Snatches moved on to conduct a search of the area around Yellow 9. The Snatches got there and came under fire straight away. The lads of C Company returned fire with their weapons as Three Platoon moved in to assist them. The Warriors pulled up and moved into a position where they could offer some protection. The dismounts in the back got out and all adopted fire positions.

The team commander of the dismounts was moving to each position to ensure his lads were covering the area correctly. Then 40m to his right he saw a sudden movement. He spun around as an insurgent appeared with an RPG on his shoulder. He dropped onto one knee and at the same time his weapon came up into the aim. The insurgent was quicker and there was a muffled bang as the RPG warhead left its launcher and flew through the air towards the Warrior. It missed by a metre and shot past and exploded on some waste ground. The team commander was not giving him a second chance to reload and fire. He squeezed his trigger and his weapon kicked into action, taking its target down with its lethal cargo. With the chilled December air, the smoke trail from the RPG hung in the air leaving its familiar smell all around the area.

The platoon commander shouted, 'Mount up' and the lads ran towards the back of their Warrior as the armoured door opened and they climbed into the safety of the back. Once they were all in the team commander shut the door with the familiar clunk and the top cover assumed their positions as the patrol moved off. Three Platoon completed their patrol before moving out of the city and back to the COB, with a job well done.

We woke up on Christmas Eve knowing what we had to do. We set about the Warriors and our personal equipment ensuring that we checked and checked again because someone's life might depend on it. With the day taken up with all the admin the OC got the company together and went over his orders just to ensure that everyone knew what we had to do. We had our evening meal and chilled out for a bit before we moved to the tank park. We conducted our final checks before we mounted up and did a radio check. When the OC was happy, we moved to the front gate where he informed the ops room that we were leaving the COB and moving to Camp Warehouse to meet up with the Iraq Army.

We headed out and moved onto the MSR and headed down to the bridge. There we turned left and went down the embankment which was very steep and took some good driving to manoeuvre down. At the river we headed left and went under the bridge before moving to the left and going across country before we entered Camp Warehouse. We pushed Three Platoon down to Green 18 to cover our entry into the camp and we moved past the Iraqi guard and pulled up just inside the gate.

We had the American Army in one of our Warriors who were flying their unmanned surveillance planes from one of the roofs. We dropped them off and they moved up to the nearest flat roof and set up. We pulled up and I moved up to the roof to see what was going on. The OC gave the command for Three Platoon to move into Camp Warehouse and they turned their Warriors around and started to move back. When they were about 40m short, they came into view when I saw the front Warrior get contacted by an RPG. It flew across the waste ground from the housing estate and went in between the front and second Warrior. Three Platoon never spotted the firing point and just pushed past the contact and into Camp Warehouse where they lined up with the company.

I was still on the roof, and I watched as Blenheim Company pushed past Green 18 and could see all the tracer and glows of the RPGs flying through the air as the insurgents tried to stop them pushing past in vain. The Iraqi army turned up at Camp Warehouse in their American Hummies and lorries and parked up next to our Warriors. The OC and 2IC got out and had a face to face with them, before coming back and briefing the commanders. We were pushing One Platoon up front with Three Platoon and HQ in the centre with the Iraqi Army with Two Platoon bringing up the rear. All we had to do now was wait for the call to come from the ops room to move once the Staffords had the building secured. It was a cold night and the lads had to keep the brews going to ensure everyone stayed warm and more important awake.

The Staffords moved up to the SCU Building and when they were 100m short they were spotted by the guards in the watchtower on the roof. Now this guard must have been mad. He was sitting in his watchtower with his AK-47 rifle when he spotted a company-strength Warrior patrol moving towards his position. Me, I would have run a mile but no, this madman brought his weapon to his shoulder and started to fire at the advancing Warriors. The bullets hit their target, bouncing off the first Warrior, but the commander of the Warrior was not in the mood to mess about and told his gunner to engage him with the main armament. The gunner got his sights onto the watchtower that was firing at them and engaged him with six 30mm rounds of high explosive. The effect was deadly as the rounds ripped through the tower like paper, destroying the guard's location instantly.

The Staffords got the dismounts out and they attacked the compound. The Warriors smashed through the gate and just drove over the cars as they moved forward to the target building. The dismounts moved fast behind and stormed the building which they took control of very quickly. Once they had the area secured, they got the prisoners who were all holed up in a little cell, counted them, and passed the information on to the ops room.

Back with Arnhem Company we got the information that the road from Camp Warehouse to the junction at Green 18 had a suspected five bombs in position waiting to blow us up. The OC called all the platoon commanders together along with me and the company 2IC. He informed us all about the possible IEDs and said that the area had to be cleared before we could move up it.

One Platoon commander bravely volunteered and got his men mounted up. They moved out with the platoon commander Warrior leading and stopped just short of the first possible IED. The lads in the back got out and started to clear forwards and as they came to the hot spot. They confirmed it as nothing more than a small fire. They mounted up and did the same again another four times with the lads of One Platoon showing great courage as they made sure that the route was safe for us to move through. With the route secure they moved back to Camp Warehouse and waited with the rest of us for the order to move.

It was 0330hrs when we got the order to move. The OC was keen to get the company moving as the December chill was starting to cut through the lads' thin desert combats. We mounted up and started to move out, with a few of the commanders looking a bit sleepy. They soon switched on as we got into the correct order of march and left Camp Warehouse. We moved down to the junction at Green 18 and moved right towards the junction at Yellow 3. We pushed past onto the Greens before moving right into Al Jameat area. We then moved up into the compound of the SCU. The engineers were setting up bar mines for the building demolition. The Iraqi vehicles moved up to the building and we got all the prisoners out of the cell and into the Iraqi vehicles. They looked please to be leaving and when we saw the shithole that they had been living in we knew why. They had a small room with about thirty men in it with a shithole in one corner and sink in the other. All they had room for was to place down a dirty blanket to sleep on. A lot of the prisoners had cuts and bruises and looked distressed.

Once they were all ready, we moved off to take the prisoners to their new home at the new police HQ (PJHQ). We moved out of the Al Jameat and started to move through the city. I looked up and could see the protection of the two Apache attack helicopters flying above us trying to keep the insurgents' heads down. It was a big operation with a lot of troops and hardware involved. When we got to the Police Station we moved in and parked up the Warriors. The Iraqi Army took the prisoners in and that was our job completed with them anyway. We left them and moved to a standby area back in Al Jameat.

The engineers back at the SCU building had now got all the explosives in place and were moving everyone out. The Staffords had taken all the munitions and IT equipment as well as any detainees and moved them to the COB. Once the engineers were happy that the place was clear they gave a countdown and told everyone to get down. We were not getting down and wanted to see what was happening. '5, 4, 3, 2, 1'. A massive explosion ripped through the Christmas morning air as we saw the roof of the building fly 20m into the air. The building was totally destroyed and there was no way it would ever be in a position to operate again. The last thing we had to do was move to the road at Yellow 3 to Green 19 and secure it so the rest of the troops could move through us and back to their bases. We moved out and headed up to the main junction at Yellow 3.

It was now about 0600hrs in the morning, and everyone was knackered. The traffic in the city was building up and the company was stretched out over a mile protecting the most dangerous part of the route. The other units started to move through with the Staffords moving on to the Shatt Hotel and our units moving to the COB. It was taking ages and the OC got on the radio and asked what the holdup was. We got told that one of Blenheim Warriors had got caught up in barbed wire and it was affecting their running gear and needed to be recovered as they had thrown a track. That meant that we had to stay in place until it was done.

Although it was Christmas morning, for us life in Basra City was no different. There were people everywhere and the traffic was the same madness as it always was. I was covering the ground to the right of my position. I was watching an Iraqi family sitting by their house. The dad was sitting outside, and the mum had just got him a coffee in a small glass cup. The two lads were trying to catch a wild dog and the youngest girl was watching and kept on running up to her dad for a hug. It could have been a family anywhere in the world and for a quick minute made me think of home. I soon snapped out of it, as when we are on the ground we have to be focused and put our family to the back of our minds and concentrate on the job.

Back at the junction at Yellow 3 the Warriors not being the smallest of vehicles were causing a problem with the traffic. The platoon commander of Two Platoon and two of his men jumped out and started to help the struggling Iraqi Police to control the traffic and get it flowing again. It was like a Carry-On movie with the mad controlling the mad. I do not know who was laughing the most, the locals or us watching.

Once the traffic was moving again Two Platoon mounted back up and the OC told them to move up to the bridge just past Green 18. Once they were there the local lads started to get a group together and the bricks started to fly towards the Warriors. With the recovery nearly completed the OC moved Three Platoon up to assist Two

Platoon who had bricks bouncing all over them. We were 100m away from Two Platoon and Three Platoon and we could see all the locals giving them a hard time. The next thing we saw a puff of flames and smoke as a petrol bomb exploded on one of the Warriors. Two Platoon commander sent his lads out the back and they gave chase for a quick 50m. This resulted in the crowd running away and the soldiers came back and mounted up.

Still watching and covering them we saw the crowd start to creep back up in the dead ground and we informed them on the radio. The commander of the Warrior that had just been hit by a petrol bomb ordered his gunner to get ready with the FRG (Federal Riot Gun) which fired a thick plastic bullet and was design to hurt the target and not kill them. The locals were about 20m away when one of them appeared to the Warrior's front with an armed patrol bomb in his hand.

The gunner brought the FRG to his shoulder and took aim at the centre of the man's body at the same time the petrol bomber brought his arm back and released the petrol bomb towards the target. A muffled bang went off as the plastic bullet left the FRG and spun towards it target. The local was a bad shot and his petrol bomb exploded 5m short of its target. The FRG gunner had more luck as he saw the plastic bullet hit its target square on the arse. The local, now nursing a dead bum, limped off in a huff holding his arse. This happened a couple more time with the Warriors getting a few petrol bombs and two more of the locals limping away with dead legs.

At last, the recovery was completed, and Blenheim Company passed past our positions and headed off towards the COB. We then received the order to move and followed them into the COB. On the way back in we got told that once we had parked our Warriors at the tank park and closed them down, that Santa and Ms Claus were waiting for us in camp. We parked up and I watched as a tired and dirty looking company moved from their Warriors in the tank park back into camp.

As we walked into camp there was one of our bigger lads dressed up in a Santa suit and our company female clerk dressed up as Ms Claus. They had a present for us which was a red box of goodies that all forces on operations got. It contained a cake, cup, toiletries and other bits and pieces not to forget a fridge magnet of the Queen. I went up to Santa and Ms Claus with my face and combats covered in dirt and dust from the patrol. They smiled as they said you can sit on Santa's knee or get a kiss from Ms Claus. I looked at the big Santa sitting down and then I look at Ms Claus who was our Welsh Company Clerk who played rugby and tug of war for the army.

It was no contest. I sat down on Santa's knee as fast as I could. They were playing Christmas songs, but best of all they had sausages and bacon butties waiting for us with a cup of gunshot (tea or coffee with rum in it). All that was missing now was a little bit of indirect fire from the locals. They did not let us down as we heard the alarm go off. We hit the deck with our gunshot drink and butties as the rockets exploded to the sound of *White Christmas*. I lay there on the floor shattered, covered in dust and dirt, stinking of sweat and looked up at Wes, who was lying next to me. He just winked and said, 'Merry Christmas Sir'.

Once the all clear was given we completed the post-patrol admin. The OC informed the lads that they had nothing on until 1700hrs where they would be served Christmas Dinner. I went to the phone where I wished my lovely family Happy Christmas and asked them what they had got. My wife Lyn, hearing how tired I was, told me to get into bed and phone later. I told them all that I loved them as I placed the phone down. We dragged ourselves back to our tents where we got a quick shower and jumped into bed as we slept through Christmas Day. We were woken up in the afternoon with the familiar sound of the rockets flying in. We lay on the floor as the two rockets exploded a short distance away.

After a good sleep, the officers and seniors moved to the cookhouse as it was an old tradition that we always served the soldiers their

Christmas Dinner. The boys and girls got their dinner without any alcohol as we were all dry in case we got crashed out. Once they were fed, they moved on to watch a DVD or phone their families as we had our dinner. The chefs had done us proud, we had turkey and ham with all the trimmings finished off with some Christmas pudding. After dinner I went and used the phone as we were given an extra 30 minutes of phone time on top of our normal 30 minutes a week.

It was hard for the families stuck at home on their own, but it was even harder at times like Christmas. After the phone call home I went around the lads' tents to make sure they were all OK before moving back to my tent to chill out for a bit. After a DVD I got into bed and fell into a sound sleep. The locals woke us up with a single rocket attack, but I can certainly say that Christmas Day Basra City style is one that all ranks in Arnhem Company will not forget.

We spent Boxing Day sorting out all the equipment and did some maintenance on the Warriors. At the company O Group, the OC passed on a well done for the last few operations that were conducted. After our O Group we moved to the cookhouse and ended up having our dinner on the floor again as we were hit with four rockets of indirect fire which exploded nearby. The next few days were spent with just platoon patrols or admin runs to SLB.

Sergeant Graham Hesketh

On the night of 28 December, I was getting into bed when again we got hit with seven rockets of indirect fire. The warning was good this time, the alarm went off, and we were not hit for 20 seconds. It was down to a RAF patrol outside the camp that spotted the flashes and radioed in. We got ourselves down and tried to get into some cover. The first two rockets were not close, but they got closer and the last one landed close to our camp. After the all clear was given, I again got into bed.

Lee, the CSM of Blenheim Company, was leaving as they were on an indirect fire patrol with the Snatches from C Company. I had been in bed for an hour when Lee came into the tent and woke me up. He told me that one of his lads had been hurt in a roadside IED explosion. I sat up and asked, 'Is he all right?' and 'Do you know who it is yet?' He answered 'Yes' and said, 'That's why I am waking you up mate. It's Graham Hesketh.'

Graham was a mate of mine that I had known for years who was a sergeant in Blenheim Company. He was engaged to one of the corporals in the fitter section called Becky. I asked Lee, 'Does Becky know? Where is she?' 'She's over the company office, mate, the OC wants a word with her.' I got out of bed and grabbed my warm kit and walked over. I walked in and Becky was standing in the middle of the room crying. I walked over and gave her a hug and she looked at me as she said, 'I can't believe he's gone.' I looked at the OC in disbelief and he nodded as he told me that he had died from his wounds a short while ago. I told Becky and one of her mates I would get them a brew to calm their nerves.

I walked out of the company office and went into the Battalion HQ room. The RSM (Regimental Sergeant Major) and the CO were talking to the ops officer by the brew kit. I just looked at them in disbelief and they asked if I was all right. I told them I was just getting a brew for Becky, and I could not believe the news. They told me to keep it to myself until his family had been informed and I nodded as I took the brew back and stayed with them for a few hours talking and keeping her company. After his family had been informed Op Minimise was lifted and I left Becky as she phoned her family and Graham's family.

It was about 0500hrs in the morning, and I phoned Lyn to let her know as she also knew Graham well. I dialled in the number and the phone rang. After a couple of rings, she picked it up and asked if everything was OK as it was 0200hrs. She could hear the sadness in my voice as I said, 'We have lost another one love.' She asked who it was and did she know him all in one question. Fighting back the tears I told her it was Graham. I heard the other end of the phone go quiet as the name sank in. She started to cry as I heard my daughter wake up crying 'Is my daddy OK?' I told her I was sorry for waking her and that I just wanted her to hear the news from me and not the local gossip down in Tesco. I told her I had to go, and she told me she loved me and to be careful. I replied with I love you too as I placed the phone back down. To be honest I just needed to hear her voice as I was hurting.

I walked back to my tent and climbed into bed, not sleeping just lying there thinking how hard this job was at times and how Graham's family must have been going through hell. The next day the padre did a service and we got told that the repatriation would not be for a few days as there was no flight available. I phoned Graham's dad Kevin as I thought hearing from one of his mates in Iraq would mean a lot to him. He told me when his body was back that he planned to see it and what did I think. I knew that he had died with a head injury and told Kevin that it was best if he remembered his son the way he was before he had left for Iraq. His dad was proud of his son and knew that he was a solider through and through and that he died doing what he loved.

On reflection, the death of Graham had a lasting effect on me as a person but also as a soldier. I had known a few lads who had died throughout my career, but this one hurt more. It was personal not only because he was my friend, but also due to the impact it had on my wife and my children. This is something I had not experience before and hearing your wife cry and daughter waking up scared that her dad was hurt, really cut to the bone. I think all soldiers old and young would agree, that it takes a special kind of family to support a soldier.

After the phone call I moved back to the tent and was soon on the floor as we got hit with seven rockets that exploded near our tank park. We had been on the floor for 10 minutes when someone ran in and shouted for everyone to get their kit on and mount up straight away. The officers moved to the ops room and the rest of us moved to our Warriors and booted the radios up. The officers were with us 10 minutes later and briefed us up on the situation. When the rockets of the last attack were fired, the firing point was seen by one of our helicopters and the insurgent firing team were followed back to a house. We were tasked to go and strike it. Egypt Squadron and Blenheim Company were providing the outer security and Arnhem Company the inner cordon with C Company doing the strike. We all moved to the front gate and moved out.

We moved down to the main junction at Green 19, and it was cleared by Blenheim Company. We pushed east and headed over the Qarmat Ali Bridge. We moved past Blenheim Company and pushed right into a housing estate and secured around the target building. C Company struck the house and within 20 minutes they had arrested three men and found all the rocket kit as well as a few maps and GPSs with all the camp details on it. We mounted up and started to move out. As we turned the corner the insurgents were waiting in an ambush and the sky lit up at their tracers and RPGs flew towards us. Luckily for C Company they were firing the RPGs at us and the small arms fire at them.

There was an explosion on the side of our Warrior, but we continued pushing through as Blenheim Company had got the insurgent fire positions and were returning fire. The tracer rounds were now pinging off our Warriors as we moved out of the contact area and moved back across the bridge. We were all soon entering the camp where the enemy rocket team were handed over and we closed down. We all grabbed a good scoff, feeling happy with ourselves for finally getting one of their rocket teams before grabbing a shower and falling into a sound sleep.

December 30th was the day that the Iraqi old leader was due to be executed. Saddam Hussein was a cruel dictator who had caused many hardships on his people. He was hanged till death for his crimes against the people of Iraq.

New Years Eve was no different and the day passed quickly with hardly a mention. There was no special dinner and there was no alcohol. With the day out of the way, we were in our tents just talking when we heard the whistle of a rocket fly in. It exploded about 150m away, we all hit the floor and tried to get into some cover but there was none. Thirty seconds later we got hit with three more rockets that exploded 100m away. We lay there hoping for the best, ten seconds later we got hit with four more rockets that again exploded closer to our camp. We lay on the ground, the explosions kept coming. You could hear the whistle of the rockets as they flew in. The deafening noise as the high explosives combusted sending its deadly metal flying in all direction. The ground shook again and again and again as the rockets flew in. You could hear the soldiers screaming as they feared for their lives. Again, and again the rockets kept coming, inching us nearer to our deaths. We lay there and no one dared moved until the all clear was sounded. We got up and all just looked at each other it was by far the worst indirect fire attack that we had been hit with in the COB so far. After that attack although we had no physical injuries, we did have one lad who broke mentally and found it hard to cope with the pressure of being on operations. We got him the best available help we could but to this day he has never been the same.

December had been a busy month with a lot of operations and firefights with the enemy. I think the most remarkable thing about December was the fact that the battalion had only lost one brave soul. It could have so easily have been a dozen. The lads had now found their feet and their performance on the ground were starting to show it. I sat with the OC on New Year's Day and asked him did he remember after our time in the Shatt Hotel he asked the question could our lads perform to the standards of the Staffords. He replied 'Yes, I remember.' 'Well after this month I think your question has been answered.' He just smiled at me and said, 'Yes Sergeant Major, the boys have done well.'

For me December and Christmas Basra City style will be one that I will remember for the rest of my days. Losing a close friend, the effect it had on my family. One of my lads being injured under my command and speaking to families back in the UK, were life-changing events. But seeing the full forces of the British Military in action under full contact with the enemy made me proud. I wanted more and this is what I joined the Army for, so bring on 2007.

3

JANUARY 2007

Different Year, Same Shit

January might have been a New Year, but the work still came thick and fast. On 2 January we got warned off for another 300km round route to Al Amara that was happening in a couple of days. We set about sorting all the admin out, with the Warriors being checked over and all the rations and water getting stored away in the back of the vehicles. At the same time the OC, 2IC and officers were going through the planning and putting the final detail into the plan. The day was taken up with all the preparation and at our company O Group the OC informed us that the orders for the operation would be at 1000hrs in the briefing tent. He asked me to get in touch with the commanders of the admin vehicles and to ensure they knew what time the orders were, and he asked as well as the commanders being there, he also wanted the drivers present. I went and informed the commanders of the admin vehicles who were based in the camp next to ours. I then went and got my evening meal and got some time in at the gym before calling it a night and getting some sleep.

The next day we got up and I completed all the paperwork for the company and grabbed a brew before moving to the briefing tent and setting the chairs out, so the right groups were sitting where the OC wanted them to. With the chairs, maps, and aerial photos all in place the company turned up and took their seats. The company 2IC gave the ground brief before handing over to our intelligence sergeant

Sam, who gave us the threat and locations of previous attacks. The OC took over and informed us of the route and told us that instead of meeting the QRL in the desert we were going to meet them in Camp Condor which was an old base south of Al Amara manned by the Iraqi Army. After the OC had finished, I got up and briefed everyone up on the equipment and medical side of the operation before the OC finished off with questions.

After dinner we moved all the vehicles to the hard standing next door to our tank park and sorted them out in the correct order of march. Two Platoon would be leading with HQ Warriors and the admin vehicles in the centre and Three Platoon being our rear guard. Once we were parked up, we got all the admin vehicles parked to our right and we left the vehicles there as the patrol was not setting off until the middle of the night. We got our evening meal early and got a little sleep as we would be travelling through the night this time. After a few hours' sleep which was interrupted with a couple of rockets of indirect fire, we got up and headed over to the tank park and booted up our radios and conducted our final checks. We again had the Americans with us who would be flying their unmanned aircraft to assist with our protection once at Camp Condor. It was a cold night, and the lads were wrapping up well to try and protect themselves from the cold. It was hard for the crews of the Warriors as they had the wind cutting into them for the whole journey and there was no way of getting out of it. They could not put on too much warm kit either as they still had to operate the Warrior and weapons. With the patrol good to go at midnight the OC informed the ops room that we were moving to the front gate, and we set of with the warm smoke of the engine loafers hanging in the cold January night. At the front gate we did one final check to ensure all the vehicles in the convoy were in place and we set off.

We left the front gate and joined the MSR heading south-west before turning right and heading north up through the oil fields. The cold was ripping through our desert combats and as we drove past the oil field flares it was tempting just to pull up next to them and warm our cold bodies against the flames. Halfway there the OC pulled the patrol over so he could use the sat phone and I went up the line to ensure everyone was getting a warm brew in them. As I got to the Warrior the Americans lads were in I started to laugh, both of them were in their sleeping bags shivering like mad. I called them a bunch of pussies as one of them said 'God damn you Brits, even your fucking vehicles are cold.' It was hard for the American Military, where us their British counterparts completed six months operational tours, they had to endure 12 months with no leave, fuck that. With the OC happy we moved off and moved through a quiet Al Qurna at about 0430hrs and managed to reach Camp Condor just after 0630hrs. It had been a good trip up with only one admin vehicle breaking down on route which was sorted out in 10 minutes.

We pushed past the Iraqi gate guard, and I looked at them and laughed as they were finding the winter chill even harder than us. They were in bits around their fire trying to keep warm. We moved past the airfield and met up with the QRL who had set up the re-supply in the old aircraft bunkers. We handed over the admin vehicles and refuelled so our Warriors were good to go. We then moved all our Warriors into an old bunker to give us some protection as the mortar team up in these parts were good, as you could tell by all the bomb craters around the place. The old bunkers were massive, and you could easily fit in a company's worth of Warriors.

They had been used during Saddam's time to protect his fighters that were involved with the Iraqi war against Iran. They were now in a state of decay but would still serve their purpose as protection to us. The QRL we were re-supplying had been hit the previous day resulting in one of their lads being hurt so we knew not to mess around in the open. The QRL soldiers at Camp Condor were kindly providing the protection and told us to go and get some rest before our trip back. We got our sleeping bags out and got some sleep as the sun rose and started to warm everyone up.

After a few hours' sleep we got up and made ourselves a boil-in-the-bag meal and a brew from the army ration packs. Everyone slags the rations off but if you get a good flavour you were sorted. I had meatballs and pasta that was done in a Bolognese sauce (which was regarded as one of the best) and I washed it down with a mug of hot tea. The OC called all the commanders together and told us that we were moving out at 2300hrs and moving through the night again. We did all our checks and were good to go. I got everyone into the correct order with the admin vehicles in the centre and said our thanks and goodbyes to the QRL. We started the engines all at the same time to try and disguise the fact that we were leaving.

The first Warriors of Two Platoon moved off and out of Camp Condor. We followed on with the main body with Three Platoon protecting our rear. We headed south down the MSR and after a couple of hours we reached Al Qurna. The patrol switched on and started to move through. Two Platoon were just in front of us as we were coming to the end of the built-up area. 'WHOOSH'! An RPG warhead flew past the last Warrior of Two Platoon and exploded to our right. We scanned the area to the left, but the firing point was not seen. It must have just been an insurgent who got woken up by the sound of the Warriors and jumped out of bed just to fire one off and then got back into bed. We pushed on and continued south before turning right going through the oil field. At about 0530hrs we reached the MSR that led to the COB and turned left as we moved down the road.

We were all knackered, freezing and covered in dust and dirt as we completed the last 30 minutes of the journey. I touched my face just to see if it was frozen or not because it was that cold. I radioed ahead and informed the ops room to get the chefs to sort out an early breakfast and hot brew for the lads so they could get some sleep as soon as possible. We reached the main gate and unloaded all our weapons before moving to the tank park and closing down the Warriors. After the post-patrol paperwork, I got some food and grabbed a shower. I just stood there in the shower with the warm water defrosting my cold tired body before I got into bed as the rest of the battalion were just getting up.

At 1500hrs we got up and ironed our best desert combats before placing them on and falling in outside. We were all attending Sergeant Graham Hesketh's repatriation that was taking place at 1600hrs. We waited on the main square in Ladysmith Lines until the coaches arrived and took us to the main terminal at the airport. We got off the coaches and fell in in two squads before moving so that we had squads of soldiers (around 100) on both sides of the plane in rows of three. Once we were in position the lads who would be lining the route marched on with ten men on both sides. The officers then arrived and fell in, with everyone in place the coffin turned up and the bearer party (six soldiers) collected it and placed it on their shoulders before marching down the centre to the plane.

I looked on as my friend passed with a heavy heart and tear in my eyes. The coffin was dressed in a Union flag and was placed down on two small stands as a short service was said. We paid our respects before the coffin was taken onto the plane for the journey home. We then got the coaches back to our camp before attending the evening meal and then attending the company O Group. The OC informed us that One Platoon was out tomorrow on an indirect fire patrol and the rest of the company would resume camp guards in the morning.

It was now 6 January. We got up and Three Platoon took over the guards, manning the two gates of Ladysmith Lines and our tank park. Two Platoon were on standby, and the One Platoon commander was getting his orders ready for his platoon's indirect fire patrol they were calling Op Tachbrook. They had their orders early and it was going to be a seven-Warrior patrol with the four Warriors of One Platoon and three from HQ, call signs Zero Bravo, Zero Charlie and the recovery Warrior, call sign 24 Bravo. After the orders they moved straight to the tank park and completed the startup procedure.

Once we were ready, we moved to the gate and moved out with the platoon commander's Warrior leading. They pushed onto the MRS heading south into the city and as they got to A Pod Bridge they stopped and had a good scan into the city. They had arranged in their plan that at the bridge they would leave the three HQ Warriors as support to the main patrol and One Platoon would move forward with the other four Warriors and do a quick circuit of the city dominating the ground. Frank, who was manning the gunner's seat for the OC, asked could he swap places with One Platoon commander's Warrior call sign 11 as he did not fancy just sitting at the bridge in overwatch. With both bosses happy the gunners swapped over, and One Platoon were ready to move out.

They set off towards the main junction at Green 19 with the platoon commander's Warrior leading, followed by one of Martin's Warriors with the platoon Warrior sergeants next and last but not least the platoon sergeant's Warrior bringing up the rear. They moved through the police checkpoint and down to Green 19 where they dismounted and cleared it before pushing on and down to Purple 1. They were patrolling a quick round route of the Yellows before moving back to the bridge going past Green 18 and 19. The city was full of life with people and cars all over the place and the patrol was doing its job dominating the ground. The patrol turned right at the junction of Yellow 3 and started to move down towards Green 18.

'BOOOM!' There was a massive explosion as the lead Warrior call sign 10 took the full blast of the roadside IED. 'BOOOM !' Again call sign 10 rocked as it took the full blast of the second IED seconds after the first. The hot melted metal from the IEDs flew through the air ripping away at the outside of the Warrior's armour. But the Warrior stood fast, doing its job protecting its crew and dismounts from the deadly projectiles. It was soon engulfed in smoke from the IED.

Back in our location we all watched from the bridge in horror as we saw one of our Warriors take the full blast of two powerful roadside IEDs. The platoon commander who was the Warrior commander of call sign 10 steadied himself and calmly asked everyone in the Warrior if they were OK and if anyone had any injuries. He soon got back that everyone in the Warrior was fine, and he grabbed his radio. With all the other call signs waiting for what seem like a lifetime to know if there were any casualties, the platoon commander broke the silence and sent a contact report to the OC. He informed the OC that they had been hit by two IEDs, had no casualties and that the Warrior was still able to move.

The OC breathed a sigh of relief before telling him to move back to his location. The OC then passed on a full report to the battalion ops room. One Platoon moved off and through the junction at Green 19 before getting to the police checkpoint. As they were moving through all the police came out and started staring with an evil smile on their faces. They were not hiding the fact that they hated us so much. One Platoon reached the bridge and the OC asked if everyone was OK before heading back north and entering the COB.

Back at Ladysmith Lines the company were all waiting for the patrol to come back in. Although they were a mile away there was no mistaking the sound of a bomb (IED) going off in the city. The patrol got back into the tank park and the crew of call sign 10 got out with their blackened faces and I asked if they were all right. Apart from a few thumping heads they said they were fine. The platoon commander grabbed his day sack which was fastened onto the outside of the turret and held it up. It had been ripped to bits. I just looked at him and said brew, and he nodded as we walked off the tank park.

The rest of the day was spent with the inspection teams inspecting the Warriors and interviewing the lads. Later at the Coy O Group the OC told us that it was assessed that One Platoon had drove into a PIR IED EFP (passive infra-red, improvise explosive device, explosively formed projectile). This was where the bomb was set off by the Warrior breaking an infra-red beam, which then resulted in the explosives being ignited causing a copper cone to melt and fly towards its target in a hot melted slug. The insurgents carrying out the attack had no respect for the lives of the people in Basra City and they were lucky that they never had people dead during this attack as they were going about their everyday lives when it exploded. The OC went onto to tell us that we had a task of escorting the GOC from the COB to Basra City in the morning and for Two Platoon and Three Platoon along with the company HQ to be in the briefing tent for 0730hrs.

After my evening meal I went and checked on the lads who had been blown up to ensure that they were OK and then moved back to my tent. Frank was sitting there, and I asked him was he OK which he replied yes. I called him a lucky bastard and he just nodded and smiled as I made him a brew. We had just got our brew when the alarm went off for an indirect fire attack. We all hit the floor as the first rocket flew in and exploded. The second two were a bit closer and the explosions were a lot louder. We were getting pissed off with the indirect fire as our camp and tents had no protection. We had been asking for bricks to place around our bed spaces for protection for weeks but what was it going to take, a rocket to land in one of our tent with mass casualties before we got them. That night it was Blenheim Company's turn and they deployed with a couple of our mortar boys who got out at A Pod Bridge and lobbed a load of 81mm illum mortars in the areas they were using as firing points. Their patrol went well, and they return to the COB without any problems.

The next day we got up and grabbed a brew and moved to the briefing tent. The OC informed us of the operation happening in Basra City that day. We had the task of transporting the GOC who was the British Army top man in Iraq from the COB to his meeting at the Iraqi Court House. Two Platoon and company HQ would be providing route protection from the main junction at Green 19 to the junction at Yellow 3 and Three Platoon would be transporting the General. With the brief done we booked out and moved to the tank park. Once all the checks were done Two Platoon and company

HQ moved to the front gate as Three Platoon went and picked up the GOC.

Once Three Platoon had its package, we moved out with Two Platoon pushing on and clearing Green 19 and then they moved down and covered to Yellow 3. Company HQ consisted of four Warriors, call signs Zero Bravo, Zero Charlie, 24 Alpha and 24 Bravo. We moved just past Green 19 and were covering down towards the bridge at Green 18 where Two Platoon had been getting petrol-bombed and bricked on Christmas Day. The OC sat on the eastern tip of the Junction at Green 19 and positioned the 24 call signs, so they were both facing west. He then informed us to move forward to the bridge at Green 18 to offer some protection there. We looked over at his turret and the OC and Frank were smiling as they knew we would get a hard time there. But the job needed to be done so our Warrior engine roared as it moved forward with us taking up a fire position in the centre reservation just 5m short of the bridge. We got our lads up in the back to give us a few more eyes and ears and the 2IC and I were scanning on top of the turret with our rifles.

We got told that Three Platoon where moving past the bridge and would be at our location within five minutes. We spotted a crowd of lads moving about under the bridge and it was not long until the bricks started to fly. They were bouncing all over the Warrior and we were doing our best to keep our eyes on them to try and spot the petrol bombers. A bottle flew through the air and smashed on the Warrior splashing its petrol over the vehicle and us. A few more hit us soaking the Warrior and our combats. I grabbed our FRG and loaded a plastic bullet into it and placed it in the aim ready to fire. What they were doing was soaking the Warrior with unlit petrol bombs. Once the Warrior was soaked, they would hit us with a lit petrol bomb turning us into a moving fireball.

We all scanned the best we could with all the bricks still raining down on us. I spotted a lad with a lit petrol bomb, so I took aim and fired just missing him, but he dropped the petrol bomb in fright causing the ground around him to set on fire. I reloaded as the 2IC spotted another and I took aim and fired. The round flew through the air and hit the lad in the shoulder, but the petrol bomb was already on the way. We watched in slow motion as it flew towards us, missing by inches and flying over the top of us before exploding behind us. The OC got on the radio and told us to get out of there. We did not need telling twice and the driver put his foot down and the Warrior moved back as Three Platoon went past us with all the lads laughing at us getting bricked and petrol-bombed.

We were about 50m back when we spotted a young lad about three years old running towards us with a small brick in his hand. He kept on running the best his little body could go until he got 20m away from the Warrior and lobbed his brick. We all fell about laughing as the brick carried for about a metre, bouncing off a passing car. He turned and ran back to the crowd of youths where he was greeted to a hero's welcome. I was not laughing for long as a brick smashed into my face leaving me with a nice little graze and red mist. The 2IC laughed as I shouted at the fucker.

We got the word to start moving back and we set off first with the OC's Warrior second and the two 24 call signs next. We were looking back as we saw the last Warriors get hit with a petrol bomb that landed at the driver's hatch. Lance Corporal Jordon, who we called Katie, was sitting there when his whole compartment was filled with flames. He jumped up and got out of his hatch at the same time the commander jumped out with the fire extinguisher and fired it towards the flames. Katie was lucky and got away with only a slight burn to his cheek, his face was all black from the smoke. We pushed on with Two Platoon and returned to the COB before moving to the tank park and closed down. The 2IC and I were covered in petrol and stunk. It had been a lucky patrol once again.

In the afternoon we noticed that Op Minimise was on, and I went to the ops room to see what had happening. They told me that Sergeant Wayne Rees of the QRL had been killed on operations up in Maysan

Province due to a traffic accident in his CVRT. It was a shame and another life lost in this place. After our company O Group, I caught up with a bit of sleep with an early night.

The next day we had the ranges and mounted up and moved out. When we got on the range, we got the Warriors weapons done first by firing the 30mm cannons and the 7.62mm chain guns. With the Warriors weapons completed we moved onto the small arms weapons and fired our rifles and light machine guns. Frank was making this a good day for the lads and also had set up the 51mm mortar and the under slung grenade launchers. With all the weapon systems done we left the locals to pick up the brass and made the short trip back to the COB.

When we got back in, we had lunch, and the OC called all the commanders together and told us we had a strike, search, and cordon operation the following night and to get all the equipment sorted out as battalion orders were going to be at 2100hrs. We grafted all afternoon and had our evening meal and then attended the orders. They told us that we were going to conduct a strike, search, and cordon operation in Basra City the following night and that the operation was called Op Cairo. Three Platoon were to assist Egypt Squadron by clearing and securing Green 19 to the bridge just before Green 18. Arnhem Company was to escort C Company into the strike and then to provide close protection as they carried out the strike and search. We finished the orders and left the commanders to their rock drills and went and grabbed a brew before hitting the sack and getting some sleep.

The next day was taken up with rehearsals and the platoon sergeants carrying out their final checks. Once they were happy, they gave me the nod and I informed the OC that we were good to go. We had our company O Group, and the OC went over the plan to ensure that everyone was happy. With the O Group out of the way we had our evening meal, and I used the phone to let the family know that I was fine and that I loved them. We moved to the tank park just before nine, where we booted up the radios and mounted up.

We watched from our turret as Three Platoon left with the tanks. The tanks were massive and the ground shook as they drove past with their powerful 120mm main guns. With all the tanks and Three Platoon out of the tank park we headed to the front gate where we parked up leaving enough room for C Company Snatches in the middle. The tanks and Three Platoon Warriors left the front gate. They pushed over the A Pod Bridge and onto Green 19 with Three Platoon leading. The patrol stopped short of the junction at Green 19 and the lads of the first Warrior got out and cleared the junction. After it was cleared, they mounted up and moved off towards Green 18. Back at the front gate of the COB, the Op Rooms informed us that Green 19 was clear and for us to move forward.

The lead call sign of Three Platoon was the platoon commander's Warrior and he stopped just after the bridge at Green 18 and got his dismounts out as protection as the area was well known for attacks from the insurgents. Once on the ground the boys started to clear the area before taking up fire positions. The young Lance Corporal who was the team commander was moving just to the front of the Warrior when he spotted a wire leading to a mound of rubbish 20m to his front. He told all his lads to go firm and went onto one knee and started to look through his weapon sight. He confirmed what he saw and then informed his platoon commander who confirmed it with the Warrior's sights before informing the squadron OC who passed the information onto the ops room.

The CO told the ops room to task ATOs (Ammunition Tech Officers), and the strike team was told to move no further forwards than the bridge. We moved into fire positions and the gunners in the turret kept watch as the ATO team moved through us and onto the location of the possible IED. ATO were the team we called for when we had possible bombs or unexploded devices. When he got to the lead Warrior call sign he got out and got a brief of the team and platoon commander about what they seen and asked them to draw a diagram. He then moved forward as close as he could and carried out an inspection. This was not easy when you were on the ground in Basra City as the insurgents were always trying to stop you doing your work. The threat of attack from RPGs and small arms in this location was high. He made his assessment and moved back and said he was going to blow it, due to the high level of insurgent activity around the area. He had it all set up and gave the count down: '5, 4, 3, 2, 1'. There was a small bang as the controlled explosion went off. He moved forward and inspected the device before declaring it safe and placing it in the back of his truck for further inspection on his return to the COB. We got the all clear to move over the radio as the area was now safe.

We move off at speed and passed the tanks at the junction at Green 19 before moving onto the area of the exploded IED and past Three Platoon's Warriors. We turned left and moved to the area of the target house and Arnhem Company Warriors moved into position as C Company struck the target house. Within 20 minutes the search was completed, and the strike team mounted up with three detainees and a small amount of munitions. We moved off and just before we got to Green 19 there was a bang as an RPG struck the side of one of Two Platoon Warriors. The lads inside were not hurt, and the patrol pushed on with a number of tracer rounds flying over the Warriors. We continued and pushed past the tanks who were returning fire with their 7.62mm machine guns. Once back in the COB we unloaded all our weapons and moved back to the tank park. After the post patrol admin was completed, we grabbed a bacon buttie before getting some sleep. We had only been sleeping for an hour when we rolled of our beds as the indirect fire alarm went off. The insurgents fired three rockets which exploded all around us. After 20 minutes the all clear was sounded and we climbed back into bed and fell into a deep sleep.

The next day we got up in the afternoon and Two Platoon and Three Platoon got told they would be out that night on counter indirect fire patrols. One Platoon was taking over guards. The short time we had, was spent on getting the platoons sorted for their night patrols. With the company O Group out the way we had our evening meal and the patrols deployed. They both went well and both platoons managed not to get contacted and both return safe. The next day was a maintenance day and was spent changing tracks on the Warriors. This was a real pain in the arse, you had to break the track then chip away the stone at the bolts before removing the track pads and replacing them with new ones. With the tracks out of the way we moved back to camp where Three Platoon were manning the guard and I completed all the shit stuff like returns and paperwork. After the evening meal we were hit with five rockets of IDF. The next few days were spent with the lads manning the guards and also, we got our wish as loads of piles of stone bricks started to get dropped off around camp.

We got briefed up that we were to brick around our bed spaces three bricks high (knee high) to give us some protection from the rockets that were flying in most days. Lee, Mogger, and Shelly were all away on operations so me, Paul, and Frank set about building up the bed spaces in our tent. We had some bricks about 10m from our tent which had been dropped off on a pallet. The bricks looked like breeze blocks but were made of high-density concrete. We were going to work together and do the tent bed space by bed space but first we had to lift all the pallets that we had put down to stop the flooding. We got all the pallets out and started to get the bricks and build them up. They were heavy as fuck, and it took the three of us all night to complete the tent. We were glad when they were completed as we had the protection that we had been asking for for so long. We called them coffins and we got told that sometime in the future we would be issued lids to add to the protection. The rain was still a pain in the arse with most of the tents flooded. The tank park was the worst with the Warriors and tanks making a real mess and making your boots dead heavy with all the sticky mud as it stuck to them.

On 13 January we got up and did some work on the Warriors. In the afternoon, the RSM got all the CSMs together and told us to get everyone on parade. We sent the message out and within

10 minutes the whole Battle Group had formed a hollow square. The RSM came out and brought everyone to attention as the CO came out and informed us that the Regiment had lost its third member in action. We got told that Kingsman Alex Green of Chindit Company had been shot by a sniper while escorting a convoy out of the city and he had died from his wounds on arriving at the field hospital. We got told that Op Minimise was now in place and that a short service would be held the next day and his repatriation would take place on Wednesday. We got up the next day and carried on with the normal stuff in camp. In the afternoon we had a service for Alex with the Padre saying a few words.

On 15 January we handed over the guards to C Company and One Platoon got warned off for a city patrol. The platoon commander got the platoon sergeant briefed up and he set about planning the orders. The platoon sergeant from One Platoon was a lad called Ray who had just come back from the UK where his wife had just given birth to their second child. It was hard for him leaving his young wife to carry on back home with a new baby and their first child. Ray was a good Sergeant who was well respected, but he never got on with his platoon commander which made it hard at times. We had our company O Group, and One Platoon did their orders and I booked them an early breakfast as they were leaving early the next day.

They got up at 0500hrs and had their breakfast before mounting up and moving to Brigade HQ to pick up the Brigade Commander. They had to take him to the OSB where he was due to meet an Iraqi officer to talk about the handover of the Old State Building to a local Iraqi Army unit. They moved out and down the MSR into the city. The local morning traffic was not as it busiest and the patrol got through the city with ease and entered the OSB. The Brigade Commander disappeared inside as the base was hit with a number of mortar rounds. With the base being so small every mortar that landed inside the wire was lethal and if you got caught in the open you could see the flash of the explosion every time. With the indirect fire attack finished the lads moved from their Warriors and moved to the safety of the building. After a few hours, the meeting was completed, and One Platoon moved outside and mounted up. As they were mounting up there was a flash that caught some of the lads' eyes over to their right. An RPG that had been fired at the base had managed to clear the fence and smashed and exploded by an old wall.

The platoon was mounted up ready to go when the Brigade Commander came out and climbed in his Warrior. He told one of the top cover to jump down and took his place on the back of the Warrior. Here he was, a Brigadier and the second highest rank the British Army had in Iraq, doing the job of a Kingsman, but the lads loved it as it showed that he was willing to do the dangerous stuff as well as them. The patrol left the OSB and moved through the city before entering the COB without any more contacts.

Back in Ladysmith Lines C Company got warned off for another run up to Camp Condor to help out the QRL. They were going to be doing it in their Snatches and would need a platoon of Warriors for the patrol. Three Platoon got warned off and they got told that the patrol would be leaving in a couple of days. They set about getting everything ready and got told that their orders would be at 1000hrs the next day. We got up the next day and Three Platoon attended their orders for the resupply mission. I went off to the office for the morning and completed the weekly returns. In the afternoon I went for a run with the 2IC and Frank before finishing off in the gym. After a quick shower I got my best combats on and attended the repatriation of Alex Green as we sent yet another one of our boys home. We had our company O Group and evening meal before hitting the sack after a DVD. In the middle of the night, we were woken up again as we were hit with four rockets of indirect fire.

We got up and Three Platoon's sergeant completed his final checks for his platoon's deployment. He was a tall lad called John who I had known for a long time. He was a good SNCO, who knew his job well. He also had a new baby which had been born during his tour, leaving his girlfriend at home alone to deal with the baby. Once he had completed his checks Three Platoon were ready, and they got some sleep as they were due to leave early the next day.

Three Platoon got up and moved up to the tank park at 0500hrs and mounted up and moved to the front gate. Once there, the Snatches of C Company were front and rear of the admin vehicles and Three Platoon moved to the front as they were leading the patrol. They moved out and headed west along the MSR before turning right and heading north through the oil fields. As the patrol reached the town of Al Medina they turned left and went around the outside of the town. The lead Warrior stopped short of the bridge and carried out a VP check. The lads dismounted and moved up either side of the bridge. When they were 50m into the clearance, one of the Kingsman stopped the patrol and dropped to one knee to check a breeze block by the side of the road 20m to his front.

He spotted that there was a fire extinguisher inside of the breeze block with wire coming out the back of it. He reported the possible IED to his platoon commander who radioed it through to C Company OC who informed the ops room who then tasked ATO. ATO was dropped off by helicopter and moved forward to where he could see the IED and carried out a controlled explosion. There was a small bang as the device was made safe. ATO got back onto the helicopter and the patrol continued until it reached Camp Condor, where they handed over the kit to the QRL.

The QRL had troops based in the desert all the time and helped with the policing of the Iraq and Iran border. After a few hours of sleep the patrol headed out of Camp Condor and started the journey back. Within a few hours they reached the town of Al Quarna and Three Platoon dismounted and cleared the main junction that the patrol had to move through. It was a cold morning and the lads edged forward with their breath hanging in the cold air. As they came to the end of the check the platoon commander shouted for the lads to mount back up. As the lads ran towards the Warrior the morning silence was broken by the sound of small arms fire and the tracers bullets flying as the patrol came under machine-gun fire.

The platoon commander spun around looking for the firing point to try and put some covering fire to cover the lads trying to get back in the Warrior. The next thing he knew there were bullets bouncing all around him as the insurgents aimed onto his position. He dropped into his turret as the back door shut with the shout from the back that they were all mounted up and no one was hit. The firing stopped from the insurgents as the other Warriors moved up and dominated the areas with the turrets moving left and right scanning the ground looking for the firing point. The firing point was not located and Three Platoon stayed in position as the rest of the patrol pushed through and on towards Al Medina.

The rest of the patrol went well with only one of the Snatches breaking down before they manage to reach the COB. As Three Platoon were on the way back the rest of the company was woken from their sleep as the COB was hit with four rockets of indirect fire. Three Platoon got back at mid-morning and after some food and a shower they hit the sack for the rest of the day.

It was now 20 January, and the rest of the company only had a few short tasks of supporting convoys from SLB to the COB as the camp was due to be handed over to the Iraqi Army in a few weeks. It went without any fuss and by 1800hrs the whole company was safely back in Ladysmith Lines. We re-cocked so all the Warriors were good to go and grabbed some sleep. We were woken the next day with a single rocket of indirect fire that exploded in the camp. Two Platoon got told that they were out that night on a counter-indirect fire patrol and the rest of the company were just on standby.

In the afternoon we noticed that Op Minimise was in place again. We got informed that a young lad from 2 Rifles had died when an IED went off in the city. Private Michael Tench was killed as his Warrior patrol was hit by a massive explosion, killing him and injuring four other members of the patrol. He was only 18 years old and had been in the army less than two years.

Two Platoon's patrol deployed out for their patrol which went well, and they returned to the COB without any contacts. The next few days were pretty quiet by Iraqi standards. On 23 January we got hit with four rockets of indirect fire which all exploded in the COB near the runway.

After the attack, we again got crashed out as the insurgents were spotted moving into a house not far from the Shatt Hotel. We mounted up and moved to the front gate ready to move. We had been there for 30 minutes when we got told to stand down as Basra City north troops were dealing with it. We moved back to camp and closed down our Warriors.

On the 25th we took back over guards and handed over one-hour and three-hour notice to move to Blenheim Company. We took over guards at midday and the first things thing the lads had to do was take cover as we were hit with a single rocket of indirect fire. Again, it landed near the A1 village that was starting to get the nickname of 'Rocket Alley'. The following evening, we were hit with four rockets from the insurgents.

On 27 January we got up and the lads went to the tank park to work on the Warriors, I went to the office and did the shitty paperwork that I hated. In the afternoon me and Carl our CQMS went to the A1 village for a milkshake and a look around the shops. He picked me up in a Land Rover and we drove the short trip and parked up. We had a look around the shops where I got a couple of DVDs for the kids and some smokes for the wife. We then headed over to the Effie where we dropped our body armour and helmets at the front door and grabbed a couple of milkshakes and a burger.

We sat down and started to watch Sky Sports News when we heard the whistle of a rocket fly in. There was no time to grab our stuff by the door, so we just hit the floor and hoped for the best. The explosion was loud but was behind a protection wall. We lay there as the second whistled in and exploded again. After the all clear we got up and got another milkshake. Me and Carl looked at each other and raised our eyebrows. The troops around the A1 village might not go on the ground but they still had it hard at times because the insurgents were hitting their camps time and time again. After our milkshakes, we headed over for a haircut and came out again looking like John and Paul of the Beatles. I posted the fags and DVDs home before we headed back to camp.

Over the next few days, we handed over guards and the platoons carried out a few night patrols to try and counter the indirect fire attacks. It never worked as the insurgents hit us time and time again with four rockets on 29 January and four more on the 30th. We were pretty lucky in the COB compared to the troops in the Shatt Hotel, OSB and Basra Palace when it came to indirect fire. We got hit with a lot of attacks in the COB and the rockets the insurgents were firing were bigger rockets than the smaller mortars the other troops were getting in the other bases. The different was the COB was massive and it was a case of miss or hit by the insurgents, you could get attacked in the COB and you would not know where it was. In the other locations when they got hit it was close every time. But at the same time, we lived in tents while most of them were in buildings, so it was a case of six of one, half a dozen of the other.

Home to the UK for Leave

January 31st was a good day for me and nine others from the company. We were flying home for two weeks' leave. I got up and did the handover to Frank who was standing in for me when I was away. Frank was an old Guardsmen who had joined the Small Arms School Corps a few years back and been attached to us as Arnhem Company Warrior CSM. He had a massive amount of knowledge on the Warriors and their weapons.

I then moved to the cookhouse where we got a brief on the journey and what to do in two weeks' time on the route back. Just like the

British Army: we were not even at home yet and they were briefing us on the trip back. After the brief we had all our paperwork checked and then got told to be at the guard room for 2000hrs for transport to the air terminal.

After the brief I got told to report to the CO's office where I had a chat with the CO as he was leaving during my leave. As well as being one of his CSMs I had also been his Recce Platoon 2IC during the first part of his command. He was a good CO who was moving on to bigger things. The day dragged but it was soon 2000hrs and we all met at the guardroom where we boarded the coach to the air terminal. At the air terminal they checked all our bags to ensure we were not taking anything home like weapons and grenades (you would be surprised what some people would do). We checked in and moved to the departure lounge and got told that our flight to Qatar was leaving Basra airport at 0030hrs.

It was just before midnight when the insurgents thought they would send us off with a bang as they fired a single rocket of indirect fire. We boarded our C-130 for the short journey to Qatar where we moved to the waiting room and again filled ourselves with butties, sweets and cans of pop from our American friends. After a short while we moved onto our charted flight and completed the journey to Teesside Airport.

We got off and there were a few families waiting to pick up their loved ones. We walked through the airport in our desert combats. I only had a daysack, so I walked straight through and was met by my wife Lyn and my little girl Kirsty. It was 0730hrs when we got to the car, and we drove Kirsty to school in Richmond and I went home. It was weird being at home with no threat of indirect fire and walking around not carrying your helmet and body armour everywhere you went. But I planned to enjoy it and try not to think too much of the shithole I had left. This turned out to be easier said than done.

4

FEBRUARY 2007

The Work Continues No Matter Who is Away

Life in Arnhem Company carried on no matter who was on leave, and the company still had the tasks of guards to carry out. They still had four days of guard duties at the start of the month and a lot of rain to deal with. The mud was a real pain in the arse and the flooding of the tents was a complete nightmare.

Back in England I was finding it hard not to think about the lads back in Iraq and I would often find myself checking Teletext and Sky News. It was also hard because you could not tell your family everything that was going on over there, as you did not want them to worry when you went back. With Lyn and the kids being at work and at school, it also gave me a lot of time to think and reflect. I tried not to do this too much, as I knew I would overthink it and it was not the reason I was at home. I was there to see my family and have some respite, so that what I tried to do.

It was a quiet start to February back in Iraq with no indirect fire attacks until the fourth day. The company were on guards when we got hit with the first that whistled through the air and exploded. We were hit with five more rockets in that attack that exploded a little further away.

On the morning of 5 February, they hit us with three more rockets. We handed over the guards to Egypt Squadron and Three Platoon were warned off for an admin run to the Shatt Hotel Base. They left and moved down to the Shatt and dropped off the package and made the short trip back to the COB.

In the afternoon we saw that Op Minimise was on and started to hear about an IED attack on our Chindit Company in the City. Around 1500hrs the RSM got the Battle Group on parade again and we knew what was coming. The CO came out and informed us that Second Lieutenant Jonathan Carlos Bracho-Cooke had died as a result of injuries sustained by an IED attack in the Sarraji District of the city. He was a talented young officer aged 24 and was the battalion's fourth fatality since the start of Op Telic 9.

Back in the UK, I was sitting at home flicking through the channels when a Sky News report flashed up stating that a British solider had been killed when his Warrior patrol got hit by an IED. I started to worry as the only two units to have Warriors in Iraq were 2 Lancs and the Staffords. I had 120 soldiers back in Iraq and wanted to know if everyone was all right. I tried to phone Carl but his phone was turned off so I sent a few people a text to see if they could tell me what had happened. I sat there for two hours worrying like mad about the company back in Iraq until Carl managed to send me a text saying that the lads were all right, and it was one of Chindit Company. I felt the sadness as losing one of ours and then it hit me. I was worrying about my soldiers after the newsflash. What was it like for the families with their loved ones over there. It must of being a complete nightmare for our families and loved one back at home. They truly were the unsung heroes

The next day the Battle Group got together, and the Padre said a few words and some prayers for Mr Bracho-Cooke and his family. The COB got hit with three rockets of indirect fire in the evening that rained in and exploded near the welfare village. The next few days were quiet with only one patrol going out to try and counter the indirect fire teams.

On the morning of 9 February, the OC, 2iC and Frank were in the company office and Frank was completing the weekly returns when the alarm went off for an indirect fire attack. They all hit the floor as the first rocket rained in and exploded. It landed near Camp C not far from our camp. It was followed up with three more rockets. After the all clear was sounded the OC was called away for a meeting with the CO, when he returned, he asked Frank to get all the platoon commanders together and once they had all arrived, he warned them all off that the battalion was taking part in a strike and search operation in a couple of days and to start getting the admin sorted straight away. The platoon commanders went into the planning with the OC and the platoon sergeants set about getting the lads in order.

In the afternoon we saw that Op Minimise was on again and we started to hear that another British soldier had been killed on the edge of Basra City. At the company O Group that night the OC told everyone that Private Luke Daniel Simpson of the 1st Battalion, The Yorkshire Regiment had died due to injuries he received when his Snatch patrol got hit with an IED. He also told everyone that the battalion orders would be at 1400hrs the next day and that all commanders were to attend. At the company O Group, we got informed that a couple of lads from Egypt Squadron had been seriously hurt in a mortar attack in Basra Palace and they had been flown out to the field hospital in the COB and after being in the operating theatre all day it was decided that they would be flown back to the UK to continue their recovery. After the O Group the COB got hit with a single rocket of indirect fire from the insurgents that exploded with no one getting injured.

Back in the UK I was sitting with Lyn when a newsflash pops up on Sky News stating that another British soldier had been killed in Iraq. It was followed by video footage of the bomb site. It was upsetting to watch as they showed medics trying to save the lad's life and another getting carried to the IRT helicopter holding his injured arm. I could see the Snatches in the video, so I had a good idea that Arnhem Company was not involved. I looked on with great sadness as another brave lad lost the battle to stay alive. That was the trouble with Sky News at times, it did its job too well with too much detail getting out too quickly. Lyn looked at me and she could see the sadness in my eyes. She never said anything, but just touched my arm before making a cup of tea.

The next day the company got woken up by one rocket the insurgents decided to lob into the COB and after the all clear was sounded they carried out an Op Wide Awake. They then went to the tank park to ensure that all the Warriors were good to go before attending the Battalion Orders at 1400hrs. All the commanders took their seats, and they began the orders. The operation was going to be a strike and search operation happening on the evening of 11 February called Operation Saddlers. The operation was taking place in the area of Green 18 and Yellow 3 and C Company would be striking the target house. Three Platoon and Egypt Squadron would be securing and clearing the route from Green 19 and Green 18, with Arnhem Company coming in after C Company to securing the target area as their close protection. With the orders completed everyone got their evening meal and grabbed an early night before the next day's operation.

The company carried out rehearsals the next day before the final checks were done by the platoons. At the company O Group, the OC checked that everyone was happy with the operation and then informed One Platoon and Three Platoon that after the patrol they would be working with the Staffords down at the Shatt Hotel and to ensure they deployed with their kit as they would move straight there after the operation. The lads had a few hours to chill before moving to the tank park at 2300hrs.

It was the first time that the company would be deploying without the CSM and Ste Tabbs our fleet manager was stepping up and deploying as the 2IC gunner. Steve was a Warrior expert as well as being the company fleet manager who looked after the company fleet. He was also a Warrior weapons instructor. He was one of the more mature lads in the company who would often offer his help and give his advice whether you wanted it or not. He was a good lad, even if he was the grumpiest twat in the company. The lads booted the radios up and the final checks were completed. Three Platoon once again left the tank park first with Egypt Squadron and they were quickly followed by Arnhem Company Warriors. When they got to the gate, they married up with C Company Snatches and once in the correct order everyone was good to go.

The first to leave was Three Platoon and the tanks and they pushed out the front gate and passed A Pod Bridge and on through the checkpoint. At the junction at Green 19, Three Platoon got out and cleared it before taking up fire positions at Green 18.

With the area secure C Company left and pushed up to Green 19, followed on by Arnhem Company. The Company had to stop at the Bridge due to a Warrior having comms trouble, but they soon got it sorted and got moving. As C Company Snatches got to Green 18 the insurgents were waiting in ambush and the night exploded with an IED going off with a blinding flash followed by a cloud of smoke that hung in the cold night air. This was closely followed by a number of RPG warheads flying through the air missing their targets by inches. The tracer was flying and bouncing off everything as Arnhem Company pushed past Green 19 and headed past the junction. As they were pushing past Green 19 the ops room were on the radio warning that there was a heat source just past the junction and for the Warriors to approach with caution.

It was too late and call sign 22 with Two Platoon Warrior sergeant in command was hit with a massive explosion. The Warrior rocked to the left as pieces of the Warrior flew through the air as the explosion ripped into it. People on the ground were trying to get on the net to try and see if they were all right but the ops room was still hogging it with their warning. Once they finally shut up, the Warrior sergeant came on the net and said there were no casualties, but the Warrior had damage to its running gear and was going nowhere. Egypt Squadron said they would recover it and the company pushed on to help C Company. Once the company had caught up with the Snatches, they escorted them out of the contact and onto the target house.

At Green 18 the company was getting hit with a lot of small arms fire and the tracer was popping off the Warriors and flying through the air. The lead Warrior was call sign 20 and it was leading the convoy down the road when it got hit with an RPG warhead that bounced of the turret and never exploded. The next one did, and the commander ducked as the WHOOSH of the warhead flew over his head, missing him by inches and exploding behind him on the face of a building. Company HQ Warriors were following behind the Snatches but were finding it hard with the turret weapons due to the confined space of the city.

The Warriors were travelling at speed when one of the corporals (Faz) who was in charge of the company signals, fired five rounds from his rifle at an insurgent with an RPG. The rounds bounced all around the insurgent who dropped the launcher and ran off, not able to get the round off. The strike team moved out of the area around Green 18 and pushed on towards the target building. At the target house the strike team struck, and Arnhem Company, again went into fire positions to offer the best protection they could.

As the strike was ongoing the tanks and Three Platoon stayed in position as the forward teams would be using the same route back to the COB. Three Platoon commander was out of his turret and ensuring all the lads were in good fire positions as they were still getting fired at with RPGs and small arms. After he had checked their positions, he moved ahead of his Warrior and took up a fire position. He had only been there for a few seconds when one of his corporals Dean started shouting at him 'MOVE GET OUT OF THERE.' He looked at the lad and shouted back 'WHO ARE YOU SHOUTING AT.' The lad replied, 'FUCKING MOVE WILL YOU.' Pissed off with the way the lad was shouting at him he left his position and marched up to the lad to give him a piece of his mind. As he got there, he asked the lad what his fucking problem was. The lad cut him short and pointed out that he was sitting on top of an IED. He blushed as he said thanks and got into his turret and reported the IED to the ops room. With the strike team due to use the route in minutes he was told to disrupt the device with the weapons of the Warrior. He ordered his gunner to fire his chain gun at the IED. The gunner placed his sights onto the device and selected the chain gun and fired ninety rounds of 7.62mm causing it to part explode with a small puff of smoke.

Back at the target house the strike teams had found a small amount of munitions and were arresting one male suspect. Outside a few of the lads had fired their rifles trying to keep the insurgents heads down as they were trying to keep the area as secure as they could. The HQ Warriors were around the target house when call sign Zero Charlie, spotted two insurgents by a wall armed with an RPG. The 2IC gave the order and Steve steadied the sights onto the target. 'BOOM.' It was too late, and the RPG warhead flew towards the recovery Warrior and exploded just short, covering the Warrior and its crew in dirt and stones. Steve had selected auto on his 30mm cannon, 'BANG, BANG, BANG', the whole place shook as the three rounds turned what was a wall into a dust pile including anything that was behind it.

With the search completed the lads all mounted back up and Two Platoon moved off with the platoon commander Warrior leading. As they left the target street there was a blinding flash as an IED exploded just in front of the lead Warrior. The insurgents were waiting and as the lead Warrior drove through the smoke of the IED like something from a Hollywood production they were met with two RPG warheads and tracer gunfire. The Warrior did its job protecting its crew from the insurgents' deadly fire.

The commander and gunner of call sign 20 spotted the insurgents who were firing at them, and the gunner did not need telling what to do. The two insurgents were firing from a low wall with the first insurgent holding a rocket launcher and the second holding an AK-47 assault rifle. Two Platoon commander seeing they had a fire position behind a wall told his gunner to select the main armament. The gunner selected the 30mm and steadied his sights onto them. 'BANG'. The Warrior rocked as the deadly 30mm high explosive rounds flew towards its target and exploded smashing the wall and the insurgents to pieces. The gunner was not taking any chances and fired two more round to ensure the threat was destroyed.

Two more insurgents appeared just to the right of the last fire position with AK-47 assault rifles in their shoulders and the AK-47 lit up with flashes as they spat their bullets towards the Warriors. Again, the gunner did not need telling what to do and selected the chain gun and fired a volley of 7.62mm bullets at the two targets. The targets went down as the lead Warrior turned right and headed off towards Green 18. Two Platoon where getting whacked with multiple RPG warheads and small arms fire but they were just pushing on trying to keep the convoy moving.

As the HQ Warriors were leaving the junction of the target house an insurgent appeared 50m in front of their position with an AK-47 and started firing at them. Now this guy was either mad or off his head on drugs taking on two Warrior fighting vehicles with a rifle. Both Frank and Steve steadied their sights and selected their chain guns. The insurgent was cut down as both guns spat their deadly 7.62mm rounds at their target throwing him through the air and dumping him on the ground. The strike group pushed past Green 18 with RPG warheads and small arms tracer rounds flying all over the place.

Once the company were past Green 19, Three Platoon and the tanks were given the order to move back, and they pulled off with small arms fire still bouncing of their Warriors and tanks. One Platoon and Three Platoon headed south towards the Shatt Hotel where they parked up before getting some food and a bit of sleep. Once the rest of the company was back in the COB, they unloaded all their weapons and fuelled up before closing down the Warriors in the tank park and moving back in camp. All the post-operational paperwork was completed and then everyone moved to get some food and a bit of sleep.

In the Shatt Hotel at about 1000hrs One Platoon and Three Platoon got told that the city was going to be closed down for a few days and a

Above: **1.** Carl Gardner CSM Arnhem Coy.

Below: **2.** Zero Charlie – Croz, Ste Tabs, John, Carl, Wes, Flemmo.

Above: **3.** A Warrior and Dismounts on the way to Al Amarah.

Below: **4.** Arnhem after their first contact with the enemy.

Above: **5.** The CSMs, Lee, Carl, Paul, and Skelly.

Below: **6.** Arnhem Search Operation.

Above: **7.** A Warrior Armoured Fighting Vehicle moving out.

Below: **8.** Basra City patrol.

Above: **9.** Wes, Croz, Marti and Sam in the back of Zero Charlie Warrior.

Below: **10.** One Platoon Basra City.

Above: **11.** Prime Mister Tony Blair talking to Carl and Paul.

Left: **12.** Operation Thyme, Christmas and Christmas Day.

Above: **13.** Ready to deploy.

Below: **14.** Everyone taking cover during indirect fire attack Christmas Day.

15. Chris eating breakfast under fire.

Above: **16.** Two Platoon.

Below: **17.** Sgt Graham Hesketh killed in action by an IED.

18. Sgt Graham Hesketh repatriation Basra COB Airfield.

19. Three Platoon Basra City.

Above: **20.** Wes, Marti and Carl, Basra City patrol.

Below: **21.** The Recce Platoon.

Above: **22.** Search operation Basra City.

Below: **23.** CSM Paul Low and that famous snore.

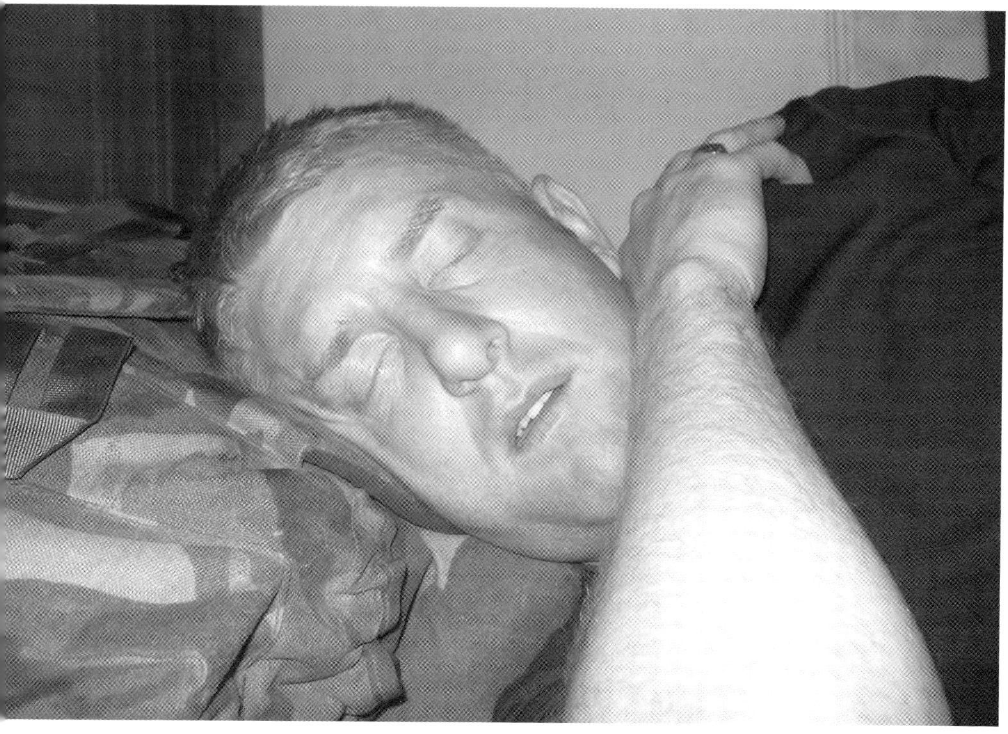

Above: **24.** Patrol Basra City.

Below: **25.** Hot, Hot, Hot.

Above: **26.** Basra JAM Commander.

Below: **27.** Basra JAM Commander KIA.

Above: **28.** Arnhem Company HQ.

Below: **29.** Dusty place.

number of high-profile targets were going to be struck and searched. This was going to happen with permanent patrols on all the main routes leading in and out of the city and they were to be manned by 0700hrs the next morning. The platoon commanders got the lads down to the tank park and they set about ensuring that the Warriors were good to go.

They had been working there for 30 minutes when they heard the first whistle of a mortar round fall in. The explosion was deafening and sent the lads diving for cover all over the place. Three lads from Three Platoon dived into an ISO container and covered themselves with a plastic garden table. What were they thinking, a plastic table! It did the job as the second mortar fell in and exploded 20m away throwing shrapnel and dirt into the ISO container.

The company signal corporal Faz and Tommy, a corporal from One Platoon, jumped into the back of the nearest Warrior as they heard a mortar whistle in. They both landed heavily in the back of the Warrior as the mortar exploded only 15m away, sending its deadly metal in all directions. They hugged onto each other for dear life as the area around them was ripped apart. A few more mortars exploded as the lads took cover under Warriors, in the hatches and even under each other. Once it had finished Faz and Tommy checked each other over to ensure they had no injuries. The three lads in the ISO container kicked the table off only to see that it had pieces of crap stuck in it. The lads all looked at each other and wondered how the hell the company never had any casualties. They quickly finished the vehicle maintenance, and all made the way inside to the safety of the main building.

The next day One Platoon and Three Platoon deployed in the city with One Platoon dominating the area of Green 19 and Three Platoon dominating the area of Red 3 where the police checkpoint was. It was an operation to close down the city and to strike the op insurgent targets. It was called Operation Troy and all the units based in Basra would be involved. The battalion also got warned off for a strike and search operation that they would be taking part in in a couple of days' time.

Back in the UK my time at home was up and I got my desert combats back on and said goodbye to my son Daniel, as Lyn and my little girl Kirsty took me the short 30-minute trip to Teesside Airport. We got there and they came inside and said a tearful goodbye. It was hard for the families and it's never easy saying goodbye knowing that a loved one is off to war. We went through to the departure lounge and laughed as the security made us take our boots off and gave us a complete body search. They said it was the war against terror and they were keeping the country safe. What the fuck did they think we were doing?

We boarded our plane, and it took off completing the trip to Qatar. From there again we boarded a C-130 and were dropped off at Basra air base in the early hours of 14 February. We got back and got into our pits as we got told that we were to be in the briefing tent by 0930hrs for an updated brief on what had been going on while we had been away. We also got introduced to the new CO who had taken over and we had a chat about what the tour had been like so far.

Tell Them to Watch *Black Hawk Down*

I got up bright and early and attended breakfast where all the lads were still telling their war stories from Operation Saddles. It is hard when you have just been on leave, and it is easy to let your head go down. I think most of us would admit that at times like this, we missed home that little bit more and were homesick. The one thing I noticed being back was that the weather had warmed up and it was all of a sudden very warm. I went over to the office and got a brief from Frank, and he gave me all the statements of the lads who had fired. The 2iC said that the OC had to leave early for his leave and that he was acting OC. He also briefed me up on the operation that was taking place that night and he told me that our Warrior was not needed for the operation tonight and asked if I wanted to stand down. I said no and told him I would be a dismount in one of Two Platoon Warriors.

I moved over to the briefing tent and saw Two Platoon commander who stood two of his team commanders down and told me that Wes and I would be in the back of call sign 23. We got our orders and got told that we would be striking a couple of target houses in the Qarmat Ali area of the city. C Company and the Recce Platoon would be doing the strikes with Blenheim Company doing the inner protection. What was left of Arnhem, which was three HQ Warriors and four Warriors of Two Platoon, would be attached to Egypt Squadron tanks covering the route from Green 20 to Green 28 which was just over the other side of Qarmat Ali Bridge.

After the orders we carried out some rehearsal and then had our evening meal. It was killing me being back and my head was wrecked. I phoned home to let them know that I was back safe and sound. I then sorted all my kit out for the patrol and made sure that my weapon was oiled up and good to go. After a few hours chilling out and catching up we moved to the tank park. I went around the lads and did a few checks of their dog tags, first aid kit, gloves, and goggles. Once everyone was good to go, we mounted up and I climbed in the back of the Warrior. We shut the door. The top hatches were open, and the dust was piling in as we drove the short trip to the front gate. In the back of my Warrior was Wes, a corporal from Coy HQ who was always in my Warrior, and Flemmo (who we called Fox's Piss due to his ginger hair) and one of the Kingsmen from One Platoon.

We left the front gate and moved to the junction at Green 19. The first two Warriors who were the platoon commander Warrior and the platoon Warrior sergeant's Warrior cleared the junction and the last two Warriors pushed through and onto Qarmat Ali Bridge. The front Warrior was the platoon sergeant's and the lads got out the back of his Warrior and started to clear the bridge, which was a good 200m long. We were in the second Warrior, so we jumped up on top cover to cover the lads doing the search.

The two Warriors followed the lads up to the bridge and then the night exploded with tracer as we were hit with small arms fire from about six different positions in an aggressive ambush. The tracer started flying over our Warrior and the lads on the bridge had to take cover as the insurgents tried to cut us down in their killing zone with their deadly fire. The gunner in our Warrior spotted one of the firer's positions and selected his chain gun. He steadied the sights onto the insurgents and opened fire with 50 rounds ripping apart the insurgents' position. The lads on the bridge carried on pushing forward with the tracer rounds flying everywhere.

Back in the second Warrior me, Wes and Flemmo were in fire positions on top cover in the back. We had tracer rounds flying past us when Wes spotted a firing point. He steadied his weapon and pulled the trigger and fired twenty rounds at the gunmen. The rounds found their target. At the same time, I felt a burning sensation in my neck that knocked me off my feet and threw me into the back of the Warrior. The lads jumped down shouting 'THE CSM HIT' over the radio. I got up and sat back as Wes got his torch on and checked my neck. I was not hit by a bullet, just a burning empty case from Wes's rifle that left a small burn.

We all jumped back up as the lads doing the check were still moving on under heavy small arms fire. We got up just as the gunner laid his sights onto another insurgents position. He started firing his chain gun when we heard him shout 'STOPPAGE.' He switched straight away to the main armament and stamped on the firing pedal. 'BANG, BANG, BANG', the Warrior unloaded three rounds of high explosive that smashed into the position, taking away the threat.

The three of us were back on top cover and the night sky was alight with tracer and the odd RPG warhead. We got fired at from about four different positions and the two Warriors and the lads doing the check were under heavy fire with tracer bouncing everywhere.

Me, Wes and Flemmo all spotted the flashes from the insurgents. We steadied our sight onto a different position. I fired first, aiming at two insurgents that had taken cover on a rooftop. They were standing firing at us with their weapons in the shoulder and the sparks flying from their weapons. I got my sights onto the first insurgent and pulled the trigger and watched as my rounds hit him, causing him to fall off the roof. I quickly got my sights onto the second and was about to pull the trigger when he jumped to one side and disappeared. Wes spotted two flashes that were firing from a third-floor window. He fired his remaining ten rounds at the position, hitting his target, before dropping down and changing his empty magazine with a new fully loaded one. Flemmo fired his rifle at a position hitting just to the right and causing dust to splatter over the insurgents' position and forcing them to go to ground.

By the time everyone had finished firing we had moved over the bridge and the four lads from the first Warrior got back in. They had all showed great courage and bravery to keep going under the immense amount of gunfire that they had been subjected to. The commander Corporal Wild would later be awarded with a MID (Mentioned in Despatches) for the team's bravery.

Once we were over the bridge, we took up fire positions with the Warriors and were joined by the other two Warriors of Two Platoon and the four tanks. Our two Warriors and the two Challenger tanks took the east side of the bridge and the other two Warriors, and two tanks took the west side.

Call sign Zero Charlie Warrior and the recovery Warrior moved over the bridge where they were also fired at by RPG warheads and small arms fire before they joined the platoon commander's Warrior on the western side. As they took up a fire position an insurgent appeared with an RPG launcher on his shoulder from behind wall 50m to their front. He was not quick enough to fire as Frank cut him down with 100 rounds of 7.62mm from his chain gun with deadly effect.

Two Platoon dismounts at this time had already got out of their Warriors and were in fire positions to try and offer the best protection they could. Corporal Baldwin's team had just got out of the platoon commander's Warrior when their position came under small arms fire. The team spotted the gunman and returned fire, suppressing the insurgent's position.

Back at our Warrior, I told the commander I was going on the ground with Wes and that Flemmo was staying on top cover to protect the back of the Warrior and to cover us. I moved around and checked the lad's positions as there was still a lot of tracer flying all over the place. On the other side of the road the night lit up as two gunmen opened fire on Two Platoon commander's Warrior with an RPG and small arms. The RPG warhead shot over his position, and we all had to dive for cover as the tracer flew past us. The gunner in the Warrior was ready and fired eighty rounds from his chain gun, hose piping his fire from one position to the other hitting both insurgents.

At the same time call sign Zero Charlie spotted four insurgents attacking their position and firing at them from behind a wall. The 2iC told Frank to hit them with the main armament. He did by whacking them with six rounds of high explosive on automatic. The wall where the insurgents were blown to pieces. Two of the insurgents who were not hit tried to move to a different position but Marti on top cover and Frank spotted them and they both engaged them with rifle fire, stopping them in their tracks.

Back on the other side Wes and I met up with Corporal Wild and was saying how well he had done to clear the bridge under fire when we heard a bang over to our left. We watched in slow motion as the RPG warhead flew down the street with the orange glow of its burner pushing it in our direction. It flew just over our heads with a massive WHOOSH as it went past and exploded somewhere behind us. We moved fast to the back of the Warrior as the RPG was quickly followed up with a burst of gunfire. The crew in call sign 23 returned fire at the position with their chain gun and the tanks fired their GPMGs from the top of their turrets.

At the back of the Warrior, I told Wes and the lads to follow me as I had seen the firing point. We ran 20m to our right and started to move down an alleyway. As we moved down the alleyway for the first time that night it had gone quiet. There was a cold chill on our bodies as the sweat made our combats stick to us. We kept on going until the firing point came into view. I stopped and turned around to give my orders. To my surprise only Wes had followed on and we were on our own.

I moved out ready to fire at the enemy position. My heart was pounding in my head as I broke my cover revealing my location to the insurgents sitting there with their deadly weapons. 'WOOF, WOOF, WOOF,' the place lit up as the enemy's tracer rounds flew past us that close that we felt the wind brush past our faces as they went past. I dropped down onto one knee as I brought my sight into my eye and fired and kept on firing for my life until the working parts of the rifle stay back due to my magazine being empty. Wes was about to step out on my right shoulder, I knew he would be stepping out into the insurgents bullets. I slammed him back into a doorway and we were face to face as the enemy's fire zoomed past us just behind my back. I started smiling as Wes looked at me: 'What the fuck are you smiling for?' We moved back until we were out of sight and just fell back against the wall and looked at each other. 'Fuck me.' Wes said it all. I turned and said to him, 'I don't know if I hit anything but you're right mate, fuck me.' We moved back just as Blenheim Company Warriors were moving off the bridge, I watched in amazement as a mad insurgent ran out 20m in front of the first Warrior with an RPG launcher on his shoulder ready to fire. The Warrior cut him down with its chain gun without even stopping. It was like something from a movie.

As the strike teams went in me and Wes started to move back into the alleyway making our way back to our Warrior. We got told over the radio that a lone gunman (sniper) was spotted down the road ahead of us. We moved up and Wes took up a fire position covering down the road where the gunman was seen. He shouted 'GO' when he was in a fire position to cover me.

I got up and started to run across the road. 'CRACK THUMP' broke the night silence as the sniper fired and the bullet shot across my body and down the road. I tried to jump into cover but ended up falling heavy and smashing my knees down on the rocks on the other side of the road. For the second time that night I heard the shout of 'THE CSM HIT' over the radio by Wes. I moved and looked back at him and shouted with a hint of moaning in my voice. 'No, you dick, I fell.' Wes started laughing as he said, 'Always the fucking drama queen.'

I got up with the pain of the fall running through my legs and got into the kneeling position to cover down the street. I shouted to Wes 'GO' as Wes got up and ran and joined me by my side. He patted me on the shoulder and said, 'Don't worry old man, stick with me and I will get you home.' As we got up and ran towards our Warrior I said to Wes, 'Come on you wanker', and he followed as we got into the back of our Warrior with a cheeky little grin on his face.

A short time later call sign Zero Charlie Warrior started to hear gunfire bouncing off their Warrior. They scanned the ground when Marti in the back shouted, 'WATCH MY TRACER.' He fired and his tracer bullets started to bounce of a wall where the insurgent was. Frank saw this and engaged the insurgent with his chain gun until the threat was gone. It was then call sign 20 Warrior's turn next and the sky lit up as two gunmen opened fire with their AK-47 rifles sending tracer bullets all over their position. Morgi, the gunner in the Warrior, was in no mood to mess around and fired three rounds of 30mm high explosive, wiping the position out.

Back at Green 19 and Red 3, One Platoon and Three Platoon were watching all the fireworks from the battalion's contacts flying all over the place and into the night air. At Red 3 call sign 30 Warrior with the platoon sergeant in the turret spotted two insurgents laying a command wire leading to an IED. The gunner lay onto the insurgents with his sights and fired over thirty rounds stopping the insurgents, hitting one and forcing the other to run away.

Back at Green 27 the strike teams had moved from the target houses where they were detaining several men. We watched as they pulled out of the built-up area and headed over the bridge. We also watched all the Iraqi ambulances coming and going into the firing positions picking up the dead and wounded insurgents. Once the strike teams were clear with Blenheim Company. We got the order to move, and we pulled off and moved over the bridge with the odd round still being fired. As we moved out of the contact area, I looked at my watch. We had been in contact for nearly five hours and the operation had flown past.

We headed back to the COB and unloaded. I got everyone together who had fired and gave the 2iC all the statements and accounts of what we had done. There were lads in the company who needed a new batch of ammo they had been that busy. We went to grab some food and I grabbed some bacon and eggs and sat down with the 2iC, Frank and a few of the lads. We started talking about the night's operation and I said, 'How the hell would you explain what has just happened at home.' Marti turned and looked at me and said, 'Tell them to watch *Black Hawk Down.*' We all looked at him and started nodding.

After our scoff we grabbed a shower and I stood there and watched as the dirt from my body ran off and turned the water a dark murky colour. I dried myself and looked at myself in the mirror and just smiled. I got into bed and turned to Mogger and said, 'Fuck me mate we haven't even been back for 24 hours yet'. He just turned and said, 'Sleep yer dickhead'. Smiling, we fell into a sound sleep, knackered.

I got up the next day and the leave blues were well and truly gone, I walked over to the company office and the 2iC said 'Well you look happier'. He was right, the busy night was just what I needed to get me back into the right frame of mind and set me up for the next few months. The day was spent with paperwork getting completed and the Warriors repaired from all the damage that was caused in the firefights. There were a few slights cracked and some of the BAR armour needed to be replaced. We had our company O Group and evening meal before we all had an early night as the company had a rare night off.

Blenheim Company were out on patrol that night with the Iraqi Special Forces. They had an interesting patrol as the Iraqis had a different set of rules when it came to opening fire. Their patrol was moving through the city when a normal car tried to overtake their patrol only for one of the Iraqis to open fire on the car with thirty rounds from his 50-cal machine gun. Luckily, the man was not hurt but his car was completely fucked.

The next day we got up and One Platoon and Three Platoon returned to the COB as Operation Troy came to an end. It was good to have all the company back in one place and I set about seeing the boys to ensure that everyone was OK. On the morning of 17 February, Two Platoon got warned off that they were going to be attached to Blenheim Company on the following night for a strike and search operation in the city. They made best use of their time and their platoon sergeant, a lad called Matt, set about ensuring that everything was good to go. Matt was in his mid-30s and joined at a later age than most of us. Because of this he had an old head on him that made him stand out. He was particularly good at his job and Two Platoon were lucky to have him.

They had their orders that night and they got told that the strike was happening around the yellows of the city. They would help with the close protection of the striking teams. The next day they got up and carried out rehearsals before they did the final checks on all of their equipment. After their evening meal they got some sleep as they were due down the tank park at about 2300hrs. When they got up, they moved to the tank park and after the radios were sorted, they mounted up and moved to the front gate.

The tanks moved first with One Platoon who were securing the route. When it was secure, Two Platoon moved out and past Green 19 and Green 18 and onto the Yellows before turning into the target street and striking the target house. Once the strike was done, they lifted off the ground without detaining anyone. They were going a different route back and moved to the junction at Yellow 3 as the route was being secured by One Platoon and the tanks. The platoon commander's Warrior was leading and as they moved past Yellow 2 Alpha which was just north of the Shia Flats.

The platoon commander heard a couple of bangs to his left. As he looked around 'WHOOSH, WHOOSH.' The two RPG warheads flew over his turret, missing him and exploding over to his right. The four turrets of the platoon swung over to the left and they started scanning the built-up area looking for the firing point. But it was not seen, and the patrol just kept pushing on out of the area and up to the bridge where they turned right and moved along the side of the river. They went past Camp Warehouse before moving back into the COB. Back in the tank park they closed the Warriors down before grabbing some food and hitting the sack.

They had been in their pits for less than an hour when we all hit the floor as the indirect fire alarm went off. The three rocket fell in and exploded a few hundred metres away. With nobody hurt the all clear was sounded and everyone jumped back into bed.

On 19 February we took back over guards for three days and One Platoon got tasked with a small night patrol to try and counter the indirect fire attacks. Two Platoon took over the guards with Three Platoon on standby. One Platoon's patrol went well without any problems, and they returned to base without being contacted. As they got back in the tank park the insurgent lobbed a single rocket of indirect fire at us that exploded near the airport (bastards, they were fucking toying with us). The next day the 2iC got warned off that Egypt Squadron had been warned off for a trip up to Camp Condor just south of Al Amara. He got told that they would be doing it in

Snatches and that a platoon of Warriors was needed. Once again One Platoon got away with it and Two Platoon were warned off that they would be part of the operation and to start sorting out the admin.

At the company O Group, we got told that after we had handed over the guards in the morning, Three Platoon would be on one hours' notice to move and One Platoon would be on three hours' notice to move. Due to Two Platoon only having three Warriors One Platoon were to hand one over to them for their trip up north. The morning of 21 February the company got up and went to the tank park as we were going to have a maintenance day as we were trying to keep the Warriors on the road as the hot weather was now taking its toll on them. All the bombs, RPGs and bullets were not helping either. We got out of our combat tops to just our t-shirts and set about working on them. Around midday the metal of the Warriors was so hot that we had to wear gloves just to touch it with the burning sun.

After our lunch, the work continued until the indirect fire alarm went off and we all jumped into the back of our Warriors as we were hit with one rocket. With all the work done at the tank park we moved back to camp and had our company O Group. The 2iC told Two Platoon commanders that their orders for the trip up north would be at 1000hrs the next day. They got up and the platoon moved to the briefing tent. It was another Op Octavia escorting supplies up to Al Amara for the QRL. They would be leaving the following morning and travelling through the day, where they would drop the admin vehicles off at Camp Condor. After the orders they did the final checks of the Warriors, and all the vehicles were moved to the hard standing and placed in the correct order. The rest of the company were still on notice to move, and One Platoon took over one-hours and Three Platoon went on standby. With the day completed we had our meeting and evening meal, and I got some time in at the gym before hitting the sack.

The next day the company got up at the normal time and Two Platoon moved to the hard standing and started up their Warriors.

When the convoy was good to go, they moved to the front gate and moved out and got on the MSR going west. They then headed north moving through the oil fields and Al Madina. They moved through Al Qurna without any problems and carried on going north until they got to Camp Condor at around1900hrs. They met up with the QRL and handed over the admin vehicles. Once again after they had fuelled up, they got all the vehicles into one of the old fighter jets bunkers and grabbed some food and a brew before jumping in their sleeping bags for some sleep before the trip back.

They had been sleeping for about an hour when they heard the whistle of the first mortar, as it flew into their position. It exploded close to them with a deafening noise. Everyone covered themselves with their body armour and helmets to try and give themselves some protection. The mortars kept falling in for about 10 minutes all landing within 100m of the bunkers where all the British units were in. The noise was unreal, and the soldiers could feel the ground shaking, with stones and dirt falling on them as the mortars ripped up the ground in the insurgents' deadly attack.

They were hit with twenty-nine rounds of high-explosive mortars during that awful attack and some of the explosions were that loud and scary that some of the lads broke down in tears with the fright. Most of the patrol slept with their body armour and helmets on after that attack but the insurgents must have used up all their ammunition as they never got attacked any more that night. At about 0500hrs in the morning, they got up and all mounted their vehicles, they turned their engines on and moved out.

You could feel the cold air rushing past your face as the Warriors moved off from Camp Condor and headed south towards Al Qurna. After a few hours, the first Warrior of Two Platoon had reached the built-up area of Al Qurna. It was still early morning and the town's build-up of traffic was still not busy. The Warriors pushed through the town and just before they came to the main bridge, 'BOOOM', there was a massive explosion that ripped through the morning silence.

The bomb had gone off a few metres in front of the lead Warrior and the blinding flash was soon replaced with a cloud of smoke that hung in the morning air.

Undamaged, the Warriors pushed on as an RPG warhead flew across the sky passing in between the first and second Warrior. The turrets were scanning everywhere but no firing points or insurgents were seen. After a few minutes, the whole patrol was out of the built-up area and the OC of Egypt Squadron pulled the patrol over to use his sat phone to inform the ops room of the attack. After he had finished the patrol continued and the morning sun was now in the air warming the place up. The patrol made good time with no vehicles breaking down and within a few hours they were entering the COB. After the short trip to the tank park, they closed down the Warriors. The dirty, tired-looking Two Platoon lads moved back into camp. They grabbed some food before hitting the sack and sleeping through the rest of the day and night.

The next day One Platoon got warned off for a city patrol that was happening the following day escorting the brigade commander to the different bases. The day was spent with Two Platoon sorting out their Warriors after the Al Amara trip and One Platoon getting ready for their patrol. Three Platoon were on one hour's notice to move and had to deploy to SLB as the prisoners there were not behaving. They made the short trip there but as they arrived, they were sent back as the situation was under control.

The next day One Platoon's patrol went well with just a few rounds of rifle fire being fired at them and the whole platoon being back in camp by 1400hrs. The 2iC and I were walking from the company office to the tank park when a rocket flew over our heads and exploded about 100m away. We had dived onto the floor trying not to land in the mud and covered our heads with our hands as the second rocket went overhead and exploded again about 100m away. We lay there for 15 minutes until the all clear got sounded and then we got up and dusted ourselves off before moving on.

On the morning of 24 February, we got told that the Battle Group would be moving up to Al Qurna in 24 hours to dominate the area and prove to the insurgents there that if they wanted to mess us about then we could and would sit in their back yard. We set about sorting all the kit out and adding the extra rations and water to our Warriors. At 1700hrs we attended the Battle Group Orders. We were given our mission and task that we would be carrying out. C Company, Arnhem Company, and a troop of tanks (four) would be carrying out town patrols. Blenheim Company would be manning permanent vehicles checkpoints with the local police and the rest of the tanks, along with Three Platoon and the Battle Group HQ would be manning a patrol base 20 miles short of Al Qurna. We got informed that we would be leaving at around 1700hrs the next day.

After the orders we all had an early night as we knew the next couple of days would be hard work. The insurgents in Al Qurna had always given us a hard time. We got up the next day and finished of our last bits of admin before checking everything one last time and leaving our Warriors good to go.

At 1600hrs we moved to the tank park and mounted up and moved to the front gate. The tanks and Battle Group HQ had already left 30 minutes ago, and Blenheim were 15 minutes behind them. We set off at 1700hrs with Arnhem Company Warriors and C Company Snatches in the middle. We had been travelling for a few hours and were halfway through the oil fields when we turned right and went down a dirt track for 10 minutes. We had arrived at our first checkpoint, this was the FMB (forward mounting base) that Egypt Squadron and Battle Group HQ would be manning with our Three Platoon. Their job was to patrol south of Al Qurna and show a presence. We got some fuel and got ready to move again.

We travelled the short two hours trip into Al Qurna and as we got to the town we moved off to the left and made our base at some old farm out buildings. We were going to be working in fire support groups that consisted of two Warriors, two Snatches and one tank (main battle tank). We had four fire support groups, and the first one went out straight away and started to patrol the town. Blenheim had moved past us and were manning their checkpoints. Each fire support team had their own outbuilding that was no more than a pile of rubble which were about 50m away from each other. We got to our location and got a brief as we were the second team out and would be patrolling for two hours from 0400hrs.

After our brief it was time to move out. We moved with my Warrior call sign Zero Charlie first, and then the tank, then the two Snatches and bringing up the rear was one of One Platoon Warriors with their Warrior sergeant commanding it. The dirt track from our forward mounting base to Al Qurna was only one vehicle wide with potholes and cracks all over it. It took us about 10 minutes to reach the town. We moved down the road and visited each checkpoint on route to ensure everything was OK. We moved through the back streets trying to give them as much protection as we could. The patrol went well without any problems and at 0600hrs we headed back to our out base location. We got there at 0615hrs and reported how the patrol had gone to our ops room (which was our Zero-Bravo Warrior and a tent). They told us that our next patrol was at 1200hrs midday and that it would be a joint patrol with the Iraqi Army.

We moved to our area and got our weapons out and gave them a clean and oiled them up good to go. We then got our sleeping bags out and got some sleep as the sun started to rise. At 1100hrs we got up and grabbed some food and a brew before moving to the ops tent for a brief. So far, all the patrols had gone well with no contacts being reported. Good to go we waited as the Iraqi Army sorted themselves out and they joined the patrol following on behind the Snatches. We did the patrol with the Iraqi army doing the VCPs and us giving them protection.

Al Qurna was a town dominated by a river running through the centre of it from east to west. It had palm trees but, like most Iraqi built up areas, it still had a lot of rubbish which was thrown all over the place. The patrol went well and at 1430hrs we headed back and booked in. Not being out until 2200hrs we moved back to our area and tried to catch up on some sleep. It was not easy as the sun was strong and there were only few places to hide. I lay on my sleeping bag outside of my Warriors but could not sleep due to the heat.

I grabbed my weapon and walked down to the next position for a brew and a chat. As I got to the next Warrior there were journalists from *The Sun* newspaper there. *The Sun* was a paper that liked to support the British Army but being a Liverpool fan I hated them after what they reported after the Hillsborough disaster, so did not talk to them. They were doing a story with Andy McNab, an ex-SAS solider who had written many best sellers. He introduced himself and asked me what I thought of Iraq. I told him it was more violent than I thought it was going to be and the number of strike and search operation we were doing was unreal.

He told me that he admired and respected the British troops so much with the hard work they were doing in Iraq and Afghanistan. I looked at him and said, 'You're ex-SAS, one of the most decorated soldiers of our time, why admire us?' He told me to think about it, 10 years ago the only troops doing strike operations were the SAS. Now you the green troop are doing it and doing it well.

I walked away feeling good, here was an ex-SAS soldier telling us we were doing a good job. Andy McNab came over like a good lad. Being an ex-SAS member and top author he could have so easily have been up his own arse, but he was taking time out to talk to the lads and sign their books when he got asked. He also dedicated his latest book to the soldiers of 2 Rifles and 2 Lancs and all the people we lost on our tour, which was sound.

It was soon 2100hrs and we started to get ready for our patrol. At 2130hrs we moved up to the ops tent to book out. We were doing this patrol without the Iraqi Army, and we moved off into the town. The VCPs were still going well, and the patrol went without any trouble again with us being back at our camp by midnight. We got told that our next patrol was at 0600hrs and again we would be joined by our Iraqi friends. We moved back to our area and in the cool night air manage to get some sleep.

We got up at 0530hrs and moved to the ops tent and waited for the Iraqi Army to sort themselves out. The Iraqi officer was getting a hard time from his men, and I went over with our interpreter and asked him what was going on. We found out that the Iraqi troops did not want to play as they had not had any breakfast. I told him to tell his men that the patrol was only two hours long and they could have breakfast on their return. They mounted up with faces like little kids in a bad mood and we moved out. We headed down to the bridge and turned left down the side of the river. When we got to the main road, we went into protection positions as the Iraqis carried out a VCP.

They had been doing it for five minutes when one of their trucks turned up with their breakfast. Every single one of them stopped what they were doing and moved to their truck and started to eat breakfast. I could not fucking believe it; we were giving protection to the Iraqi Army as they ate breakfast. Once they had finished, we mounted up and moved back to base. That was the last patrol of the operation for us and a few hours later we headed south away from Al Qurna and moved into the Battle group's FMB. We got some fuel and headed back through the oil fields before reaching the COB a few hours later. Every time we had been to Al Qurna in the past, we had been in contact with the insurgents but the whole two days we had been patrolling there was not even one bullet fired.

On our return into our camp, we started to hear about an ambush in the city involving 2 Rifles. Op Minimise was in place and we heard that a young lad had been killed. At the company O Group, we got told that a patrol had been ambushed by gunmen and that Rifleman Daniel Lee Coffey had died as a result of his injuries back at base. He was only 21 years old and was on top cover when he got hit.

Over the next two days the insurgents hit the COB with six rockets which exploded around the camp. That was the last indirect fire attack we got in February, and at the end of the month the OC returned from leave and the 2iC went home for his two weeks break. We briefed the OC up on all the operations that the company had been involved in his absence and he went and got a brief to see what was on the agenda for March.

February was a strange month for me with two weeks' leave at the start of the month. Once home I thought I would just be able to relax and forget about everything. I soon realised that this was easier said than done. I always had the troops on my mind and then reality bites. The shocking truth of what we put our family and friends through. We deploy and get on with it and get into the zone. They have to sit playing the waiting game to see if their loves ones are dead or ripped apart. A lot of the military feel the wrong people get the medals and I totally agree and understand why. The best thing for me was getting straight back into it after leave and the five-hour night battle was just what I needed. It really was something special being involved in such a professional operation. It was soldiering at the highest level and something I had be yearning for my whole career. I think we can all say, February was one hell of a month.

5

MARCH 2007

The Al Qurna Prisoners

The insurgents started March off by hitting the COB with rockets which exploded near the A1 Village. Zero Charlie call sign also said goodbye to Sargeant Sam Jono as he was tasked to go and work with the Americans up north for three months. Something he would later be awarded the American Bronze Star for. This saw a new member of the team come in from One Platoon, Cpl Tommy Whittingham. Tommy was a quality soldier and had just passed the PSBC and was a great Cumbrian lad with a wicked sense of humour. Chris would also leave in a week's time to be the CO's driver and Flemo take his place in the driver's seat.

It was now starting to get warm and when we went on patrols, we would often come in soaked in sweat. Because of this it was important that the platoon sergeants kept an eye on their lads to ensure they were drinking enough water. There were bottles of water situated all over the camp and if you went to the right place, it was also chilled.

The next day we got up and went down to the tank park and mounted up. We were going to the range to fire our Warrior weapons and ensure the sights were set correctly. We got there and fired our chain guns and 30mm cannons and then moved back to camp were we greased and oiled them all up again so that they were good to go. After lunch I was in the company office and the lads were doing some first aid training when a rocket flew in and exploded a short distance away. In the company office there was me, Lee and the two company clerks. We all hit the floor as a second rocked landed and exploded about 50m away. It was quickly followed up with a third that exploded a short distance away. After the all clear was given, everyone got on with the day-to-day routine.

At the company O Group, the OC informed us that we were taking part in a Battle Group strike and search operation in three days that was happening in the Al Hyyaniyah area of the city (the Shia Flats). After the O Group I got some time in at the gym and laughed at all the lads pumping the weights. When I went to the gym, I did the running machine or bike with a few press-ups and sit-ups to try and keep myself toned but a lot of the lads were on what we called Op Massive. They were trying to get as big as they could in seven months using powders and weights. After the gym I phoned home before hitting my pit.

The next morning, we fired our rifles on the range and ensured that the sights were on target. As we were on the range the COB got attacked with one rocket of indirect fire. After this we did a bit of training, with the lads going over all the paperwork that we needed on the ground for things like arresting someone and searching them. At the company O Group, the OC informed us that the Battle Group orders would be at 1000hrs the next day and that all commanders needed to be there.

That night we had to move to Brigade HQ for a Time Sensitive Task (TST) operation. This was an operation being controlled by surveillance soldiers on the ground who were watching a target. We moved up and the officers were soon moving out of Brigade HQ to brief us up. We would be conducting the route security with Blenheim Company escorting the Iraqi Security Force (ISF) patrol in the city. We moved out and secured the route and Blenheim Company moved through us and onto the target house.

They struck the house, and it came over the net that they wanted to move to PJHQ. This was the Iraqi Police HQ for Basra, and we also had a number of British soldiers based there. We set out and secured the route and they had soon moved through us. Blenheim Company thought that they were just going there to touch base with the local police. So, they got a bit of a shock when the ISF started to storm the place, hitting each sanger in turn and forcing all the police to the floor. They stayed there for an hour before releasing the police and moving out. We all moved back to the COB and completed all the post patrol paperwork before getting some sleep. That patrol caused more problems that night than any other patrol we did, but at the end of the day it was their forces patrolling in their country.

The next day we got up late morning and we grabbed a brew before moving to the briefing tent and receiving our orders. We got told that we were striking two houses just off Green 38 in the Shia Flats. Egypt and the Recce Platoon's Warriors would be securing the route with the rest of us breaking down into two strike groups. Strike Group 1 would consist of Arnhem Company Warriors and half of C Company Snatches. Strike Group 2 would consist of Blenheim Company Warriors and the other half of C Company Snatches. We were leaving at around 2200hrs with the strikes hitting at around 2300hrs. After the orders we had lunch before all the final checks were done in the afternoon.

In the afternoon we heard that a young lad from the Staffords had lost his fight to live. Private Jonathon Wysoczan, aged 21, had been injured by a single shot from a gunman on a patrol earlier in the week. He had been evacuated back to the UK where he later died from his injuries.

We had our company O Group and grabbed some food before chilling in our tents before moving to the tank park. We got to the tent, and I made all of us a brew and we were just sat on each other's wall talking when we heard the whistle of a rocket fly in. We all jumped for cover and landed hard grabbing our helmets and body armour as the first rocket exploded 150m away. Thirty seconds later as we lay there, we heard the whistle of two more rockets flying in and they exploded even closer with the noise being deafening. As the next two flew in we heard screams from some of the other tents as some of the lads started to panic. They exploded even closer with the explosions rocking the camp and shaking the very ground we lay on. There was no doubt that they were walking them in with somebody watching where they landed and directing them onto our camp.

We all stayed where we were and hugged the cover the best we could as we heard another whistle in that exploded just outside of our camp. You could hear the panic in the camp but there was nothing anyone could do but stay down and hope for the best. We heard another whistle in and we all braced ourselves sure that this was it and at any moment our tents would be ripped apart with hot metal flying everywhere. Again, it exploded just outside of our camp, deafening us and forcing the ground to shake again.

As we lay there, I heard one of the lads shouting out in panic in another tent. We shouted for them to stay where they were and to keep calm (easier said than done). We lay there for 20 minutes, but no more rockets came. The all clear was sounded and I sat up and just looked around the tent. The heads of all the other crept above their walls and we looked at each other without saying a word. There was no movement at Mogger's wall and Lee asked if he was all right. He got up and sat on his bed and just placed his head in his hands, we all knew how he felt.

They hit us with multiple rockets during that attack and it definitely felt like we were their only targets but being in tents, the fear of a rocket ripping through and killing everyone was a surreal experience. It is near impossible to put these attacks and events into words which do the cruelty of the attack justice. The scream of the rockets, the deafening explosions, the shaking of the ground, the deadly silence which follows with only a slight ringing hanging in your ears. It really is something which will stay with the soldiers for the rest of their lives. Me and Lee grabbed our kit and went and checked on the soldiers in our companies just to make sure that everyone was OK.

By the time we got back we had time for a quick brew before placing on our kit and moving up the tank park. With the 2IC being away I was stepping in for this patrol as the acting 2IC. As the lads went to the tank park, I went to the ops room and made sure all the flap sheets and checks were correct. I checked the main map board to ensure there was no more out of bounds areas and moved to the tank park. Instead of me being call sign Zero Charlie's gunner, I was the commander tonight with Steve Tabbs joining me in the turret as my gunner. Our driver was Chris Squires with Tommy, Wes, Marti, Coz, and the Phil the Medical Officer, in the back. We did the comms check and I then reported to the OC that the company was good to go. We moved out and met up with our Snatches at the front gate.

The Recce Platoon and Egypt Squadron moved out first with Arnhem strike group moving second and Blenheim strike group moving third with BGHQ. The patrols moved out and down the rubbish tip (Old Trafford) before moving down the road we called route Anfield. We all stopped just short of the bridge at Red 1 until the route was secure.

Once it was secure, we got 'GO, GO, GO' from the CO over the net. Our Warriors moved with Three Platoon leading, then company HQ Warriors, then the Snatches of C Company followed on by Two Platoon and One Platoon. We moved over the bridge and went through the police checkpoint at speed. We moved down the Reds with the odd round of tracer flying through the air until we reached Red 5. At Red 5 we turned left and moved towards Green 38, I was head height in my turret as we got to Green 38.

'BOOOM'

There was a massive explosion that engulfed the first Warrior. We all stopped and waited as the smoke started to clear. I heard the OC send the initial contact report stating that our front Warrior had been hit by an IED. It took a few seconds until the commander got on the net. He told us that himself and the driver had got knocked out by the blast but came to seconds later and that apart from a thumping head they were all right. He also told us that they had two more IEDs to the front of their Warrior.

The OC told him to try and disrupt them with his chain gun. The gunner steadied his sights onto the IEDs and fired fifty rounds, with the tracers bouncing all over the place and into the night sky. He reported back that it had not worked and the IEDs still looked intact. At this time, the CO was pushing for the patrol to get moving and we had started to get small arms and RPG fire on our position. He told the front Warriors to push on, but the commander, dazed from the blast, was not happy and the Warrior did not move. I heard the CO come on the net again and saw some tracers fly past the Snatches.

I turned and looked at Steve and said, 'Fuck it pull out to your right Chris.' He pulled out and our Warrior moved past the four Warriors of Three Platoon. As I got to the front I shouted to the commander and told him to move back. As they moved back, I saw the two IEDs on the corner of the road and reported back to the OC that I could see the two bombs and that I was pushing past them and onto the target house. I shouted to everyone in the Warrior to get down and hold on and told the driver to place his hatch down and to push forward and drive over the two bombs!! He did without question, and we moved forward, all braced up ready, towards the two IEDs waiting for the bang. It never came and we roared down the road to the target house. The young driver was simple outstanding and showed an amazing amount of courage (how he never got a bravery award I will never know). The Snatches pulled up and the strike team went and struck the target house. Three Platoon pushed past us and moved to secure the bottom of the street. We were joined in the middle by company HQ Warriors with One Platoon and Two Platoon securing the other end of the street. The company started to receive gunfire at our positions. Everyone looked out, but no firing points were seen as the night sky lit up with more tracer bullets.

Down at Three Platoon position the lads who had just been hit by the IED were still shaken up and trying their best to cover their arcs. Fifty metres in front of their Warrior an insurgent appeared with an RPG on his shoulder. The gunner steadied his sights as the RPG warhead flew down the road and exploded on the side of their Warrior covering them in dirt, with the noise not helping their already thumping heads. It was the last thing the insurgent did as he was cut down by the chain gun of the Warrior. He was soon replaced with another insurgent who started to fire his AK-47 rifle at their Warrior with the bullets bouncing and pinging all over it. The gunner had him and fired at him again with his chain gun hitting him and sending his AK-47 flying through the air. They watched as he crawled to the side of the road where another man carried him away.

Our strike team returned with one male they were arresting and a small amount of munitions. The same happened at the other target house with one being arrested. With both strike teams finished we mounted up and moved off. As we made our way out of the Shia Flats there was the odd round of rifle fire seen, but we just pushed on with the job done and headed back to the COB.

Back at the COB we unloaded and fuelled up before returning to the tank park. The MO checked over the lads who had been knocked out and I got all the lads together who had fired and completed all the post-operational paperwork before reporting to the OC and letting him know what the company had fired. I turned to walk out BGHQ office when the OC grabbed me and said, 'Well done tonight, Sgt Major.' I smiled and walked over the cookhouse. I grabbed some food and sat and joined the lads from my Warriors. They all looked at me as I told them the OC said to say well done to them all but singled out the driver for praise. After our food we grabbed a shower and hit our sacks and fell asleep.

We got up for lunch and then completed the rest of the paperwork and checked all the kit over to ensure we were good to go. We did the company O Group on the floor of the briefing tent as the COB got attacked with one rocket of indirect fire. One Platoon got told that they would be working from SLB for the next few days supporting 1 Yorks with their operations. The following morning, we took over guards for four days with Three Platoon going on first. One Platoon left the COB and moved over to SLB where they met up with the company with who they were working with. They were based on their own in port-a-cabins and would be patrolling two times a day in their Warriors with their Yorkshire Regiment colleagues in their Snatches. The rest of the time was their own, so they were happy.

In the afternoon, the insurgents hit the COB with three rockets of indirect fire. Over the next few days, we started to see pallets of bricks arriving again. We got told at our O Group that we would be bricking around our tents to give us extra protection. The QM came up with a mad plan that would see us having it all completed in a day. We were to start the following morning at 0600hrs, and he was convinced that we would be done by lunch. At the end of the O Group the OC told me I had to go and see the Regimental Sergeant Major (RSM). The RSM is the most senior enlisted soldier in the unit and one of the most respected and feared. I had known him my whole career and he was someone I respected and looked up to. I caught up with the RSM at scoff and he asked me to command one of the Warriors in the CO patrol group as they were going to SLB to see One Platoon. He told me to be at the tank park at 0830hrs and that we were leaving at 0900hrs.

I was made up because that meant I would only be lugging bricks for an hour before I had to deploy. The next day we got up early and set about the bricks, but things were never straightforward in the army and most of the bricks were at the wrong end of the camp. Which meant that we had to carry them 200m. It was hard work, and I was made up when I had to fuck off on patrol. At the tank park we mounted up and made the short trip to SLB were we stayed for a couple of hours with One Platoon before travelling back. We closed down and were back in our camp by 1300hrs. The QM's mad plan had been a success and the lads had completed 90 per cent of the bricks in camp with only a few to do. The wall was the same height as the bricks around our bedspaces and were three high, around knee height. The lads looked knackered and had worked their socks off.

On 11 March Blenheim Company were out on a counter-indirect fire patrol that went well apart from the fact that Lee who was in the next bed space to me had to crawl through a river of shit. This resulted in him stinking out the whole tent on his return as he left his combats on the tent floor as he got a shower. I laughed as his ironed combats looked in shit state. They were soon bagged up with Lee spraying some spray before jumping into bed with a sick smile on his face.

The next few days were the quietest of our tour with only a few little patrols happening and no attacks of indirect fire. A week later Two Platoon took over One Platoon in SLB and One Platoon returned to the COB and went onto standby. Back in the COB we had a new welfare village that had opened up just behind our camp. The 2IC Jon, Carl and I went to have a look around. It had a NAAFI shop and café, a couple of local shops selling the dodgy DVDs. It had a Subway and a Burger King and an Effie Café. We had a look around before grabbing a milkshake and walking back.

Before we knew it was 15 March and we had not been on patrol for a few days. Two Platoon returned from SLB with a platoon from Blenheim Company taking over them. In the afternoon, the OC called for the platoon commanders, me and the 2IC and then warned us all off that the company would be involved in a TST (time sensitive target) operation the following night. He told us that there would be no orders and that we would move down to the Brigade HQ and wait for the go from other agencies. We moved over to the tank park at 2100hrs and at 2200hrs we were outside Brigade HQ with all the Warriors good to go on the road with all the lads sitting there tooled up ready.

The OC, 2IC and the platoon commander were in the main building so they could get briefed up as fast as possible and move back and brief us up, so we were all good to go. I went with the OC just so I knew where they were and then moved back to the lads. We sat there for six hours before the officers came back and informed us that it was a no go for the night, and we all mounted up and moved back to our camp.

We slept through most of the next day and got up in the afternoon and checked the kit over. We attended the company O Group and the OC told us that the reason we were not getting any indirect fire attacks was because the insurgents had run out of rockets and were waiting for more to arrive. Just as he finished, we hit the floor as a rocket screamed overhead and landed somewhere in our camp. The explosion was deafening and the ground shook with the force of it. A few seconds later another screamed in and the explosion was close again. A third flew in and exploded, rattling the very tent we were in. We waited 30 seconds and I looked at the OC as we lay on the floor and said, 'Fuck this sir, I cannot wait for the all clear we need to check on the lads, they were close'.

He nodded as I told the platoon sergeants to check on their platoon and report back to me at the HQ companies tents. We ran from the briefing tent and checked on the soldiers in their tents, the platoon sergeants reported that they were all all right and that the rockets had exploded just outside of our fence. I reported to the ops room and reported that Arnhem Company were all accounted for and informed them where they had exploded. I reported back to the OC and smiled as I said to him, 'I take it the insurgents have taken delivery of their new stock of rockets sir.' He just smiled as the all clear was sounded. The next few days were pretty busy with a couple of patrols taking place with One Platoon and Three Platoon carrying out counter indirect fire patrols and the rest of us spending most nights sitting outside of Brigade HQ waiting for the go that so far had never come.

In the afternoon Blenheim Company deployed to conduct a counter-indirect fire patrol and as they were moving through Green 19. They came under sniper fire resulting in one of their lads being shot through the arm. He was extracted off the ground by Lee and Northey his medic and handed over to the hospital staff. In the evening, the insurgents hit us with three rockets that exploded in camp.

Arnhem Company were also on standby for a TST operation and the officers went off to Brigade HQ and I stayed behind and was in control of the rest of the company. At midnight we got crashed out and we moved to Brigade HQ. The officers were waiting with our Special Forces who we got told would be travelling in the back of our Warriors. We got told that Egypt Squadron would be doing route security with Arnhem Company providing the inner cordon. With C Company assisting the Special Forces with the strike. After the strike was complete Blenheim Company would pick up the strike teams and move them back to the COB.

With everyone briefed we moved out at 0030hrs. The tanks moved first and secured Green 19. We pushed through and moved past the Shatt Hotel, before moving towards Yellow 7 with a few rounds of tracer being fired at us. At Yellow 7 we moved onto the target street and there were a couple of RPG's that exploded against our Warriors but with no firing point being seen we just pushed on and the strike teams moved out on foot. The Special Forces moved up to the gate and attached their explosives and told everyone to take cover. 'BANG!' There was a massive explosion as their entry charge blew the gates off. They stormed in and kicked in the door only to find out that they had hit the wrong house and the target house was next door.

We watched them like a scene from the Benny Hill Show as they all move out and kicked in the next door. This time, they had got the right house with three men being detained. With the search completed Blenheim Company moved in and extracted the strike teams. We followed on and within 20 minutes we were all back in the COB where we dropped off our guest and completed all the post operational paperwork before grabbing some food and getting a bit of sleep.

On 20 March, the OC warned us off that we would be taking part in a Brigade operation that was going to be happening in a couple of days and that all commanders had to be in the briefing tent at 1400 hour for our orders. We got the word out to everyone and continued with our work.

In the city our Chindit Company were handing over the Old State Building (OSB) to the local Iraqi Army. Since they had taken over the base in late October it had become the most attacked base in Iraq. They had been under daily attack with the insurgents hitting them with all they had. They were leaving with their heads held high after every single one of them performing to the highest of standards. They had a motto for the OSB base which was 'Where the metal meets the meat'. Chindit's performance was simple amazing and on any other tour, they would have walked away with a bucket full of bravery medals. They would be moving from the OSB to Basra Palace for the remainder of their tour.

After our lunch we all moved to the briefing tent. It was hot and we all grabbed some bottles of water to see us through the orders. We got told that it would be a strike, search and detain operation that was taking place in Al Qurna. We were all moving up to the place where Egypt Squadron did their patrols from a couple of weeks ago. From there, the Special Forces and our Recce Platoon would be dropped off by helicopters and strike a couple of target houses. Blenheim Company and C Company would be in next hitting the town from the south and striking a number of target houses with the Danish Army doing the same in the north of the town. Arnhem Company had to secure a helicopter landing site (HLS) and set up a detaining centre for the prisoners just on the southern edge of the town.

After the orders I got told to stay behind for rock drill where the CO informed me that I would be in charge of the detainee centre and responsible for the processing of the detainees. I would have two ISO containers dropped off near the HLS and once all the paperwork was correct. I would organise the prisoners into chalks for flights back to the COB where they would be taken to the detainee centre. The rest of Arnhem Company under the OC would be responsible for town patrols and the picking up of the prisoners before dropping them off at my location. At the company O Group, I informed the OC that I would need the company search team for my part of the operation, and he informed me that I would have two Snatch Land Rovers and two lorries to drop off my ISO containers.

The next day we set about sorting all the kit away with the company checking all the Warriors and the search team sorting out the ISO containers. The containers had holes drilled in the side and were fitted with mats on the floor and sandbags for them to sit on. With the containers done I checked on the paperwork and ensured we had extra paperwork and things like zip ties, blacked-out goggles and ear defenders. The next day we got the containers onto the back of their trucks, and I covered off my four vehicles in-between Arnhem Company Warriors.

At 1600hrs we all mounted up and completed the three-hour trip up north and pulled in at the old FMB. We stayed there a few hours where we fuelled up and got some food down our necks. At 2230hrs the whole Battle Group was mounted up good to go and in the right order of march ready to move off.

Once completed it was 2300hrs and we moved off again heading north. An hour later we made our final approach to Al Qurna. With a mile to Go Blenheim Company Warriors speeded up and roared past us heading into the town at speed. We heard over the radio that the Recce Platoon had been hit in their target house by three RPG warheads and they had got a couple of casualties. We headed at speed to our area as we had to set up the HLS to get the injured lads out. We turned left and the 2IC went forward and cleared the area for the HLS. I waited on the road and saw the flashing light that we attached to our Warriors to signal that it was carrying injured soldiers.

It was Lee's Warrior from Blenheim Company, and I led them forward to just short of the HLS. As I got to the back of the Warrior the MO and the medics were working on the injured lads. It was LCpl

Freddy Lungburg who had been hit in the face and arm and Kingsman Scott Siner who had a leg injury, I knew both lads well from my time as the Recce Platoon 2IC. They got moved forward to the HLS and I moved back to my Snatches and watched as the helicopter came and lifted the injured lads. Once the lads had been lifted everyone jumped in the vehicles and headed off to their area. I was just about to head off when I noticed a lad still on the ground on his own. I went up and noticed it the Battalion Intelligence sergeant, so he jumped in our Snatch, and we headed off and set up the detainee centre.

The first Warriors returned with six prisoners, and I moved them into the ISO container with the arresting lads. I had to ensure that all the paperwork was done correctly and that it was clearly marked what house they had been arrested in. They needed to have been arrested correctly with their hands bound to their front, blindfolded with blacked-out goggles and earmuffs placed on their heads. Once done I had to mark up the munitions that had been found in their house and ensure that the paperwork was all placed together and given to the arresting solider.

I was halfway through the first lot when the second lot arrived with four from the second house. I placed them all to one side until I had finished the first lot. Once they were done, they were placed in the second ISO container where they would await a flight to take them back to the COB. It was like a sausage factory, and I got the first ten out with the detaining soldiers and all the kit found.

I had AK-47 rifles, a shitload of ammunition, paperwork, IT equipment and all sorts. The lads back in Arnhem Company had been in and out of the town a few times now. They were often picking up the prisoners while the other subunits were under fire and most of the platoons had small arms fired at them as they were leaving the town. I was well into my twenties on the prisoner's side and had already flown out two chalks. The Danish Army turned up with a few more and I check them over and flew them out. With most of the target houses completed, the flow of prisoners came to an end. It had been a mad few hours and the units started to lift of the ground and move back to the FMB. As they were moving there was a massive explosion in the town. We all took cover in case it was indirect fire, but no rockets or mortars came our way, and no reports of any contact were given.

One Platoon who had been manning a VCP on the edge of the town stopped a car that had two men inside with a couple of bits of munitions in the boot. They were arrested and I processed them through just managing to get them on the last chopper. We closed down our area and the ISO containers got placed onto their trucks and we started to move back to the FMB. As we reached the forward mounting base, daylight was breaking and after a quick check of our kit, we completed the rest of our journey to the COB. We got in at breakfast time and I reported to the OC that none of the company had fired and that all kit was accounted for. We slept through the day before attending the company O Group where a well done was passed on by the Brigade Commander. After some food we all hit our sacks still knackered from the previous night.

The next day we got up and I had to attend another briefing at Bridge HQ on the IED threat. It was only a day long this time and I could not moan as I got to have lunch in their cookhouse again. When I got back the OC warned me off that the company was going to be evolved in a Battle Group strike and search operation in the Qarmat Ali area of the city again. I did not like the sound of that as the last time we were there, we were in contact for nearly five hours.

The next day was spent sorting all the equipment out and attending orders. Blenheim Company would be securing the outer area with Arnhem Company the inner and C Company doing the strike. The next day we did our rehearsals before the final checks were completed. At 2200hrs we went to the tank park and mounted up and moved to the front gate.

Two Platoon moved out first and secured Green 19. As we move through, One Platoon and Three Platoon dropped off on the way securing the route before, we secured the ICP location at Green 32.

Blenheim Company pushed past us and secured to our right as C Company struck their target. So far so good, we had broken into the area without a round being fired. The insurgents were quiet tonight and we waited for the attack to come. Ten minutes later the first rounds of the night were fired with tracer flying over our Warrior. We scanned around but no firing point or insurgents were seen.

Blenheim Company got contacted by an RPG warhead but the all-out attack that we got last time never came. With the search complete we moved off and back over the bridge without arresting anyone. At Green 19 they fired four mortar rounds at us that exploded near the road and Two Platoon Warriors, but it was more of a token attack than anything deliberate. Back in the COB we attended breakfast and the lads started talking about how two patrols in the same area could be so different. They were saying the last time we were there it was mad but this time it is dead quiet. I laughed to myself: we had just been on a patrol and got fired at with gunfire, mortars, RPGs, and the lads were calling it a quite patrol, but when I thought about it, it showed what a long way the company had come and what a lot they had been through. After our food we slept through most of the day before attending the O Group and the OC informing us that we had no patrol planned for that night and to make the most of it.

The next couple of days we resumed guards, and all was quiet until the afternoon of 27 March. It was about 1600hrs when we heard the rocket fly in with some force and land in the camp next to ours. The explosion was frightening, and the flames shot through the air as it exploded ripping apart a couple of vehicles. Carl our CQMS was driving past the camp when it exploded on his right. He jumped from the Land Rover and took cover in a ditch as the second one flew in. Again, it was loud as the insurgents hit the right area again. The unit in that camp had a couple of injured lads but luckily it was not life threatening. The next day we got woken up with one rocket of indirect fire falling in at around 0700hrs but again no one was hurt, and the day continued with little happening.

The following day the OC warned us of that company HQ Warriors and Three Platoon would be on a counter indirect fire patrol the following night (Op Tashbrook). He told us that we were to be in the briefing tent at 1900hrs for our orders and that we would be deploying straight after them. We spent the next day sorting all the equipment out before moving to the orders. At the orders, the OC told us that we would be moving from the COB to Yellow 1 where Three Platoon would be going off road to the area around Camp Warehouse. With the orders completed we moved to the tank park and mounted up and moved to the front gate.

We left the front gate with Three Platoon leading and us following on. We moved through Old Trafford and came out of the rubbish tip by the bridge at Yellow 1. Three Platoon cleared the bridge, and we pushed through going firm just short of Yellow 2 Alpha.

HQ Coy covered the ground as Three Platoon Warriors moved toward Camp Warehouse. They were halfway there when the sky lit up over to our right. We had come across a rocket firing point, and we all scanned the area as the OC informed the COB that they were under attack. The rockets flew through the air, sounding like a fighter jet taking off, and shot past Three Platoon who thought that they were under attack as the rockets shot past them into the sky. We scanned the area, but no insurgents were seen and with it being on the edge of the Shia Flats it was no use going in there with such a small force on the ground.

With all the activity going on the eye in the sky was working overtime and they spotted an indirect fire team setting up and moving back to a house near Green 18. We got the order to stay in our position and to act as a distraction using the ground the best we could to give us cover. The rest of the Battle Group deployed and struck the house, catching all three insurgents and all of their equipment. Once the Battle Group had lifted, we got the order to move back into the COB. Once there we unloaded and moved back to the tank park before completing all the paperwork and getting into bed.

March had been a strange month and with reflection it showed just how much the indirect fire can affect you mentally. The fear of a rocket screaming in, is something words simply don't do justice to. The whistle of the rockets as it flies in, the deafening explosion that leave a ringing silence in your ears and pounding shake of the ground as you lie there excepting to get ripped apart at any moment is something you don't get used to. The consent threat that wears you down can leave invisible scars that can crumble a person to the core. Some of the IDF attacks during March had been so intense, I would say these are attacks that will stay with the soldiers for a lifetime, bonding them together in a way you just can't explain.

During April and May, Arnhem Company soldiers got multiple rocket and mortar attacks EVERY DAY AND EVERY NIGHT. The Basra insurgents just never let up. To save the reading becoming repetitive I will only write on the big IDF attacks during the next two months. But please remember as well as all of the other attacks I write about, the soldiers on Op Telic 9 were under constant rocket and mortar attacks both day and night.

6

APRIL 2007

Yellow 2 Alpha and Op Rattlesnake

On 1 April it was April Fool's Day, but we were in no mood to fool around as reports started to come in that another member of the battalion had been killed in the city. The CO got us all together and the first thing we had to do was to take cover as the insurgents lobbed a rocket at us that exploded a few hundred metres away, but with no one hurt and the all clear being sounded we got up and fell back in. The CO informed us that Kingsman Danny Wilson of Chindit Company had been shot on patrol in the city and had died of his injuries. He had sustained a gunshot wound when his patrol had been ambushed by insurgents and despite being given immediate first aid at the scene he died of his injuries. He was the fifth member of the battalion to have been killed in action.

After the parade we got warned off for a Battle Group strike and search operation that was taking place on the following night. We attended the orders and got told that we would be striking a house just off Green 18. C Company strike teams in their Snatches would be striking the target house. Arnhem Company Warriors would provide the security and Egypt Squadron's tanks with our One Platoon would be clearing Green 19 and protecting our route in and out. After the orders we had our evening meal, and I got a bit of time in at the gym before getting some sleep.

The next day we got up and carried out our rehearsals and completed all our checks. Just before our evening meal we noticed that Op Minimise was on again and at the company O Group we got told that a young Rifleman from 2 Rifles had been killed in the city. His patrol had been contacted by small arms fire and the firing point was seen. On the follow-up the patrol was just about to strike the building where the fire had come from when they were fired at from a different position with Rifleman Aaron Lincoln being hit. They evacuated him to the field hospital but sadly he later died from his injuries. He was only 18 years old.

The OC went over the plan for the night patrol before we got a bit of down time and rest before moving up to the tank park. At the tank park we sorted out the radios and we all mounted up and moved to the front gate. One Platoon and the tanks moved out first and then we followed but went firm at A Pod Bridge while they cleared the route and junction at Green 19.

Once it was clear and they were in position we moved off at speed with Two Platoon leading, followed on by the company HQ Warriors. Then the Snatches containing the strike teams with Three Platoon bringing up the rear. We moved past the junction at Green 19 before heading right and coming to the built-up area at Green 18. There was a flash to our right as the first RPG warhead flew through the air towards us and exploded on the second Warrior.

It was soon followed by a load of tracer that was being fired at us from the alleyways. The tracer rounds smacked into the side of the Warriors with the usual sound of pings ripping through the vehicle as the metal and bullets met each other. With the firing points not being seen we pushed on and turned right into the street where the target house was. Two Platoon pushed past and secured the bottom of the street with Three Platoon securing the top. The OC Warrior stayed near the junction at Green 18 with our Warrior being given a free role to move down the west side of the houses covering the alleyways.

The strike teams went in, and the house was struck. Outside the dismounts had all taken up fire position to try and counter the RPGs and small arms fire we were still receiving. On the ground Cpl Park was a team commander and was covering down the street with Cpl Raistrick (two outstanding JNCO and soldiers). An insurgent appeared 50m to their front with an RPG on his shoulder and fired. The RPG warhead flew down the street, right in between the two lads with the wind brushing past their faces as it shot past them and down the street. They steadied their sights onto the main mass of the insurgent's body as he dropped his RPG launcher and grabbed his AK-47 rifle. They both fired, sending their tracer bullets from their rifle into the insurgent, throwing him off his feet. With the threat gone they stopped firing and covered down the street.

Call sign Zero Charlie Warrior was moving up and down the west side of the housing estate stopping off at each alleyway and scanning down it. We stopped as we saw some movement and the 2IC popped his head up to have a look. I looked on using our thermal image sight. The next thing we knew the sky was lit up with a volley of tracer bullets that flew just over the 2IC's head. I spun the turret around, but the firing point was not seen.

With the strike completed we all mounted up and moved to Green 18 and started to move out. The insurgents were waiting, and the sky lit up again as they tried to hit us with RPGs and gunfire. The Warrior's armour did its job as the RPGs and bullets smacked into it with no effect on us. We broke out of Green 18 and pushed past Green 19 before completing the short journey back into the COB. We did the normal after patrol stuff like unloading our weapons, fuelled up and all the paperwork before hitting the sack and getting some sleep. It had been a quick patrol, lasting from start to finish less than three hours.

The following day after some rest we set about ensuring all the equipment was good to go. In the afternoon all the Warrant Officers moved to the cookhouse where we dined out the old RSM with a meal and a few words of thanks. He had been 2 Lancs' first RSM and had taken us through our build-up training and most of the operational tour. A proud man with high standards who would go onto be an outstanding officer in the future. He was to be replaced by another very good soldier who was on the tour already and being promoted into the RSM position.

After the meal we moved back over to our company offices where we set about with the work we had to do. The OC warned us off that the night of the 5 April the Battle Group would be involved in another strike and search operation and that the orders would be at 2000hrs in the briefing tent. We did as much of the admin as we could and had our evening meal before attending the orders. At the orders we got told that C Company would be striking the house with Arnhem and Recce Platoon Warriors securing the area and BGHQ Warriors being in command. The strike was taking place in the built-up area around Blue 8.

With the orders completed we moved back to our tents and got our heads down. The next day as usual was spent doing rehearsals and checks. In the afternoon we got into our best combats and attended Kingsman Danny Wilson's repatriation. He was the fifth person we had sent home in this way. Once the repatriation was over, we had our evening O Group and meal. We were not due at the tank park until 2300hrs, so I managed to phone home and chill out for a bit before the patrol began. At 2300hrs we moved up to the tank park and started to get sorted before we moved to the front gate.

At midnight we moved out onto Op Rainin with the Recce Platoon moving first and securing Green 19 and Green 18. The strike group containing Arnhem Company, C Company and BGHQ pushed past and moved down the Yellows. At Yellow 4 we turned right and then left on towards our target house. We secured the area, and the strike went in.

After a few minutes we started to spot movement on the rooftops. We scanned using our thermal Warrior sights and the commanders scanned from the top of the turret. We started to get gunfire onto our Warriors with the familiar ping sound ringing out as the bullets hit the metal. The gunfire was soon followed by the RPGs as they flew through the air. At Three Platoon's location the platoon commander's Warrior started to get gunfire onto his Warrior and the platoon commander spotted a group of insurgents on the rooftop armed with AK-47 rifles and RPG launchers. He dropped into his turret fast and orders his gunner to open fire. The gunner selected his chain gun and stamped on his firing pedal. He suppressed the insurgents with over forty rounds of 7.62mm, hitting one and forcing the others to go to ground.

At Two Platoon location the Warrior sergeant's Warrior came under fire from two gunmen, one with an RPG and the other with a rifle. The gunner did not need telling what to do and engaged the gunmen with a lethal volley of shots, cutting them down where they stood. On the ground the dismounts were having just as much a hard time as the Warrior crew with bullets flying all over the place. One of the dismounts ran around the corner to come face to face with a gunman 50m to his front. He reacted first and fired ten rounds from his rifle, hitting the insurgent, and then moving back to his Warrior. With tracer still flying everywhere the strike teams finished and everyone mounted up and we moved off.

As Arnhem was fixed in a firefight, the Recce Platoon broke out first, followed on by Three Platoon then Company HQ Warriors and the Snatches. This left Two Platoon, One Platoon and the COs Warriors bringing up the rear. The patrol pushed up to Blue 15 before turning right and heading towards Yellow 4. At Yellow 4 we turned left and moved towards Yellow 3. A few hundred metres past Yellow 3 we went firm as we heard a massive explosion to our front.

The Recce Platoon had been hit by an explosion and had come under intense RPG and gunfire. We waited for the platoon commander from Recce Platoon to send a report and Matt, Two Platoon sergeant, was standing by as he had the Battle Group's medical officer (MO) in the back of his Warrior. We waited for what seemed like a lifetime before the radio silence was broken. The Recce Platoon commander sent his report.

> 'WE HAVE ONE WARRIOR THAT HAS BEEN HIT BY A MASSIVE EXPLOSION'
>
> 'THERE IS AT LEAST FIVE DEAD IN THE BACK AND TWO INJURED IN THE TURRET'
>
> 'WE ARE STILL IN CONTACT RECEIVING SMALL ARM FIRE AND WE ARE ENGAGING'
>
> 'THE WARRIOR IS BLASTED TO BITS AND WE NEED THE MO AND A RECOVER WARRIOR STRAIGHT AWAY'

Our hearts sank, especially mine as Paul the HQ Company CSM was in their patrol and he was one of my best mates. Before I became Arnhem Company CSM I was the Recce Platoon 2IC and most of the lads in the platoon were my old boys. The 2IC looked at me and told me to keep my head up and keep focused. Matt's Warrior flew past us with the MO in the back.

The Recce Platoon was in a fierce firefight with the insurgents running around on the rooftop all firing and doing what they could to try and fuck up the lads in their killing zone. The Recce commander and the 2IC had jumped out of their turrets and were getting the platoon moving the best they could. It was not easy as the road was narrow, and they just had to throw body parts and all sorts into the stricken Warrior and get the platoon out of the area. They moved out of the contact point fighting all the way to a safe location firing down a lethal amount of firepower, hitting the insurgents with everything they had and putting a stop to their attack.

We got told that an IRT helicopter was inbound, and that our Warrior had to move forward and secure just past the Recce Platoon

Warriors so they could land and extracted the two injured lads. We moved up with all the Warriors scanning like mad into the built-up area. As we moved past the blast site the Warriors had to move to the right to move past the hole in the road caused by the explosion. There were bits of the Warrior blown everywhere. As we reached the Recce Platoon, the Recce Platoon commander and the 2IC were doing a fantastic job, they had all their lads pushed out so that only a few were able to see the carnage inside the back of the Warrior.

With our recovery Warriors doing all they could to link up to the broken Warrior there was not much room to pass. I told the 2IC I was jumping down and would walk the Warriors through. I grabbed my weapon and jumped down. As I moved up to the broken Warrior, I could see the medical officer checking the dead bodies in the back and the medic was helping the injured lads in the turret. It was a mess and the dead in the back had been hit hard. Their bodies had been blown to bits. It was such a bloody mess. How the MO and medics were working in there I will never know. It was complete carnage and one of the worst things I have ever seen in my life. As I got to the back there was movement inside of the Warrior and the RMP lad somehow had survived. They said later it was the floor plate which had been blown up that forced the blast away from him. He was covered in blood and diesel and looked a mess, but he was lucky to be alive. As I looked in the back my heart sank as I noticed that the interpreter was one of the dead. Paul my mate was always in the same Warrior as him as he controlled him on the ground, so the chances were he was one of the other dead in the back.

I got the Warriors past and as we were securing the area there was another explosion that rocked the night. I jumped back into my Warrior and asked the 2IC what the explosion was. He informed me that another IED had gone of near Two Platoon's location, but no one was hurt. The helicopter flew in, and the medics jumped off and ran towards the stricken Warrior and started working on the injured lad who was in complete pain as his legs had been shattered. They grabbed the two injured lads and placed them into the helicopter. It took off and headed towards the COB. Two Platoon's commander was scanning the ground when he noticed a heat source near the blast area. He asked on the radio if everyone was accounted for. The call came back that the gunner of the stricken Warrior had fallen through the hole in the Warrior and was not there (the place was in such a mess it was not easy for the lads working there at night). Two Platoon's platoon commander went over to the body with a couple of his lads and checked it. They reported back that he was dead, and they carefully placed him into a body bag before he was air lifted out.

The names of the dead were sent over the radio, and it was confirmed that they were two medics, the female searcher, the gunner, and the interpreter, five in total. I was hit with mixed emotions, relieved that it was not Paul but gutted at the loss of such fine soldiers in this shithole of a place. Because the blast had been so different than any other IED we had been hit with we secured the area and waited for ATO to move out and examine the scene. The Recce Platoon moved off with the stricken Warrior with the four dead still in the back and moved to the COB where the Warrior was taken to a hanger where the police could deal with the bodies and keep as much of the forensics in place as possible.

Back on the ground we got the order to collect as much of the Warrior parts that had been blown off as we could. We set about picking up all the bits we could see, with the lads finding pieces of body parts as well. It was turning out to a life-changing night. The explosion happened just past an Iraqi police station and Two Platoon's commander got the task of entering the police station and collecting all the ID cards as they must have seen the bomb getting laid. They went inside and were met by a bunch of scared policemen. They collected all the information and passed it onto the brigade ops room.

ATO arrived and we were all in positions to try and offer the best protection we could as daylight was starting to break, and we were sitting on the edge of the Shia Flats. He set about trying to find out all the details of how the insurgents attacked us and was collecting wires and pieces from the blast area. After a couple of hours, he was finished and at 0730hrs we moved back to the COB. With the Warriors having all the bits in the back we moved straight back to the tank park.

As we parked up, the OC gave instructions for all of the body parts and pieces of the Warrior to be moved just in front of our Warrior. I set about down the company line to check on the soldiers. I saw the MO and the medic first. They were covered in blood and dirt, and I just gave them a hug without saying a word. Next, I went to Two Platoon's Warriors and saw them washing the blood out of the back of their Warriors. There was lads just sitting down with tears rolling down their faces. There was a few with blood on their combats and boots and the CQMS was going to be busy replacing all the kit. Two Platoon's commander got given the task of collecting all the pieces in of the broken Warrior and dropping them off at the forensic hanger. He was in no fit state and clearly upset by what he had to do on the ground. I told him to go check on his platoon and I would sort it out. He thanked me and went to check on his lads.

I grabbed the driver of Zero Bravo Warrior, and we placed all the bits in the back of the Warrior and moved to the forensic hangers. As we got there because some of the pieces were big and heavy, we got told to back our Warrior into the hanger and unload it. The people working in there all had the white suits on with the hoods, face masks and gloves. The area was all secure. We backed in and started to unload all of the stuff in the back. With it now being daylight I looked at the Warrior and it was a complete mess. For some reason, I looked in the back of the Warrior and it was the worst thing I ever did. The bodies were still inside and with it being daylight there was nothing left to the imagination. The images in the back of the Warrior would haunt me for the rest of my life. With my eyes filling up with tears, I mounted up and moved back to the tank park.

Back in camp the CO got everyone on parade. The Battalion all stood there with all the lads who had been on the ground looking like death warmed up with blood and dirt all over them. He stood there and confirmed that four soldiers and one interpreter had been killed during the night by an IED and he named the following, Second Lieutenant Joanna York Dyer of the Intelligence Corps (who had been working at our battalion int cell). She was 24 years old. Corporal Kris O'Neill of the Army Medical Corps (who was attached to the patrol as med cover). He was 27 years old. Private Eleanor Dlugosz of the Army Medical Corps (who was attached to the patrol as med cover) was 19 years old and Kingsman Adam James Smith (who was the gunner in the Warrior and in the Recce Platoon) was also only 19 years old. He did name the interpreter, but sadly I cannot remember his name. The padre said a few words and a prayer. After he had finished, the CO told the soldiers from the patrol to move back and get cleaned up and some rest.

At the tank park, me and Bish cleaned the Warrior of all the blood and dirt before we started to head back into camp. As we walked in, we saw the Bn on parade and started to walk towards the parade. The MTO who saw us approach, came running over and led us away. It was only then that I realised that we were covered in blood, diesel, and dirt. I checked on the lads before moving back to the tent. On the way back I spotted Paul and just walked up and gave him a hug, he understood why. Once I got in my tent, I just sat on my wall staring into space. We all knew that Op Minimise was on, but I still sent the following text home on my mobile.

'I am OK and safe I love you all.'

I took off my dirty bloodied combats and placed them into a plastic bag and then gave them to Carl to get rid of. I moved back to the tent and grabbed a shower before getting into bed. It had been the hardest night of my life and one that we all would never forget. After a day of broken sleep, we got up and I completed all the paperwork, and we attended the company O Group. At the company O Group, the OC informed us of the details that were in the ATO's report. The insurgents had been planning a big attack aimed at killing as many targets as they could. They had laid an IED under the road and covered over it. When the third Warrior of our convoy was over it, they exploded the device. The second device that exploded a short time after the first was designed to hit the dismounts clearing through the area. Luckily with the amount of firepower the Recce Platoon had fired back it caused the insurgents to withdraw saving many lives, but once again it showed what a determined enemy we were facing.

After the O Group I phoned home and spoke to my wife Lyn. It was big news back at home and everyone in Catterick was talking about it. She asked was I OK and how everyone was coping. I told her we were fine and she than told me that she knew I was on the ground and thanks for the texts as the day would have been unbearable with all the news coverage. I said my goodbyes and moved back to my tent.

Arnhem Company and Recce Platoon had been given the night off, but the Battle Group was still working with everyone apart from us out on another strike and search operation. They had to move past the site of last night's explosion to get to the target house and they moved out only to be stopped by the Iraqi police at the checkpoint as they had the barriers down. As they were doing this the call came over the radio that there was digging and insurgents placing something into the hole of last night's explosion site at Yellow 2 Alpha. They pushed forward with caution. As they moved forward, the front vehicle which was a tank got hit at the same point at Yellow 2 Alpha by an IED dug into the road again resulting in the driver's legs been blown apart. We were lucky not to have more people killed and the insurgents in that area were proving to be worth their salt. The day was finished off with the insurgents lobbing a couple of rockets at the COB that exploded without anyone getting hurt.

The next day everyone got up and set about our work. The place was sombre with everyone's morale being hit hard over the last couple of days. The commanders were working overtime to try and keep on top of the lads and keep their heads up.

The next day we saw another base handed over to the Iraqi Army as the Staffords handed over the Shatt Hotel Base. It had been another base that had been under attack almost daily. The Staffords had done a great job and their good name as an armoured infantry battalion had only been enhanced during this tour. In the afternoon we set about upgrading the Warriors with new armour that had to be fitted to our fleet. It was a big job, and we would be working when we could on getting the fleet ready.

In the late afternoon we all got our best combats on again and moved down to the airfield to carry out the repatriation for our four fallen comrades. The two medics coffins were being carried by their friends and colleges from the field hospital and ours were being carried by the Recce Platoon and the officers. The sight of the four coffins with their Union flags draped over them was upsetting and with a lot of the medics being females it hit home hard (men do not like seeing ladies cry). At the end of the repatriation the alarm went off for an indirect fire attack as we were hit with two rockets. The fuckers could not even let us send our fallen off in peace. With the all clear sounded with got on our coaches and moved back to our camps.

In the evening, we got tasked with another TST operation and by 2100hrs we were all lined up outside Brigade HQ with the offices in the building waiting for the orders. We sat there in the warm Basra night just chatting when we saw and heard the first rocket fly over that exploded somewhere in the COB. We all took cover as the second one flew in but again it went over our heads. The all clear was sounded but we were soon taking cover in our Warriors as they lobbed a single rocket in. With the all clear given we sat there waiting but were soon joined by our officers who quickly briefed us up and informed us the we were moving out.

We moved out and it was Arnhem Company's job to move forward and secure Green 19 and Green 18 for the other troop to move through but as we got to the Iraqi police checkpoint, we got told to go firm and then move back as the operation had been called off. So, we moved back and closed down our Warriors and got some sleep.

The next day all the OCs and the CO got called away to Brigade and when they returned in the afternoon. We got a warning order that a big operation was going to take place on the evening of 13 April and that we were to be involved. At the company O Group, the OC informed us that Battle Group orders would be taking place at 1000hrs tomorrow morning and that all commanders had to be there. We had our meal and then got some sleep.

In the morning, we got up and got ready for our orders. At the briefing tent we sat down, and they informed us that we would be carrying out a seek and destroy mission (ambush). We would be moving troops into two ambush positions and then deploying troops from Yellow 1 towards Yellow 2 Alpha to try and draw out the IED team that had been so successful against us over the last few days. Once they had been tricked into setting up an IED, we would hit them with everything we had.

The smiles around the room were evident and it was about time that we took the fight to them for a change. Arnhem Company HQ, Two Platoon, Three Platoon and half of C Company with a troop of tanks (four tanks) would be the feinting troop moving down from Yellow 1 towards the IED were we would stop short with the tanks at the front ready to use their powerful 120mm guns if needed. The Recce Platoon would be setting up one ambush line in the dead ground just in front of Camp Warehouse with their Warriors and C Company with some of our lads would be setting up an ambush line to the right of us with Javelin missile launchers. As well as all this we had artillery in support with their 105mm light guns. The last thing we were reminded of was for everyone to remember the importance of security because if the operation got out it was doomed to fail. It was to be called Operation Rattlesnake.

In the afternoon, the OC got us all together and told us that before Operation Rattlesnake was taking place on 13 April that eight Warriors would be needed to take the Brigade Commander up to Al Amarah on 12 April. We would be using Zero Charlie as the command Warrior with the company 2IC in overall command with four Warriors from Two Platoon and three Warriors from Three Platoon, backed up with the two recovery Warriors. With our orders being the next morning we all set about getting as much work done as we could.

We were down the tank park when the alarm went off for an indirect fire attack. We all got into cover fast with lads crawling under the Warriors and jumping into the turrets and the back of the Warriors. The first four rockets rained in and exploded. A minute later a couple more dropped in shaking the ground with the force of the explosions, this was quickly followed by three more, the explosions of which were deafening. We waited and stayed still as four more fell in and exploded. They followed these up with another five rockets that again exploded in the camp. We all stayed in our cover not daring to move until the all clear was sounded. We got out of our positions and continued with our work. At the company O Group, we were told that the COB had been hit with eighteen rockets in that afternoon's attack.

We had our meal and moved back to our tent. As soon as we got inside, we were on the floor again as the alarm went off for another indirect fire attack. The explosions were loud and scary as the insurgent hit us again with another seven rockets. As the all clear was sounded Frank turned on the kettle as he cursed the Iranians for giving the insurgents so many munitions.

The next day we attended the orders for the move up to Al Amarah and the 2IC informed us that Two Platoon would be leading the patrol with Zero Charlie Warrior in the centre with the recovery Warrior and Three Platoon bringing up the rear. The Brigade commander would be travelling in the back of our Warriors, and he had to be at his meeting by 0700hrs on the morning of 13 April where his meeting was going to last an hour before we escorted him back.

There were a few unhappy faces and the 2IC asked what was wrong. One of the lads turned around and said, 'This is shit, sir, we're going to miss out on Operation Rattlesnake.' The 2IC soon placed everyone's mind at ease when he told them to think about it. We were escorting the Brigade Commander and Operation Rattlesnake would not go ahead without him here in Basra. The rest of the day was spent sorting out all the admin and getting as much completed as we could. In the evening, the OC confirmed to us that both operations had been confirmed and for people to get an early night as the next few days would be hard going.

We went back to our tents where we got a bit of sleep in the afternoon as the night patrol was due to leave at 2200hrs that night. Things like an afternoon sleep were not always as easy as they sounded in Iraq. The insurgents attacked us twice with one rocket each time, giving us hardly any sleep. It was like they knew when to attack us, we were always sleeping or having our meal or a shower, they were complete twats. At 2000hrs we moved to the tank park and got ready before moving to Brigade HQ and picking up the Brigade Commander. He did not travel light with over ten people being in his party for the move up north. With them all squeezed in we moved to the front gate and booked out.

We set off and gave Two Platoon a minute's head start before joining the MSR and heading west. After 40 minutes Two Platoon turned right and started to head north. As they moved through the police checkpoint, they noticed one of the policemen running to use his mobile phone. The front Warrior with the platoon commander in charge was spooked by this and halted the patrol as they scanned the area. The main body pulled over to the right before deploying the dismounts as protection. Back with call sign 20 the gunner was scanning the ground to his front using the Warrior's TI sight when 200m to their front they spotted a couple of insurgents digging in an IED and laying a wire. He ordered his gunner to engage them with his chain gun. The gunner laid his sights onto the first insurgent and stamped on his firing pedal. The night lit up as the first insurgent was cut down with the deadly 7.62mm tracer. He switched onto the second insurgent, but it was too late. He had already gone to ground.

With the ground not cleared to their front, Two Platoon's Warriors moved back to us and we went a different route, pushing further west before heading north again. We were heading through the oil fields for about an hour when one of the Warriors went off the road, nearly killing everyone in it. We all moved into positions to offer the recovery Warrior as much protection as we could and me and the 2IC went to find out how long we were looking at and what had happened.

The recovery was a bad one with the Warrior stuck in a ditch off road and was going to take at least a couple of hours. This was leaving it tight for the Brigade Commander and we asked the ops room was there any chance of a chopper to drop the package off. We got a 'wait out' and I went to speak to the driver. I asked what had happened and he said he was driving tactically trying not to set patterns. The commander of the Warrior, John, was going mad. I had to grab him to stop him killing him, as he shouted 'You are lying fucker you fucking fell asleep, you nearly killed us all'. I calmed them down and told them to leave it to later and not to embarrass themselves in front of the Brigade Commander.

We got a call back from the ops room telling us that a helicopter would be with us in 30 minutes and to set up a landing zone (LZ). I got all the dismounts together and moved forward and cleared a section just to the side of the road. Once it was clear the Brigade Commander's bodyguard came up to me and started to direct what was going to happen. I was a CSM in the Infantry with 18 years of experience behind me and this twat was a sergeant in the RMP who thought he was Kevin Costner. I gave him a clear message to fuck off before he got decked and pushed the lads out and marked up the landing zone.

With five minutes to go I got the Brigade Commanders party together and we all knelt down as we heard the helicopter fly in. It was a Merlin that had a rear-lowering ramp and I shouted to everyone to put on their goggles and to protect their faces. The downforce of the Merlin helicopter was powerful and out here in the middle of the desert the stones and sand would rip your face apart. It flew in and landed, knocking a couple of the lads of their feet, including Kevin Costner which made my day. The back ramp was lowered and the loady gave me a flash of his green torch. I patted the Brigade Commander on the back, and he shook my hand as they all went forward and boarded the chopper. Once they had all boarded the back ramp raised and the Merlin took off heading north, firing its anti-missile flares pods as it went.

With the Brigade Commander gone I closed the lads in, and we moved back to the recovery, which was turning out to be a pain in the arse. After a couple of hours, the lads had the Warrior out and had hooked it up onto the back of the recovery Warrior. We all turned around and started to make the trip back to the COB and in a few hours, we were entering the front gate. Once the Warriors were closed down, I completed the statements for Morgie who had fired and we got our heads down as we knew we had a long night ahead of us with Operation Rattlesnake.

We got up the next day and everyone was busy sorting out all the kit for the nighttime operation. Once they were all completed, all the vehicles were placed on the hard standing. It was going to be a big operation but one the Battle Group was looking forward to. Taking the fight to the insurgents for a change instead of having to wait for them to make the first move. With everything done we had our O Group where the OC went over everything and wished everyone the best of luck as the company was split up all over the place. He informed me that I would have the combat cameraman in our Warrior and to pick him up on the way to the tank park. He would be waiting for me at the guard room.

We moved up to the tank park at about 2100hrs and sorted everything out, so we were good to go and then moved to the front gate. One Platoon who were dropping off the Javelin teams had already left, as had the Recce Platoon. At the front gate, the cameraman was out with his video trying to show that the British Army was fighting back after its recent setbacks as his video footage was going to be used on Sky News. He moved up the line of Warriors showing us all ready to move out.

One Platoon dropped of the Javelin teams who would be completing the last mile by foot to not give away their position. They moved across the hard ground trying to keep a low profile with the heavy launcher and its missile digging into their back with the heavy weight. Once they had reached their bund line they got down and the two firing posts were set up. The first firing post was manned by lads from C Company and the second was manned by lads from Arnhem Company. With both posts good to go they reported back that their ambush was set and with Recce Platoon also reported that their position was also good to go and the ambush was set.

We got told over the radio that the ambush lines were in place. We moved out with Two Platoon and the tanks leading. Half of C Company Snatches in the middle, with Three Platoon bringing up the rear. We were trying to look as much like a strike group as possible to try and trick out the bomb teams. We moved over the rubbish tip and Two Platoon took their time clearing the bridge at Yellow 1 to try and give the insurgents enough time to set up their deadly IEDs.

It was working and our surveillance was picking up heat sources and the ops room was getting a live link through showing the insurgents setting up. We moved just past the police checkpoint when the Javelin team came on the radio stating that they had a clear target of insurgents in two vehicles unloading their IEDs. Our hearts were pounding as we waited for the order to come, but we got a wait out, we could not believe it.

The target were there, the twats that had killed and maimed our mates were in our sights and someone was saying wait out, surely they were not shitting out at the last moment. Then the silence was broken by the ops room. 'Shot out Javelin post to fire in fig 30 seconds'. That was great new, the artillery had fired, and their shells would be falling in less than a minute. I told the camera man to get ready as the ambush was about to go live, and he got out and set up.

In the Javelin post the lads had steadied their sights onto the vehicles with Javelin post one taking the first vehicle and Javelin post two taking the second vehicle. With ten seconds to go they got told to fire. 'THROOSH'. We watched from the road as the first missile left its post going high in the air and flew towards its target. Five seconds later we saw a massive flash as it hit its target. 'THROOSH'. the second was away and again within a few seconds it too had hit its target with devastating effect, both killing everything within their vehicles.

The tanks had already moved past us and took up firing position at Yellow 2. Once there they confirmed that they had a target and the ground shook as the first Challenger fired its massive 120mm gun. The artillery was dropping in but because of the built-up area they were landing 100m short. It did not matter as we all watched as the Javelin posts fired again with the tanks' 120mm guns pounding away and the Recce Platoon chipping in with a deadly amount of firepower from their 30mm cannons and 7.62mm chain guns. But it was the tanks' main armament that must have been doing the most damage.

Down at the contact point it was devastated with massive flashes and smoke clouds dominating the area. Any insurgents in that area at the time did not stand a chance. Once all the targets were hit, we got the order to hold our fire. We watched from our position as the smoke went into the sky and the area was checked by the eyes in the sky to confirm that they were all taken out. We got the order to withdraw, and we stayed in our location as the Recce Platoon and Javelin teams moved out. Once they were clear we moved back and moved through the checkpoint. The Iraqi police just stood there as they knew that this time, they had all been outthought and that their phone calls to their mates were the last time they would ever speak to them. Once back in all the paperwork was done, I went into the cookhouse. I could see that all the lads had been lifted by the ambush. It was a relief to have taken the battle back to them after all the losses that we had suffered over the last few days. We were glad to have got some of the people responsible for their previous attacks.

The next day it was on Sky News with the Iraqi Police confirming that at least ten to twelve insurgents had been killed setting up an IED in the area. They showed us at the front gate ready to move and then showed us firing in at the insurgents. It was a good night for the British Army, but it was also needed to show the insurgents that we were more than just about protection patrols and strike operations.

After a bit of rest, it was work as normal with Arnhem Company getting warned off for another trip up to Camp Condor to support the QRL on Operation Octavia. We set about sorting all the admin out until the middle of the morning when we got attacked by four rockets. To be honest, we thought after Operation Rattlesnake we would have got a lot more.

At the company O Group, the OC walked in and looked like death warmed up. He informed us that the 2IC would be taking charge of Operation Octavia and that the orders would be at 0900hrs the following morning. We got up and attended the orders and got told that Two Platoon would be leading with Coy HQ in the centre with Three Platoon bringing up the rear. One Platoon would be moving up with a spare recovery Warrior but would turn around halfway through the oil fields as they were needed on a patrol the following day. The patrol was not leaving until later that night, and we would be travelling through the night. We spent the rest of the day completing all the checks and confirming that we were good to go. We moved up the tank park at 2200hrs and got ready and moved to the front gate.

After everyone was in the correct order of march we booked out and pushed forward and away from the front gate. It was a warm night and we had boxes of frozen water to try and keep ourselves hydrated. We made good time and were soon pushing north through the oil fields. One Platoon stayed with us until their release point and then we pushed on heading north as they turned around and headed south.

On their route back to the COB they spotted what they thought was a group of insurgents. They were carrying what looked like an IED from one vehicle to another at 0230hrs in the morning, in the middle of the desert. They were also moving from their cars to the compound 100m away and they were carrying weapons. The platoon commander had seen enough and informed the ops room that he was engaging. The platoon sergeant stood by to fire up some flares and to turn night into day. Two gunners from two different Warriors laid their sights onto their targets and stamped on their firing pedal as the flares got fired into the sky and popped open. The sky lit up as the flares went off and the tracer flew from the chain guns towards their targets. The tracer did not reach its targets and fell a few feet short, covering the insurgents in sand and dust.

They all dived for cover and One Platoon stood by for some incoming fire back at them. It never came, and the chain guns kept firing until all the cars put their lights on and they all stood up with their hands in the air. The platoon commander could not believe what he was seeing. The Warriors and dismounts moved forward and placed everyone down and away from the weapons. The platoon commander jumped out of his turret and moved towards the insurgents with the interpreter. The detainees were gobbing off in Arabic and the platoon commander told the interpreter to tell them to keep quiet. The interpreter stopped him and said 'Sir, they say they are not insurgents but just thieves'. After inspecting the cars, it was clear that they were thieves just robbing an oil compound. They were lucky bastards, and it was a good job that the two gunners were shit shots firing over 200 rounds of 7.62mm from their chain gun and not hitting even one but at least it scared them and taught them a lesson. After the Iraqi oil police had turned up and they had been handed over, One Platoon pushed on and finished their journeys to the COB where they closed down.

The rest of the company carried on pushing north and had reached the town of Al Medina. Again, we turned left and looped around the west of the town. We reached the bridge and Two Platoon got out and started to clear it. As they finished, they were mounting back up when the last Warrior got contacted by gunfire. The dismount on the back of the Warrior spotted the flashes from the insurgents and returned fire with ten rounds of 5.56mm from his rifle. They reported it over the radio and told us that the dismount had fired ten rounds from his rifle and the commander one 9mm round from his pistol (we started laughing: one 9mm round, what was it, a mistake?). On reaching Camp Condor the commander got some stick for that one round.

Once over the bridge we turned right and started to head east towards Al Qurna. After a couple of hours, we reached the town of Al Qurna, and we went into overwatch as Two Platoon cleared the main junction that we had to move through. It went well and within 30 minutes we were clear and heading north towards Camp Condor. After a few hours we had reached Camp Condor and once all the kit was handed over, we took cover in our old bunker.

After a quick brief from the 2IC the company got their heads down apart from the 2IC and me that were needed in an hour for a brief from the CO from the QRL. We were knackered and got some coffee to try and keep awake. At 0730hrs we put on our body armour and grabbed our helmets and moved over towards their bunker. We walked the short 100m and got told that the brief would be in 10 minutes. So, we moved outside to take some fresh air and try to stay awake.

I turned around to the 2IC and said, 'We're lucky to have these old bunkers here as the mortar teams up here are rather good'. I had just finished the sentence when we heard the first 120mm mortar screaming in. We dived onto the ground as it landed less than 50m away, throwing dirt and stones all over the 2IC and me. The noise of the explosion was deafening and the ground shook as the high explosives ignited. How we never got hurt with that one only God will ever know. We got up and ran into the bunker and dived for cover as the second one fell in and exploded between our bunker and the one with the lads in. The third screamed in and hit the bunker but the old building did its job, just dropping a bit of dust on us, but no one was hurt apart from a load of ears ringing. It was followed by a fourth mortar that again dropped in and exploded between the two bunkers. It was an aggressive attack by the insurgents' mortar team, who dropped all of the 120mm high explosive mortars into a small space of just 50m, pretty impressive. We lay there for another 10 minutes but no more mortar rounds came falling in. We had the brief, with everyone speaking loudly due to their ringing ears, and after the brief we ran back over to our bunker where most of the lads were sitting up just looking at each other. They were soon lying back down and in the land of nod getting some sleep before our trip back.

Back in the COB One Platoon patrol was placed on standby and they were left on 1-hour NTM. In the afternoon they came under attack by two rockets, but it was nothing compared to the attack they received during the evening when the COB was hit with thirteen rockets in five minutes that exploded all over the COB but again lady luck was on our side with no one being hurt. After this attack their patrol was cancelled and they were stood down.

Back in Camp Condor after a full day's sleep, we got up and got some food and water down us before we started our journey back. At around 2200hrs we headed out and started heading south towards Al Qurna. In a couple of hours, we were past Al Qurna and we kept going south. In a few hours, we were heading into the COB after a good journey back.

When we got back in, we noticed that Op Minimise was on again and we got informed that two people had been killed when two Puma helicopters had crashed. They were Colour Sergeant M. L. Powell of the Parachute Regiment and Sergeant Mark J. McLaren of the RAF.

With the paperwork done we grabbed some food before hitting the sack and slept through the day. At the coy O Group, the OC informed us that we had a rare night off and to try and catch up on some sleep. The next day the British Army made a massive stride with the handover of Maysan Province to local Iraqi control. We spent the day doing maintenance on the Warriors. In the evening, I had my evening meal and then went and phoned home. I had just started speaking to Lyn my wife when the first rocket flew in. It exploded close by with a deafening explosion. I quickly told Lyn I would have to phone her back, put the phone down and hit the floor. They hit us with a further three rockets which exploded a bit further away.

After the all clear was sounded I phoned back and said sorry about that love something came up. She turned as quick as a nail and said, 'Don't you mean something came down.' I just laughed and said it was a door being slammed as she replied 'Whatever.' After my phone call home, I got changed and went the gym, but we could not even do a workout as we got hit for the fifth time that day, with a single rocket this time.

The next day we got up and all went up to the tank park and got ready and left for the ranges. We left and went down the range and fired all our Warrior weapons followed by our small arms. Once done we moved back and cleaned all the weapons so that they all were good to go.

The following day we took over guards and for a change and we never got any indirect fire attacks against us which was a welcome break as they had been hitting all the bases hard lately and it was hard going.

In the evening, we noticed that Op Minimise was on again and we found out that two lads from the QRL had been killed when their CVRT was hit by an IED up north. They were Corporal Ben Leaning who was 24 years old and Trooper Kristen Turton who was 27 years old.

After a good night's sleep, we got up the next day and handed over the guards duties and moved onto one hour and three hours' notice to move. Three Platoon got warned off for a short counter indirect fire patrol that was happening that night and everyone else was just on standby.

At the company O Group, we got told that four lads from Chindit Company had been seriously hurt in a mortar attack in Basra Palace. They had been in the smoking area wearing their helmets and body armour when a 120mm mortar round fell in but luckily for them it hit a wooden beam above them and exploded, otherwise they would have all been dead. They were still in a bad way with their bodies been cut to bits by the deadly mortar and it was going to take some of them months or years to recover, if ever. Chindit Company CSM, a good friend called Lee Hamley who they were lucky to have, was also there with Sergeant Pete Reid when the round flew in. They both dived for a doorway and somehow never got injured in the blast.

At the evening meal, the officers and SNCOs were in the cookhouse having their meal. The football was on the TV and the Padre walked in and changed it over to the rugby. I turned to the Padre and said, 'Oh, it is like that is it?' The Padre exploded, slamming his plate down shouting at everyone. I looked at the Padre and said, 'Not in here, get the fuck outside now.' As we got outside, I looked at the Padre who was a friend and said, 'Really in front of everyone, what the hell was that about?' The Padre broke down in tears, the news of some of his soldier being hurt again in Chindit Company had been the final straw on a long and hard tour and showed he was only human like the rest of us.

He looked at me before he spoke: 'Oh no, what do I do now?' I told him to go wash his face, come back in the cookhouse, and come straight back and sit with me. He went to wash his face and I went back into the cookhouse. Everyone was laughing and smiling at me as I walk back in as Lee said, 'I cannot believe you offered the Padre out for a fight.' That was the talk of camp, it was all in good humour and what squaddies are all about. Even if I did end up in front of the RSM with him asking 'Carl, why did you offer the Padre out for a fight?' Once I explained to the RSM I was protecting him in front of everyone, he smiled and explained he already knew and was part of the wind-up. In the evening Three Platoon patrol went well and they all returned safely to camp.

The next day was 23 April and St George's Day, and we got woken up by the insurgents lobbing in a single rocket. It was also my 36th birthday and I had managed to keep it quite or so I thought. We had a parade in the afternoon as it was an old tradition on St George's Day that all members of the regiment get presented with a single red rose by their officer commanding. We formed up in our companies and Lee the CSM of Blenheim walked past and said, 'Happy birthday big boy.' I do not know how he found out but now everyone knew. A few of the boys sung Happy Birthday and we marched on. Once the CO was on parade each CSM got their roses and escorted the OC around and each member of the company was presented with a rose.

Halfway through the parade the battalion 2IC got called away and at the end of the parade the CO got us all together and gave us a speech about how we were on the final stretch of the road and now was the time to keep it going. The battalion 2IC came out and pulled the CO to one side. When he came back, he informed everyone that the battalion had lost another member in action and that Kingsman Alan Jones had been killed by a gunshot wound to the head. He had been on top cover in the back of a Warrior that was escorting the Brigade Commander around the city when his patrol came under fire near Basra Palace. Once he was hit, they got him into the medical centre in the palace, but he fail to survive. The Brigade Commander took his place on top cover for the rest of the patrol.

I was gutted as Alan was one of my old Recce Platoon boys. The company 2IC grabbed me and took me to the company office and made me a brew as he could see I was upset. Some fucking birthday this was turning out to be. We had our evening meal and I got given a birthday cake from the company which was a nice touch. After my meal I phoned home and then moved back to my tent.

I had been in the tent for less than a minute when the alarm went off for an indirect fire attack, they fell in and exploded around the COB. Within 10 minutes the all clear had been sounded and we carried on watching TV. A minute later we all dived for cover as we heard the whistle of two more rockets fly in, the explosions this time were closer and louder as they landed not far away. Again within 10 minutes the all clear had sounded and we carried on watching TV. Five minutes later we again had to dive for cover as more rockets flew in. The explosion were close and the ground shook as the first two exploded just outside of our camp. They were followed up with four more that exploded just by our tank park with the flames flying up in the air as they impacted on the desert ground.

They were definitely aiming for us as we were one of the main units hitting them on the ground. When the all clear was sounded this time we all thought fuck this it is safer in bed, and we got changed and got into our beds as they were behind our brick walls. We were not there for long as the insurgents finished off my birthday with a single rocket. I fell into a sleep thinking this is one birthday I would not forget in a hurry.

The following day I woke and had some breakfast before I moved over to the company office. The OC was waiting with the platoon commanders and he warned us that we would be involved in an operation that was happening the following day and that all commanders needed to be in the briefing tent for 1400hrs. I went off and informed all the commanders. In the morning, we saw another base being handed back to the Iraqi Army as we gave them control of the Shiba Log Base. We were slowly but surely giving them back control of their country which could only be a good thing.

At 1400hrs we were all seated in the briefing tent when the orders began. The patrol was a company-strength operation called Operation Howson. With the OC still bedded down, the company 2IC would be in command again. It was a route protection patrol where we had to secure the road on the south-eastern side of the city. The road was the first part of the route that led into Basra Palace. We were to secure it for a convoy that was dropping off supplies for the troops in the base. Once it had moved past our positions, we would hand it over to the troops who were securing the second part of the route. We would then move back to the COB until the next night when we would do the same for the convoy's move back out of the city.

With the orders done I manage to get to the welfare village where I got Lyn some fags and the kids some DVDs, not forgetting a milkshake. The rest of the day was taken up ensuring that all the kit was good to go for the night patrol and as we were not due to leave until 0100hrs that night, we managed to get a few hours' sleep before we began. At midnight we moved to the tank park and got all the Warriors ready. The 2IC was commanding Zero Bravo Warrior so I was commanding Zero Charlie Warrior with Steve in the gunner's seat. Once we were ready, we moved to the front gate and were good to go by 0100 hour. We waited for 15 minutes just sitting on top of our Warriors in the warm Basra air, watching the flares from the oil fields burn high into the night air until we got the order to go from the ops room.

The Warriors roared as we left the front gate and moved through the rubbish tip and down route Anfield. We stopped just short of the bridge at Red 1, where we went firm until we got told that the convoy was only 20 minutes away. We moved out and crossed the bridge. Three Platoon Warriors secured Red 1 and Red 2 including the police checkpoint. Two Platoon securing Red 3 and Red 4. One Platoon securing Red 5 and the handover point of Red 6. Call sign Zero Bravo stayed near Red 4, and I stayed near the bridge where I would pick up the lead vehicle of the convoy and escort it down to Red 6 and hand them over.

The dismounts of Two Platoon had jumped out the back and were taking up fire positions when one of the lads noticed an IED to his front. He ran back to his Warrior and informed his platoon commander. With the convoy moving up they had no choice but to disrupt it. Their gunner Morgi steadied his sights onto the device and stamped on the firing pedal. He fired with tracer bouncing all over the place and into the dark night air. He kept on firing until he saw a puff of smoke and the device slowly burning. Back on the bridge the first truck of the convoy came into sight. I placed our four way on, so they knew that they were to follow me. With all the convoy following on we moved off and passed through the police checkpoint. It was all going well until we got to Red 5. The night lit up with the flash of a massive explosion that smashed just on the back of my Warrior. The Warrior rocked to the left as it took the full force but kept on going through the attack.

I checked that everyone was OK and then looked behind to ensure that the first truck was still moving and no one was hurt. Seeing that everyone was fine I sent the contact report to the 2IC that we were all OK and that the convoy was still moving. The 2IC passed it on to our ops room. We pushed through the smoke and continued until we came to a Bulldog Fighting Vehicle who took over leading the convoy and the handover was completed. Once the convoy was clear the 2IC gave the command and we moved back the long route, moving past the old SLB camp and back into the COB. We closed down as quickly as we could and got some sleep as the second part of the patrol was taking place later on that evening.

We got up late afternoon and checked over all the kit and ensured that we were good to go. We got told that as well as our Op Howson the Battle Group was also conducting an ambush onto the insurgents that kept on blowing us up at Red 4. Blenheim Company was doing the inner cordon and C Company would be moving in on foot to hit the insurgents. With the brief completed we got all the paperwork done and chilled out for a bit as we were not due down the tank park until 2300hrs. At 2300hrs we did all the final checks and moved to the front gate. At midnight we got the call from the ops room to move, and we moved out heading the long way around, passing SLB again.

As soon as we got to Red 1 we got told to take up our positions. We moved up dropping off Three Platoon first and then moving onto Two Platoon's position. Just as call sign 20 was approaching their position they stopped the patrol. They spotted another IED set up ready to go. With the convoy ready to leave Basra Palace they again got told to disrupt it using the Warrior's chain gun. The gunner, again set his sights and fired at it with over 100 rounds of 7.62mm. The device this time let of a little bang as it part exploded, and it was passed as safe. At the same time the Battle Group's ambush went in with a firefight taking place at a compound where the insurgents were. They managed to escape but were followed back to a house and arrested.

We pushed on with the odd tracer flying past but going way too high to bother us. Once we were all in position the convoy left the Palace, and all our dismounts were deployed to try and give maximum protection. Back with Two Platoon, two of the dismounts spotted two insurgents with two AK-47 rifles. One of the lads dropped onto one knee and fired seven rounds of 5.56mm from his rifle. He missed the insurgents and they managed to make their escape. At Red 6 the convoy was handed over and we started to lead them down the road and out of the city. At the bridge we moved over, and they pushed on past and headed off towards the COB. Once they were all clear we got the order to move back and this time we headed back the quick way and were soon safely back in the COB, closed down and back in our beds.

On 28 April we took back over guards for a couple of days and the insurgents hit us with twelve rockets that all exploded near the airfield. In the evening, they were a right pain in the arse, attacking us five times with five single rockets. They were purely trying to piss us around, but they got what they deserved when they were spotted by a fighter jet that dropped a 500lb bomb on them, wiping out most of the indirect fire team.

The next day Op Minimise was on as the sad news came through that a young Rifleman from 2 Rifles had been killed in the city. He was Rifleman Paul Donnachie who was 18 years old and had died from small arms fire in the city.

In the evening, we were on standby for another TST operation, and we had the same set up as before with the officers up at Brigade

HQ and the rest waiting in camp under my command. We got the call from the ops room, and we all crashed out. The officers were waiting, and we got briefed up. Egypt and Arnhem would be clearing the route with Blenheim escorting the Iraqi Special Forces into their strike.

We pushed out and secured Green 19 and Green 18 and Blenheim Company and the ISF in their Hummies pushed past us towards Blue 16. They pushed up to the target house and Blenheim Company secured the area. They got hit with a number of IEDs and also a lot of small arms fire and RPGs but luckily no one was hurt. With the strike complete the Battle Group moved out of the area and we all moved back to the COB where we closed down and got some sleep.

Back in the COB we all started to hear of an attacked on one of Chindit Company Warriors not far away from the PJHQ base. One of the platoon sergeants called Pete Reid was in command when the whole of his Warrior was hit with a massive explosion that blew the armoured vehicle to bits. The call sign behind reported that he had spotted something flying in from the air, which came down into the Warrior which was very unusual. With a thumping head and blackened face, Pete radioed the contact report through only to be told to wait out. It came to light that a British soldier from PJHQ had mistaken Pete's Warrior for an enemy 4x4, how I will never bloody know. The Javelin missile is an anti-tank weapon designed to take out main battle tanks. The only reason Pete and everyone in the Warrior survived is that the missile came down in top mode and hit the engine block. Half a meter either side or a side attack would have killed all nine of them out right.

They had to increase the guard on the PJHQ gate as Pete tried in vain to go and speak the soldiers who had fired. Pete was having a mare of a deployment, not only had he lost three soldiers through no fault of his or his platoon commander, but he had now only just survived a blue-on-blue attack by the skin of his teeth.

April had been a hard busy month with a lot of good soldiers losing their lives in Basra City. The insurgents had hit us hard with some blistering attacks. We had also taken the fight to them and left them with some great sucker punches. It was also a bit strange for us as normal operational tours only lasted six months but because they did not want to do two changeovers at the same time (Afghanistan was changing over at the end of April as well) someone would be missing out. So instead of going home at the end of April we still had another month to go. Ah well, maybe it would be a quiet month but that was just wishful thinking.

Personally for me and I think a lot of the soldiers in Arnhem Company and the Recce Platoon April would be a month that changed us as human beings for the rest of our lives. The insurgents' attack on the Warrior at Yellow 2 Alpha resulting in five deaths was by far the worst of the tour. The pure carnage in the back of the Warrior and having to pick up pieces of a person who had been blown apart is something no one should ever have to do. I do wish I never looked into the back of the Warrior during the day, but hindsight is something we all wish for.

Seeing my soldiers once back in camp just breaking down in tears and not knowing what to do was so hard. Thinking one of my best mates is dead and what his wife and kids were about to go through, was heartbreaking. We train hard for these tours, but no amount of training can prepare you for a patrol like Yellow 2 Alpha. It was a life changing night. It took strong and brave leadership to realise we needed to take the fight to the enemy. The Brigade Commander of 19 Light Brigade was just that leader and one that understood just what his soldiers needed. The armoured ambush was needed to save life and to ensure the soldiers were re-cocked ready for the last month of the tour, which after the ambush we were.

7

MAY 2007

The JAM Commander and the Last Patrol

The seventh and last month of our operational tour started with the insurgents lobbing another four rockets into us to wake us up. Three Platoon took over the guards and One Platoon got warned off for another Operation Howson that was taking place the following night but this time they were to be attached to Blenheim Company. The day was spent supporting One Platoon so that they were good to go for the following night. We had our company O Group and got some sleep.

The next day we got up and One Platoon attended their orders. They got told that they would be escorting the convoy down the Reds as Blenheim Company secured the area. After the orders were complete, they carried out their final checks so they were all ready to go. They then moved back to their tents before they were due down the tank park. In the afternoon we started to hear about someone that had been killed by a bus in the COB. Op Minimise was soon but in place and it was confirmed that Major Nick Bateson of the Royal Crops of Signals had been killed in a road traffic accident.

At 2300hrs One Platoon moved over to the tank park and once they were good to go, they moved to the front gate. At midnight they moved out, following on the back of Blenheim Company and completed the long route around moving past Shiba Log Base. As soon as they got there Blenheim Company secured from Red 1 to Red 6 and One Platoon waited at the bridge for the convoy to arrive. The platoon commander decided that call sign 21 would lead and as the convoy arrived, Martin placed on his four ways and started to move down the bridge.

As the lead Warrior was moving past Red 4, there was a blinding explosion that broke the nightly silence and rocked the Warrior to the left, throwing the crew all over the place. The commander steadied himself and asked if everyone was OK. They were but the Warrior had a lot of damage to its BAR armour on its right-hand side. It was still able to move, so they pushed on. The HGV behind had also managed to get caught up in the explosion and they had one injured lad that they were taking into Basra Palace where he would be flown out to the hospital at the COB. They pushed on to Red 6 where the handover was completed.

With all the convoy past Red 6 they got the order to withdraw and moved back into the COB where the damaged call sign crew worked through the night with our REME to ensure that the Warrior was good to go.

On the following night Blenheim Company and One Platoon again moved up to the tank park for the second part of Operation Howson. The patrol went well this time with only a few tracer rounds being fired as they moved down the Reds. With the mission completed Blenheim Company and One Platoon moved back before closing down and getting some sleep.

The following morning the OC informed us that we would be involved in another TST operation that night and that we had to be down at Brigade HQ for 2200urs. The afternoon was spent with the company sorting out all the kit and, in the evening, we confirmed with the OC that we were all good to go. An hour later the OC informed us that we were now stood down for the night and not needed down at Brigade HQ. After our evening meal I got some time in at the gym and then chilled out in the tent before grabbing some sleep.

The following day was spent in the tank park as the surveillance troops attached some kit to our Warriors to help track our targets. In the evening, we got warned off that we would be involved in a Battle Group strike and search operation that was happening the following night. It was soon becoming obvious that any thought we had about the last month being quiet was way off the mark and if anything, it was going to be busier.

We attended the company O Group, and the OC informed us that the orders for the strike and search operation would be at 1400hrs the following day and to ensure that all commanders were present. We had our evening meal before we moved to the tank park and completed all our pre-patrol checks. Once done we moved up to Brigade HQ and once again the officers moved inside. We all sat outside in the warm Basra air waiting once again for an operation that might never happen. We had a cutoff time of 0300hrs for tonight's operation. So, there was a lot of waiting about to do.

I had ordered the lads a packed meal and they sat there with their shitty sausage roll, pack of cheap crisps, pack of nuts with raisins and apple. Half the time they just ended up throwing it at each other. By the time it was 0300hrs half the lads were sleeping in the back of the Warriors. I woke them all up as the officers came out and headed towards us. My driver turned around and said 'Looks like another waste of time', but as the officers reached us, they shouted 'Close in, we are moving out in five minutes.' He briefed us up that the tanks were providing route protection from Green 19 to Purple 1 and we were providing route protection from Purple 2 to Yellow 7 with Blenheim Company doing the protection around the target house.

We mounted up and the tanks moved first and secured their area. We pushed past them and secured our area. The strike teams moved past and struck the house. We had to stay in position, to keep the route open for the return journey and after five minutes we spotted movement from the houses to our right near Yellow 7.

The nightly silence was broken as the insurgents fired their AK-47 rifles at us with the tracer flying through the air and pinging off our Warriors. We spotted a couple of the firing points, but we had to hold our fire as our friendly troops were just behind them and the chances of shooting up our own troops with a blue-on-blue was high. So, we just sat there for a couple of minutes pointing our weapons with the insurgents' rounds flying everywhere. With the strike completed the strike teams passed through our position and then we got the order to move ourselves.

We pushed off and as we were moving past Green 19 the insurgents lobbed three mortar rounds at us that exploded just to the left of the road sending their sparks and deadly shrapnel all around us. It was not a problem for our Warriors, and we just kept on pushing past and moved back into the COB. Our fuel trucks were waiting, and we fuelled up and moved back to the tank park and closed down. After a quick bite to eat we got our heads down as we were needed for the Battle Group orders a few hours later.

We got up the next day and attended our orders and got told that it would be a Battle Group strike and search operation called Operation Pluto. It was taking place in the north-west part of the Al Hyyaniyah (Shia Flats) near Green 16. We would be taking the long route in moving down the Reds. Egypt Squadron and Recce Platoon would be securing the Red's with Arnhem securing from Red 6 to Green 5 and Blenheim Company providing protection for C Company who would be doing the strike. After the orders we left the officers to do their rock drills and we used what little time we had to check the kit over and carry out any rehearsals. We were not up the tank park until 2300hrs, so we tried to get a bit of shut eye before the operation began. At 2300hrs we moved up to the tank park and completed all the checks and booted up the radios. Once we were ready, we moved out of the tank park and headed towards the front gate and slotted in behind Egypt Squadron and the Recce Platoon.

With all the subunits good to go the Recce Platoon and the tanks moved out and we followed on. We went the long way around and pushed past SLB before going firm just short of the bridge at Red 1. After a few minutes, the Recce Platoon and the tanks got given the order to move and they moved out and secured from Red 1 to Red 6 receiving a few round of tracer on the way. Once they were in position, we moved with Two Platoon leading, followed on by Company HQ with Three Platoon and One Platoon following on behind us. We moved down the reds with the odd tracer flying through the air until we reached Red 6 were we turned left and headed down the Greens. As call sign 23 Warrior was moving past Green 4 the sky lit up as two explosions ripped through the nightly silence with their deafening bangs.

'BOOM, BOOM'

The deadly projectiles smashed into the side of the Warrior, rocking it to the right as it took the full force of the two blasts. We all went firm as the flashes turned into a smoke cloud and we waited for the commander to report. I got ready to move as I had the company medic and would have to move forward if there was any casualties. Matt the commander was soon on the radio confirming that they had been hit by two IEDs and that they had no casualties. He informed us that they had a bit of damage to the Warrior, but they were still able to push on.

So, we all moved forward and took up our positions in our Warriors. Back with call sign 23, the Warrior took up a firing position and Matt had got his dismounts out. They were checking the area when a young lad noticed a mound of dirt to his front with a wire coming out the back of it. He turned to inform his team commander when the mound exploded, sending the lad flying through the air. The team commander turned around just as the explosion had gone off and saw one of his lads in mid-air being thrown by the blast. He landed heavily and Mick the team commander picked him up and asked was he OK. He informed him that his leg had been hit and he was a bit dazed. They moved him back to the back of the Warrior were on inspection they noticed that he had been hit by a piece of shrapnel. Mick dressed the wound and reported to Matt that they had one T3 casualty. We got the message through and call signs Zero Bravo and Zero Charlie began to move forward.

'BOOOM, BOOM, TROOSH'

Within a few seconds we were engulfed in a massive ball of flames as both Warriors got hit with a couple of IEDs. I had my eyes just by the Warrior's weapons sight and I looked to my right without moving my head and could see the flames as they moved inside and licked every space. Within a second, they had been replaced by smoke. This was an incendiary device where the insurgents place some explosive on a large container of petrol which when ignited throws an intense fireball to the killing area.

I looked at the 2IC who for some reason was remarkable calm and he raised his eyebrows before asking on the radio is everyone in the Warrior OK. It was then that we got the message from the back that Marti could not see and he had burns to his face. The 2IC reported the situation to the OC who then sent a report back to the ops room. They asked if we needed the IRT helicopter and we told them to wait out as we made an assessment. The young lad with the injured leg was classed as a T3 casualty and so was Marti in the back. The medic said he was keeping an eye on him and that he would be OK to move back with us. We reported to the ops room that we did not need the IRT helicopter, and we continued with the operation.

We arrived at Matt's position and Croz got out and checked the injured lad's leg. He moved him into the back of our Warrior to keep an eye on him. We moved forward and took up our positions and covered the ground as the strike team moved past and struck a house near Green 16. I sat there covering the ground with my sights and thanked God that we were in Warriors not Snatches as we would have been blown apart in those explosions.

Back with call sign 23 they were having a busy night. Not only had they been hit with three IED in three minutes, but Matt's gunner also spotted another team laying a IED and rolling out the wire. The gunner who was a CSM from the ops room and a guest of Arnhem Company for the night. He steadied the sights onto the insurgents and stamped on the firing pedal, firing forty rounds of 7.62mm from his chain gun that fell just short of their target and smacked into the ground. He did admit later that even though he missed, he did scare them. A bit further down the road the Warriors were coming under small arms fire and the gunners scanned the ground for possible firing points. They never spotted the firing points, but they did spot an insurgent on his mobile phone dicking the patrol from a rooftop. With a new rule that had come out they were allowed to fire at him. They again steadied their sights and fired over forty rounds between them, but the dicker jumped behind a wall and lived to fight another day.

The insurgents were mad tonight and another Warrior had to open fire as his call sign was hit with small arms fire but again the insurgent was not hit. Call sign 33 who was the commander who got blew up at Green 38 a month ago spotted an IED team who were on a roof who had a wire that was leading to their Warrior. He did not fancy another thumping head, so he ordered his gunner to engage. The gunner steadied his sights onto the insurgents and fired with over forty rounds of 7.62mm from his chain gun. The chain gun's deadly rounds flew into the insurgents, causing one of them to fall of the roof and for the other to hang over the roof bleeding down the wall.

At the same time, our Warrior and Three Platoon commander's Warrior came under contact from a couple of RPGs that flew just past our turrets and exploded behind us. Three Platoon commander spotted one of the firing points and his gunner fired fifteen rounds at the position, but the insurgent was gone. Five minutes later the sky lit up again as another two RPG warheads flew towards us and bounced off the Warriors but did not explode. I scanned using my TI sight and spotted heat sources on a rooftop to my front. I steadied my sight onto the heat sources and was convinced that I had my insurgent in my sight. As he popped his head over the wall again, I fired thirty tracer rounds that smacked into the wall and started to break it up. I soon had a nice hole and could see my insurgent. I told the 2IC I was not messing around and switched my weapons to main armament and steadied the 30mm sights onto my target. I was just about to stamp on the firing pedal when the 2IC shouted 'STOP, he's sleeping on the roof'. I checked my sight again and watched as the cheeky little fucker shook his blanket off where the wall had fallen and lay back down. I muttered 'You lucky bastard' as I applied my safety back onto the weapons.

We got the word that the strike had lifted and would be moving back through our position in the next few minutes. I checked if Marti was OK, and the medic told us that we needed to get him off the ground as soon as possible. The strike team moved past us and as we moved off as we got contacted with a load more tracer rounds as the insurgents gave us a parting gift. We moved back to camp by he fast route, moving down Anfield and Old Trafford. As we approached the front gate, we got told that Lee's Warrior was waiting for us with the MO and to move there so the MO could assess the casualties. We pulled up behind the Warrior and the doc jumped out and had a look at the lads. He upgraded them both to T2 as their conditions had become worse and told us to place them into his Warrior and that they would drop them off at the field hospital. With the lads handed over we moved back to camp where all the statements were completed, and we got a meal.

After my food I got my mobile and phoned Lyn. It was 0300hrs and Lyn woke with a fright and she asked what was wrong. I just told her that I was fine but for some reason just wanted to hear her voice and tell her I love her. It was one of those nights where you felt lucky to be alive. I said my goodbye and went and got into bed. We were not in bed long as the insurgents lobbed in three rockets that exploded forcing us all to take cover on the floor.

After a few hours' sleep I got up and went and saw the lads in the hospital. The lad with the injured leg was sitting up with his leg all bandaged up and he was pretty happy as the pretty nurse looked after him. Marti was in the bed next to him and had his face sorted and had a thick bandage on his head. He still could not see out of his eyes. We treated him as normal and started to take the piss. I told him not to worry at least he could watch the Manchester derby on TV. We all fell about laughing as he called us all twats. Just before we were leaving the doc told him he would be flying home the next day to continue his recovery in England. He was not happy as he did not want to leave his mates behind for the last few weeks. I told him not to be daft and to get home and see his little family.' Sorry, sorry,'

I said, 'at least you can touch their face.' We left laughing as Marti was shaking his head. Some of the lads took him some stuff later that night and it was the last we saw of him in Iraq. He was a good lad and an outstanding soldier who had saved a few of us with his brave soldering throughout the tour, he was going to be missed.

When I got back, I phone Marti's wife and the other lad's mum and assured them that their injuries were not life-threatening and told them how well their loved ones had done. After I had finished, I phoned Lyn and said sorry for phoning her so early and that I hoped I had not frightened her. She had already heard about the injured lads and asked was I OK? I told her I was fine but could not wait to get home. We also got informed that Private Kevin Thompson, who was the lad who got injured a week ago on an Op Howson with One Platoon, had lost his fight to live and had died in the UK. He was 21 years old and had been serving with 19 Combat Service Support Battalion. I went back to the room and was soon on the floor taking cover as a couple of rockets fell in and exploded just past our camp. After the all clear, I went back over to the tent and got into bed and fell into to sleep.

The next day I went over to the company office. The OC asked me to go and get the platoon commanders and the 2IC for a brief and within five minutes we were all in his office. He warned us off for a Battle Group strike and search operation that was taking place in a couple of days and informed us that we would be carrying out the strike with our search team doing the search. We set about sorting all the kit away and I got all the paperwork ready for the search.

At the company O Group, I informed the platoon commanders who I needed for the search and told them I was breaking it down into two half-teams with myself commanding the first and Morgi commanding the second. I told them that I needed the teams for the morning but would be at their platoon rehearsals in the afternoon.

The next day we got up and attended the orders. The operation was going to be a strike and search operation that was taking place at Green 18. Egypt Squadron and the Recce Platoon would be doing the route protection and Arnhem would be doing the strike and searches. The operation was to be called Operation Freetown.

After the orders we sorted out all the paperwork and tools that we needed for the search and in the afternoon we did all the rehearsals with the platoons. I was with Two Platoon and was striking and searching a shop and building just off Green 18 and Morgi was with One Platoon who was striking and searching a dwelling house 100m behind us. At the end of the day the OC confirmed that everyone was happy, and we retied back to our tents. After a DVD we jumped into bed and tried to get some sleep, but like every other night, that was not possible with the insurgents.

The next day we got up and the final checks were completed in the morning. We rested in the afternoon before moving down the tank park at 2200hrs where all the checks were completed. I went and saw Morgi and wished him good luck before jumping in the back of our Warrior. The door shut and we moved to the front gate. It was warm, and we cracked open the frozen water and tried to keep ourselves hydrated. At the front gate we waited for the Recce Platoon and the tanks to move out before we were told to move by the ops room.

We moved through the main gate and onto the MSR. Just after the A Pod Bridge we turned left and moved down the ramp towards the river. We headed under the bridge before moving across country towards Camp Wear House. We stopped short of the housing estate and waited for the ops room to tell us that the tanks and Recce Platoon were in place at Green 19.

We got the go and the Warriors roared as we launched forward at speed. We stormed into the housing estate and stopped just short of our target house. We dismounted and got into the correct order with the strike teams in front of us. All the search team put on rubber gloves to help protect the evidence. We moved forward and struck the first building. The door was knocked down by the hammers and they went inside and cleared it. Once it was clear the strike team moved out and we moved in and completed the short search of the first outbuilding.

With it completed we moved onto the shop, and we all took cover by a short wall as the lads set to work on the front door. The insurgents had spotted us, and we scanned with our sights as an RPG warhead flew past us with a loud WHOOSH and kept on going down the street where it exploded. It was followed by tracer rounds that lit up the sky as they flew past us. The door was at last opened and the strike teams went in. With it being a small shop it was soon clear, and the search team moved in. They had a cans of pop and a load of cigarettes as well as some other strange snacks. We did a quick search and were soon completed.

Outside call sign 21 had spotted some insurgents and our ears started ringing as his gunner opened fired with thirty rounds of 7.62mm. It was frightening stuff in such a small built-up area and must have scared the shit out of the insurgents.

Back at One Platoon location they broke in the door and found that no one was at home. So, the search began with four rooms to search and one back yard. Morgi set about the task, splitting up the lads into search pairs.

Back at our location we were striking another group of out building and the strike team broke down the gate as we came under fire from a single shot that cracked over our heads and made us all dive for cover. We were soon in the back yard as call sign 21 again responded back at the insurgents with a volley of tracer. We searched the new outbuilding and got told that fast air (an attack aircraft) was on its way to support us. The sky lit up as the fast jet roared overhead about 30m in the sky, dropping a trail of flares to let the insurgents know that he was there. It was so fucking loud and the dust from the road flew into the air as it shot past. The insurgents must of shit themselves.

One Platoon had found one male hiding and a small amount of munitions and informed the OC that they were detaining him. With both searches completed the Warriors moved back and Three Platoon covered us as we were about to mount back up. The Warrior crews lobbed a load of phosphorus smoke grenades to cover us, and we ran out as a few rounds were fired into the smoke. The fast air again roared overhead as we shut the back door and began to move. As we were about to move call sign 31 reported that it had a problem, and his Warrior would not move. We moved into all-round defence to protect the recovery and within 20 minutes we were moving back towards Camp Wear house.

On the route back we had a problem as we needed to move over a steep ramp that had a disused railway track on top of it and we were not sure if the recovery Warrior towing the damaged Warrior was going to be able to get over it.

He told the OC that he was going to go for it, and we watched as the two Warriors speed up and left the ground as it flew over the ramp, the mad twat, but with everyone over we headed back to the camp were the detainee and munitions were handed over. Back in our camp the paperwork was completed, and we got our heads down.

You could tell when you had pissed off the local insurgents because they always lobbed some rockets at you after the operation. We slept through the morning but were woken up with four attacks on the COB. Sleeping most of the day, we got up and checked all the kit off and completed all the paperwork. At the company O Group, the OC informed us that we were to be on standby for a TST operation that night but instead of all the company going down to Brigade HQ only the officers would. The rest of the company would stay in camp with a lad in the ops room and all the Warriors standing by good to go with a driver staying with them. It was a great idea as the lads could chill out in their tents instead of sitting on a road all night. By 0100hrs the operation was stood down and everyone was back in our camp.

The next day Egypt Squadron and the Recce Platoon were deploying on an Operation Octavia to Camp Condor but were going left out of camp and heading past Green 20. This meant that Arnhem Company was tasked with clearing the junction at Green 19 and the road up to Green 21. The day was spent getting ready and by 2000hrs we were down the tank park completing the final checks. With the company good to go we all moved to the front gate and waited for the nod from the ops room.

We were told to move out and One Platoon headed out and secured the area around the Iraqi Police checkpoint. Two Platoon pushed past and cleared the junction at Green 19 leaving two Warriors there and the other two moving up to Green 20. Company HQ and Three Platoon started to move up to Green 20 when we were told to go firm by Two Platoon's commander. They had spotted an IED just past Green 20 and with the convoy moving up they were told to disrupt it using the Warrior's chain gun. The gunner steadied his sights onto the IED and stamped on the firing pedal. The chain gun spat out its deadly rounds that smacked into the device. After 100 rounds it had still not gone off. So, the platoon commander told his gunner to try again. He again steadied his sights and fired a further fifty rounds of 7.62mm, with tracer bouncing off the ground and flying into the air. There was still no reaction from the bomb. The OC ordered us to clear the other side of the road which we did, and we moved on. We informed the convoy of the situation at Green 20 and told them to use the far road as it was safe.

Within 10 minutes the convoy was moving past us and once it was over Qarmat Ali Bridge we moved back to Green 20. Call sign 22 and 23 who were back protecting the junction at Green 19 started to come under fire from mortar rounds that were falling in and around their Warriors. They got their dismounts to get back into the Warriors and waited for the company to move. The platoon commander of Two Platoon wanted to see what was going on with the IED and went to have a look. On inspecting the device, he asked the OC could he place in on the back of his Warrior and hand it over to ATO. We could not believe it, was he some kind of madman? Rightly so, the OC declined his offer. We moved back through Green 19 with the mortar rounds still dropping in but having no effect on us and we all moved back to the COB were we refuelled and closed down.

The next day we took over guards and were warned off for an Operation Howson in a few days' time. After the Operation Howson we were to move into Basra Palace where we would be involved in a Brigade operation. We set about the admin and at the company

O Group we got told that the orders would be at 1300hrs the next day but before that we would also be involved in another TST operation tonight. I set about and informed Paul the camp CSM that we needed to be replaced on guards. We did the same set-up for the TST operation with the officers moving up to Brigade HQ and the company staying on standby back in camp. Again, we were not needed, and we took back over the guards. We got up late the next day and by 1300hrs we were all seated waiting to receive our orders in the briefing tent.

They informed us that it was going to be a brigade strike and search operation called Operation Rasputin. We had two big buildings that were going to be struck. The first was a block of flats which the Special Forces and C Company would be hitting and the second was an old hotel which Arnhem Company was going to be striking. One of the Rifles' companies from Basra Palace and Blenheim Company would be securing the area.

The next few days we studied the lay out for the Hotel and practised how it was going to be done. Three Platoon would be doing the break-in and securing the ground floor and then Two Platoon would push through and secure the second floor before One Platoon pushed past and secured the third floor and the rooftop. We worked hard ensuring that every man knew what he had to do and before we knew it, it was the day we were due to deploy. In the evening, we attended the O Group and the OC walked in with his arm in plaster. He had broken it in a fall earlier in the day and the hospital wanted to send him back to the UK but there was no way he was going to leave his lads with just a few weeks to go so he stayed and supported the company the best he could. This meant that the 2IC was going to be in command on the ground.

We also got informed about Blenheim Company who had been crashed out earlier in the day to assists a Danish patrol who had been blown up with an IED and needed help to extract out of the area with their casualties. Blenheim Company moved up and under fire they extracted them out back to the COB. With the O Group out the way we had our evening meal before a bit of down time. I phoned home and told the wife I would be away for a few days, and I would phone her when I could. At 2330hrs we moved down the tank park and ensured we were good to go. Just after midnight we were at the front gate ready to move.

At 0030hrs we moved out and headed down the rubbish tip. There were a lot of fires in the tip, and it was causing a few problems with the front Warrior leading us. It soon became a nightmare when call sign 31 Warrior decided to see if he could cross over the oil pipes (the madman, what was he thinking?). Of course his Warrior got stuck with the threat of oil bursting out a great possibility. We left one of the recovery Warriors to sort him out with the commander getting the nickname the ‘Pied Piper of Arnhem’, taking the recovery Warrior four hours to get him of the pipes. We pushed on with call sign 32 leading us and as we broke out of the smoke at Y1 Alpha we noticed a Warrior moving over the bridge on his own heading towards Y2. We got on the radio and told all call signs to go firm and informed call sign 32 to stop and move back towards the rubbish tip. He later informed us that he was not lost, just covering the ground. Covering the ground my arse, he was lost or just the hardest twat ever, doing a city patrol on his own. We pushed down Route Anfield before again stopping short just before Red 1.

We got the go from the ops room, and we pushed on with Three Platoon covering the Iraqi Police checkpoint and Two Platoon securing Reds 3 and 4, with One Platoon and Company HQ covering Reds 5 and 6. Again I waited at the bridge ready to pick up the convoy and lead it to the handover point at Red 6. The convoy turned up and I led them down the road with the odd tracer round being fired at us but with no firing point being seen I just pushed on and handed them over at Red 6. Once all the convoy had passed through the company collapsed from their position and joined on the back and we all headed into Basra Palace.

We moved in and got met by some lads from 2 Rifles who showed us where to park up our Warriors. We parked the Warriors up in one of Saddam’s Hussein’s palace’s car park and the officers went and booked in at the ops room.

Carl and I moved forward and took over the accommodation. We then got the lads and got them into the safety of the building. We were staying in one of the old building that used to be occupied by the Romanian Army when they used to have troops here. Most of the soldiers had bunk beds that were three high, but others just had a mattress on the floor. It was a tight squeeze with bodies all over the place, but the lads were not arsed as they stripped down to their underwear and got their heads down.

It was hot and being so near to the Shatt Al Arab River a lot of us placed up our Mosi nets to try and stop being bitten. It was the early hours off the morning when we finally got all the company into their beds, and it was 20 minutes later that the company nearly lost a few lads. We got hit with some mortar rounds that landed just outside of our building that exploded with a deafening noise, but two of the seniors Frank and Ray forgot that they were on the top bunk of a three-storey bunk instead a low cot bed. The silly fuckers rolled off their beds only to fall ten feet and hit the ground smacking the floor with their girly moan. If you think that was bad, I was on the bottom bed in my Mosi net when I rolled off only to land with a bump, looking like Spiderman on speed caught in his own net. The room fell about laughing as everyone sorted themselves out and got back into bed and fell asleep.

As we tried to drop off to sleep, we all heard the loudest snoring that was ever known to mankind. I heard movement and got out of my bed and turned the lights on. I could not help to laugh as around twenty soldiers were around Paul (HQ Coy CSM) just looking in amazement at the noise coming from Paul's head. I told them to get into bed, as I turned off the lights to the deafening sound of Paul's snoring.

The insurgents hit us again a couple of hour later dropping in four mortar rounds but this time we were more prepared and also remembered that we were in the safety of a building. It still did not wake up Paul who was still snoring away. We got up in the afternoon with a couple more rounds falling in exploding with one exploding behind our building and the other dropping into the water.

We walked over to the other building and paid our respects to 2 Rifles' RSM before having a good look around. The compound had a number of palaces that were all fine-looking buildings with wooden carvings all over the outside. They also had sandbags all over the place and a couple of the buildings had a number of blast marks where rockets or mortars had exploded. On the inside they showed the marking of buildings that had been built up to protect them. There were sandbags everywhere and all the windows had been removed and boarded up. The main building had a hole where a rocket had gone through the outer wall and landed in some lads' bedroom but lucky for them it never went off. It was also the building that had the cookhouse in it and the food was good. It had a little shop in there that sold everything. As well as the shop it had another barbers, turning all the soldiers into more Beatles lookalikes.

I went to the ops room and booked the skills house for rehearsals the following day so the company could practice and fine tune everything for the strike operation that was happening in a couple of days. The skills house was an old shell of a building that we could practice our strikes and knock the doors in. It was a good way to fine tune our training and iron out any mistakes.

We got a shock in the evening when we got told that we would be used in the second part of Operation Howson as we thought we had the night off. We got to our Warriors at 2200hrs and at 2240hrs we moved out and secured the first part of the route from Pink 25 to Pink 19. The convoy moved out and within 10 minutes they were past our positions, and we got told to move back into Basra Palace. As we got in, we got into bed for some well-deserved sleep. The next day we woke up with a couple of mortar rounds exploding and once the all clear was given we got washed and shaved and had our breakfast. As a company we then moved over to the skills house and spent the day storming the house ensuring that everything was good to go. Once the 2IC was happy we moved back and had lunch. The rest of the battalion who were taking part in the operation had turned up from the COB and were in the palace.

We had the night off and spent the night watching TV that someone had kindly set up for us. After watching TV, we got into bed for a good night's sleep. The following day was spent with the commanders going over the plan and then the lads getting briefed again just to ensure everyone was happy and good to go. In the afternoon we did our final checks and just before our evening meal the 2IC got called away and on his return, he informed us that the operation had been delayed by 24 hours and that the company was not on patrol that night and to tell all the lads to make the most of it and get a good night's sleep. The following morning, we got some more time in at the skills house and spent the afternoon waiting for the operation to start.

At 0100hrs we got told that the operation was a go and we all moved to our Warriors and got them ready to go. At 0200hrs we moved to the front gate and waited for everything to be put into place and for the word from the ops room telling us to move out. It was a warm night and we sat by our Warriors with all our kit on sweating our arses off. I moved down the line and ensured that the boys were taking on water and keeping themselves hydrated. The call came from the ops room at around 0330hrs, and we all mounted up and waited for our turn to move.

The first to move from Arnhem Company were Three Platoon who moved out through the northern gate and were dropped off by Warriors at Pink 20. The platoon commander got his men sorted out and they set off on foot moving down some of the most dangerous streets in the world heading towards our strike building. The streets were full of litter and the lads moved down trying to make best use of the shadows as they could to try and keep out of sight of the deadly insurgent sharpshooters. The Special Forces were doing the same, but they were heading towards their target. With the first part of the operation under way we got the order to move, and we pushed out of our gate and moved past Pink 24 on the way toward our target building near Pink 19.

Three Platoon had completed the short and nervy move on foot and they were now securing the outside of the building. As we arrived, they had the building secure. We dismounted and got ready to move in once the door had been broken down. The Warriors with Frank in charge were scanning everywhere to try and give us as much protection as they could with most of us being exposed on the ground. We were scanning around us, up at the building scanning the windows in case anyone tried to stop us entering. Three Platoon got the nod from the 2IC, and the door was smashed in with a chain getting cut and then the hammers smashing against the part-metal and part-glass door, sending glass flying all over the place. The doors gave way sending them flying inwards with one nearly coming off its hinges. Three Platoon stormed inside, and they soon had the lobby and ground floor secure.

Two Platoon pushed past and started to take the stairs. At the top of the stairs, they secured the corridor and told One Platoon to move. One Platoon pushed past and then did the same for the third floor. With each platoon in position the company started to clear the building. The doors to each room were kicked open and anyone inside was told to face the wall and place their hands on their heads in the kneeling position. Once a room was secure, we left one lad in each doorway and continued to do this until all the room were secure.

The 2IC who was controlling the strike soon got the messages back that the ground floor, second floor and third floor were secure, and that One Platoon were moving up and securing the roof. 'ROOF CLEAR' came the shout down the stairs and the 2IC reported over the radio that the building was secure and that the search was now taking place.

This was my ball game and as I was already on the second floor. I set the lads about searching the rooms and Morgi did the same for the third floor. I walked to the first room and started the search. It had two young Iraqi men in the room who were about 19 years old, and they were not going to be any problem as they were shitting themselves (to be honest so would I if I was in their shoes). Their hand were tied to their front, and they were kneeling down facing the wall. I got them off their knees and sat them down and signed to them to relaxes and that they would not be hurt. I stepped out into the corridor and shouted to all the rooms to sit the locals down and to just keep control of them. I got some of the soldiers to go get a few boxes of water and instructed the soldiers to give each local a bottle of water and to just calm them down.

The rooms were small and were no bigger than ten foot by ten foot. They had a shower in the corner that looked like it had never been used and a hole in the floor for the toilet, it was just an old hotel room. With nothing been found I moved on to the next room and did the same until all the rooms had been searched. As the search was going on all the ID cards were collected in and the information was passed onto the ops room. With the floor completed I moved back down to the lobby where Three Platoon had it cleared and secure. It had a toilet in the back where an Iraqi man was being questioned. Three Platoon had stopped the local who had tried to run as the building was stormed. We looked at him and it was clear this was the man we had been looking for.

With all of the building having been searched we noticed that there was another part to the hotel that was locked and had not been cleared. Three Platoon moved outside and again they broke the door down and moved inside. I followed them straight in and had a look around. It was full of offices and stunk to high heaven with a few dead rats around the place. There was also rat shit and piss everywhere with the smell stinging your eyes.

With the old hotel completed the 2IC reported back that the building was no longer a hotel and was just full of squatters. He informed them that we had one male that we were detaining and that we were ready to mount up on their call. We untied all of the locals and shut the room doors to keep the area secure inside of the building. The call came five minutes later, and I stood by the door and counted everyone out to ensure that no one was left behind. With the whole company out of the building I informed the 2IC that we were good to move. He nodded and I ran and jumped in my Warrior. Frank was in the gunner's seat and passed me a bottle of water as I got myself sorted. With all the Warriors good to go we got told to move out. We pushed on towards Red 18 where we went firm and waited for the Battle Group to catch up. The deadly morning silence was broken with a few rounds of tracer that flew at our Warrior and pinged off, flying into the sky.

Frank turned the turret looking for a firing point. It was at this point that there was a muffled bang, and I felt a burning sensation on my leg. I informed Frank we were hit by an RPG and that it had broken through and that my leg was wet. I shouted down to the boys to open the turret cage and to have a look as I had no room to bend down. It was strange as I had no pain, and the bang just did not sound right. One of the lads in the back shouted up, 'No you're all right it was just a can of WD40 that had got caught in the turret and exploded onto your leg'. What a dickhead I felt and when we got back, I got a bit of stick of the lads about the insurgents attacking us with cans of WD40.

The Battle Group had now caught up and we pushed on moving forward following one of the platoon from the Palace. We went a different way out of the city, one we had not been before. It was down a vehicle-width track moving through the oil fields. We kept checking the maps but soon we were that far north we ran out of maps. The convoy was around 100 vehicles long and if we had a breakdown God only knows how we would get out of this one. The platoon commander who was leading was a Lancs officer and after that extraction the route became known as his surname. The patrol managed to get back on track and was soon moving back into the COB. We refuelled and closed down the Warriors in the tank park. After all the paperwork was done, I went and had my normal fry-up and moved back to the tent. I had a long shower as I felt even dirtier than normal coming from the old hotel and then jumped into bed and slept most of the day.

In the afternoon I went over to the office and completed all the paperwork. In the evening, I phoned home and told Lyn that I was now back in the COB. She told me that Daniel and Kirsty were looking forward to me coming home and I smiled to myself thinking at last we were into the last two weeks. On the way back to my tent I had to jump into the dirt as the COB got attacked with a few rockets of indirect fire, after the all clear was sounded I moved back to my tent and got some sleep. The following day was spent in the tank park working on all the Warriors. They had been smashed over the last few weeks and needed a bit of maintenance.

It was good to see soldiers of the Royal Welsh turning up getting ready for the handover and it reminded us that our time was nearly done. In the evening, the OC warned us off that we would be on standby for a TST operation the following night and that all the officers would be needed to move down to Brigade HQ from 2100hrs. At 0330hrs it was called off and everyone was stood down.

The next day was spent ensuring that the company was good to go for the possible operation that night. At 2200hrs the officers were all at Brigade HQ and we had all the Warriors running and ready to go in our tank park. At 0100hrs we got crashed out and we all moved up to Bridge HQ and waited to get our brief. The officers came out and told us that we were supporting a strike onto a target house at Yellow 9. Three Platoon were moving out first with Egypt Squadron and then we would be moving as the protection to C Company who were to strike the building.

Three Platoon and the tanks moved first, and they pushed forward and past Green 19. At the front of the convoy was Three Platoon's commander's Warrior and he was being followed by a tank. They had just got past the first part of the junction when the sky lit up with a massive explosion. It had missed their Warrior and Three Platoon commander looked back to see the tank surrounded by a fireball as it took the full blast of the device. The tank commander reported that the tank was still working and that they were all OK apart from himself who had a number of cuts to his face, but he reported that he was fine and would dress the cuts himself.

Three Platoon commander was the person to go on the ground with. His Warrior had never been caught by an IED and he had often drove past one with the second vehicle getting hit (he definitely had someone watching over him). They pushed on and secured the junction. We pushed on and moved through their position and turned left at Green 18 and onto the target area. We positioned our Warriors to offer the best protection we could offer using street corners and our dismounts to cover the dark alleyways. The strike went in and within 30 minutes they had completed the search and had detained a couple of men as well as a small amount of munitions.

The strike teams pushed through and as One Platoon started to move the sky lit up as the insurgents were waiting with their AK-47s in aggressive ambush. It was like Road Runner and the Coyote with One Platoon Warrior flying past us followed on by the deadly one in one tracer. We pushed up in our Warrior to just outside of a bakers to try and offer some protection. The locals in the bakery were watching the show by their front door. We spotted the flashes of the insurgents' AK-47s, and I steadied my sights onto the target. I stamped on the firing pedal and the sky lit up as the deadly 7.62mm tracer flew from my chain gun and smacked into the area of the insurgents forcing them to go to ground and stop firing. The 2IC started laughing and told me to pop my head up. I got up and looked down from the top of the turret. I saw the poor locals who had been watching crawling into their shop on their bellies. I do not think they expected our Warrior to fire and when the chain gun went off, they shit themselves and dived for cover. With all the company through we moved off and pushed on past Green 19 before entering the COB. We closed down and completed all the post-patrol admin before getting some sleep.

We got up the next afternoon and prepared and re-cocked so we were all good to go. In the evening, we were on standby for another TST operation. We all mounted up at midnight and moved up to Brigade as we got crashed out. The offices came out and briefed us but as we mounted up the radio sparked into life as we got told to stand down as the operation had been called off. We moved back and got some sleep.

The next day we got up in the afternoon and got warned off for another TST operation. We went down the tank park and started to sort out the Warriors. My Warrior was broken, and I got told it was not going to be on the road for at least 24 hours. I informed the 2IC and asked him what job I could do. He told me to have a night off for a change as since we had been in Iraq, apart from leave, I had not missed a company operation (to be fair neither had he). I agreed but it did not feel right being stood down with the lads all on standby.

C Company 1 Yorks had come to the end of their tour and had handed over to A Company 4 Rifles. C Company had been an outstanding part of the Battle Group and their men had balls of steel following our Warriors into the city time after time in their Snatches which had no protection from an IED. They had done more strikes on their seven-month tour that any subunit before them. We were saying goodbye to some good friends and an outstanding group of men. Later their OC would be awarded the Military Cross for his and his men's leadership and bravery.

The 2IC and the officers moved to Brigade HQ and the lads stayed in camp waiting to be crashed out. The call came just before 0330hrs, and I watched as the lads mounted up and moved out. They got to Brigade HQ and the officers came out and briefed them up. They were to move out first and secure just past Green 18 for the Battle Group to move through with the help of a few tanks.

They moved out and at A Pod Bridge they turned left and headed down the ramp. They turned left moving under the bridge and then went across country towards Camp Warehouse, before moving down towards Yellow 2 Bravo. At Yellow 2 Bravo the sky lit up as two rockets were fired from the Shia Flats area. They passed over the heads of the company's Warriors and flew towards the COB. Back at the COB the OC and me were soon on the floor as the rockets exploded near the airfield.

Back on the ground Two Platoon moved forward towards Green 18 and with it being 0730hrs it was already light. Their Warriors moved forward and stopped just short of the junction. The lads in the back of the Warriors dismounted and they moved out into the morning air that was becoming very warm in the sun.

The first part of the junction was cleared without any fuss but as they got onto the other side of the road movement was spotted ahead on the rooftops and ally ways. The morning silence was broken as the first insurgents' AK-47 rifles kicked into action, spitting out their deadly rounds towards the dismounts. The ground around one of the lads kicked up all around him as the 7.62mm bullets struck the ground.

In the platoon sergeant's Warrior, he spotted two insurgents with AK-47 rifles and an RPG launcher. His gunner steadied his sight onto the RPG man, and he stamped on the firing pedal. The chain gun kicked into action firing its one in one tracer, cutting the RPG man down where he stood. The second man went to ground and disappeared. The 2IC a little further back seeing Two Platoon under heavy fire, sent the tanks forward to assist. Their big engines roared as they moved forward. As they got to Two Platoon, they pushed to the front were they got their 7.62mm machine guns working straight away cutting down the insurgents' positions.

The Battle Group pushed through Green 18 with the RPGs and small arms fire still flying all over the show, but they carried on reaching the target area striking the house. The tanks that were with Two Platoon just forward of Green 18 had both spotted a group of insurgents firing and taking cover behind a wall. Their big 120mm guns spun around. 'BANG, BANG.' The ground shook as the impressive main armament fired, smashing the wall to pieces. The insurgents behind it flew through the air and landed with the rubble. The Warriors from Two Platoon and call sign Zero Bravo were still getting whacked at Green 18 and a number of Two Platoon's Warriors had opened fired on different firing points and dickers on the rooftops.

Over the radio news started to come through about casualties from Blenheim Company and A Company. The 2IC got told to set up the HLS and he informed Three Platoon to sort it out. The platoon commander moved forward and got the area ready for the IRT helicopter. Back in the COB I could hear all the bangs going off and when the Tannoy call for the IRT crew I moved up to the ops room and listened to what was going on. Blenheim Company had four lads injured and A Company had two that were being moved back by their Warriors to the HLS.

At Two Platoon's location the Warriors were still under heavy fire and there was a loud bang as the tank on the right-hand side of the road got hit full whack by an RPG warhead. It pulled back as the warhead pieced its fuel tank, spilling diesel out onto the road. As the tank started to move back it was set on fire and there was little the tank commander could do as his radios were down. So, he just had to keep on moving to a safe area and sort it out. Two Platoon regrouped and set up their Warrior to cover the main junction of their position. Call sign 33 who had secured the HLS with his platoon moved forward to assist Two Platoon.

As they were moving to their position their Warrior turned into a fireball as it took the full force of an IED.

'BOOM, TROOSH'

The flames soon turned into smoke and the Warrior started to reappear through the smoke. The commander steadied himself and asked was everyone OK. It was the shout from the back that alerted the commander that something was wrong. One of the lads in the back of the Warrior grabbed the headset and informed him that the two lads who were on top cover had been knocked out but were still breathing although still down on the floor out cold. Within a few minute they came to but had a few cuts on their faces. The commander reported that he had been hit by a roadside IED and that he had two T3 casualties that needed extracting. The first IRT helicopter had left with the first six casualties and the report went over the radio that there was more moving to the HLS. As well as our casualties, Blenheim Company had three more and A Company had another two that were all moving back to the HLS.

Back in the ops room it was being controlled well but there was no way I was ever going to miss another patrol as I felt as useless as a priest in a whorehouse.

Call sign 20 who was facing south-east noticed that the road to their front had gone quiet. All of a sudden, the placed exploded with RPGs and small arms fire zipping down the road. The gunner in the Warrior spotted a gunman and quickly got him in his sights. He fired, cutting the gunman down where he stood and switched onto another target who just got out the way of his deadly bullets. They spotted some movement to the right-hand side of the road and watched as an insurgent crawled from a wall and took up a fire position behind the car. The platoon commander told his gunner to select high explosives and he switched his sight and stamped on the firing pedal. 'BANG, BANG, BANG', the Warrior rocked as the 30mm rounds left the barrel, and exploded smashing the wall and causing the car to set on fire. The insurgent did not stand a chance and was struck down with the force of the attack. The place was becoming untenable with every Warrior on the ground coming under RPG or gunfire. The strike teams had nearly finished, and the Warriors were still covering the grounds the best they could.

At call sign 22's position they were coming under heavy gunfire when the turret exploded as it took a direct hit with an RPG warhead. The warhead went through the metal and exploded into the gunner's face, causing the inside of the turret to burst into flames. The gunner grabbed his face and shouted, 'AM HIT.' The commander George, who was the platoon's Warrior sergeant, jumped out of his turret with gunfire flying all over the place and pulled his gunner out of the turret and placed him in the back of the Warrior through the open hatches on the roof. The commander then jumped back into his burning turret and informed the 2IC that they had taken the full blast of an RPG and that he had one T2 casualty and they were moving him to the HLS. George showed amazing courage leading the Warrior out of the firefight and passed over the casualty to the waiting med team in their helicopter. Bravest thing I had seen in my time in Iraq and that is saying something.

Call sign 21 seeing what had happened moved forward only to get hit by the full force of an IED explosion that ripped through the sunny morning air.

'BOOOM'

The blast hit the Warrior with such force that it sent bits of the armour flying off as well as the lamp post next to it. The commander checked that all his crew were not hurt before he got on the net and reported what had happened and that they needed help to get the armour picked up. In the back of Warrior, one of the new lads who was attached to the patrol started to lose control and started shouting, trying to get out. He was calmed down with a right hook from one of the Fijian lads.

The second group of casualties got picked up and taken to the hospital in the COB. At the same time the strike team started to move up to the junction. When they were 200m short, they got hit with an IED that blasted into the side of the Warrior. It was still able to move but the Snatch behind it was disabled. The first part of the strike team went through the junction but there was no sign of the second part that were hooking up the broken Snatch. Two Platoon's commander placed his head up to see what was going on when two rounds smacked into the sight next to his head. He thought fuck this and jumped down straight away.

The second group started moving and as they were moving through the junction a Snatch took the blast of an RPG. One of the Warriors and tanks moved either side to try and give them some protection as they sorted themselves out. They took longer than Two Platoon's commander wanted with a lot of insurgents still engaging the troops. So, he again put his head up and shouted to them 'GET FUCKING MOVING NOW.' They got the message and moved on and out of the killing area. As they started moving out the insurgents upped the amount of firepower and the call signs had to fire and manoeuvre out of the killing area with an unbelievable amount of fire being thrown at them. Bullets were pinging of the metal of the Warrior and the tanks as they moved back. RPGs were flying everywhere and a couple of them bounced of the vehicles and carried on bouncing down the road.

Everyone managed to break free from the deadly firefight and the patrol continued towards the COB. Once inside of the camp they refuelled and moved back to the tank park. I grabbed all the lads who had fired their weapons and did all the paperwork. My office was full. Once they were done, I sent them for some food and to get their heads down. It had been the first patrol I had missed, and I promised myself it would also be the last. The Battle Group had sixteen of their soldiers in hospital receiving treatment. The operation had been an all-out firefight between our forces and the insurgents with both sides showing great courage.

Arnhem Company had three lads in hospital and me and Carl got some of their stuff together and went down to see how they were getting on. The two lads from the back of the Warrior were sitting up and apart from being a little shaken we got told that they would both be fine and let out of the hospital later that day. The young lad whose Warrior had been hit by an RPG had burns and cuts on his face and we got told that he would be flying out the following morning so he could get treatment back in the UK and continue his recovery there.

Most of the other lads from the Battle Group had minor cuts or burns or had been knocked unconscious by a blast but they would all make a full recovery with only a few lads being sent home for treatment in the UK. The Battle Group had been lucky, and on another day, we could have had half a dozen lying dead. That evening once Op Minimise was lifted, I phoned the three families and ensured them all that their loved ones were going to be OK, and we told them how proud we were of what they did on the ground that day.

The OC called for all the platoon commanders and told them that a platoon was needed to assist Blenheim Company on an Operation Howson. Two Platoon got the short straw and their lads moved down the tank park and mounted up. I took over one of the commanders and also deployed onto the ground as a Warrior commander. We moved out once we were ready and pushed up to the front gate. We were then released by the ops room and moved out stopping short just before the bridge at Red 1. We got told that the convoy was 20 minutes away and moved out and took up our positions.

We had been there for 30 minutes when we got told to hold our positions as one of the HGVs in the convoy had broken down. Three hours later we were still in position trying to stay awake in the warm Iraqi night air. We had received a few tracer rounds that flew over our head, but it was pretty quiet which was a bit alarming. Call sign 23 with Two Platoon's sergeant in command spotted that they were being dicked by a couple of males from a nearby rooftop. He ordered his gunner to engage, and he steadied his sights onto the males and fired. The round smacked into the wall by them and by the time the gunner had readjusted they had gone to ground and were not seen again. The convoy at last came past our position and once it had been handed over, we got the order to move back to camp. We got back into the COB as daylight was breaking from what seemed like the longest Operation Howson ever.

We slept through the day and got up and washed and shaved before we moved to the company O Group for a brief from the 2IC. He told us that we would be picking up the convoy at Red 6 and escorting it down to Red 1 where we would release them. Three Platoon would be the Warriors that were doing the handover and escorting the convoy down the Reds with Two Platoon securing from Red 1 to Red 3 and One Platoon securing from Red 4 to Red 6 with Company HQ in the middle controlling it. We also got briefed that Corporal Jeremy Brooks from 4 Rifles had been killed by small arms fire in a city patrol. He was 28 years old and classed by his unit as a top soldier. With no questions we went and had our evening meal and then moved back to our tents before moving down the tank park at 2100hrs.

An hour later we were at the front gate and were ready to go. We moved out and completed the long route out, again moving past SLB. We pushed straight on and over the bridge and managed to get all the way from Red 1 to Red 6 without any rounds or devices going off. We were in position at 2330hrs and radioed through to Basra Palace and told them we were good to go.

Three hours later we were still sitting there as the new units in the Palace had spotted heat sources and did not want to push on. It was always hard for a new unit when they came to theatre because the unit that had been there for so long had all their drill sorted and knew the ground well. They finally got moving and our Warrior moved up 100m to get eyes onto the handover. As we pulled up, I noticed a heat source on the ground 50m to my front, I told the 2IC and he told me not to take a chance and to engage it with my chain gun. I steadied the sights onto the heat source and fired over twenty rounds of 7.62mm into it. There was no explosion but whatever it was, it was now safe.

The convoy got picked up and we started to move down the Reds, and we soon had it over the bridge and on its way. Back at Red 6 one of the Warriors from Basra Palace had got bogged in. We moved down and moved into position to offer some protection. We deployed our dismounts and the recovery started. We were soon coming under small arms fire as the insurgents realised what was going on. The bullets were soon joined by RPG warheads. A few hit our Warriors with a couple exploding and some getting caught in the BAR armour. They managed to get the Warrior out and they headed off towards Basra Palace and we mounted up and headed our own way back up the Reds. Once we were past the bridge we headed left and moved back down route Anfield before pushing through the Old Trafford rubbish tip and entering the COB. We did the normal refuelling and closed down the Warriors before grabbing some food and getting some sleep.

The following morning, we got up and entered our last week of the tour and we went down the tank park to start getting the Warriors ready for handover. We were leaving the Warriors in Iraq for the

Royal Welsh which made a lot of sense. The Warriors had all of the armour on, and comms and ECM which worked in these conditions. It meant the handover for both units would be twice as easy than seven months before. As the company were down the tank park One Platoon got called away as they were told that they were supporting Blenheim Company on an Operation Howson that was taking place that night. They all left and attended their orders and started to sort all the kit out ready to deploy.

We had our O Group and the OC informed us that we were not out that night and to make the most of it. He also told us that the first party of men from the company who were taking over us were arriving tomorrow. That made us all smile as he said it was a party of five men that would be taking over the CQMS store. With the evening done I phoned home and wished my wife happy anniversary, we had been married for 15 years and she had always supported me, as had my two amazing kids, Daniel and Kirsty. It took a special kind of family in the forces to put up with all the work and shit that we did, and I had one of the best.

One Platoon moved down the tank park at 2300hrs and got sorted out and moved to the front gate. At 10 minutes past midnight the patrol moved out and they headed the long way around moving past the Basra Oil Field. After 30 minutes they stopped short of Red 1 and waited for the call to move forward from the Basra Palace ops room. After 10 minutes they got the order and the Warriors moved over the bridge. Blenheim Company secured from Red 1 to Red 6 with their Warriors and One Platoon moved forward to Red 6 where they were picking up the convoy and escorting it out of the city.

As they were waiting the Warriors took up fire positions and they covered the ground around the junction. Call sign 21 with the Warrior sergeant in command spotted some movement to their front and he dropped down into his turret and looked through his sights. What he saw was beyond belief: there were two insurgents about 100m to his front in full view of his Warrior setting up an IED and rolling out the command wire. They must have thought they were protected by the darkness of the night and did not realise that the Warrior had night and TI sights.

The gunner did not need telling and already had his sight laid onto the first insurgent by the device. He got told to engage and he stamped onto the firing pedal and the chain gun kicked into action firing out its tracer rounds at the insurgent. They hit the insurgent full in the chest, knocking him of his feet and dumping him on the ground. The gunner switched onto the second insurgent, but he was too quick, and he was already off on his toes out of sight of the Warrior.

The Warriors from Basra Palace were soon at Red 6 and the handover was completed. One Platoon led them down the Reds and past the location where the insurgents had been setting up the IED but there was no explosion and the convoy just kept on pushing through. They were soon at the bridge at Red 1 and One Platoon moved over and let the convoy past and on their way. OC Blenheim gave the order and their Warrior moved off and everyone moved back to the COB, where they refuelled, closed down and got some sleep.

The next day we were all on standby during the day for a TST operation. There was surveillance troops deployed in the city that were watching out for the commander of Basra JAM insurgents. They were watching the places where he had been sighted and looking out for his car. Abu Qadir was the head of Basra JAM insurgents and the British Army had been trying to arrest him for the last three years. He had always been one step ahead of us and his early warning system had always resulted in us failing.

We sat by the front gate with the hot burning sun baking us in the warm sunny day. I did not mind as I had been working on getting a tan for going home. We sat by the front gate and tried to keep ourselves hydrated necking bottle after bottle of water. For our dinner we had packed meals which consisted of a sausage roll (which in this heat looked and tasted like a dry flipflop), an apple and some nuts. If the saying was right that an army marched on their stomach, then we were fucked.

In the afternoon we all had to take cover as the COB was attacked with three rockets. By 1600hrs we were stood down and we moved back to our camp. We went straight into the briefing tent where the OC informed us that Arnhem Company would again be at the front gate from 1000hrs the next day and for us all to make the most of the night off. I went and saw the chefs and told them that the packed meals in that heat were killing us and was there any chance of our CQMS picking up a load of sausages and a few loaves of bread and bringing them up to us. They agreed and I went and briefed Carl up for the next day. In the evening, we got an early night, but we were still woken up with two indirect fire attacks from the insurgents.

The next day we got up and got all our kit ready and headed over to the tank park, grabbing our boxes of frozen water on the way. We moved out and by 1000hrs we were again sat waiting for the go from the ops room. At midday Carl turned up and we moved down to grab a buttie. About half the lads had gotten through when the shout came down from the turrets for everyone to mount up and that we were moving out. We jumped up and Carl fucked off with our dinner still in the back of his Land Rover. We sat there for five minutes before the order came to move, we could hear Three Platoon on the radio who were dropping off the Iraqi Special Forces (ISF) at Basra Palace.

We got the order to move and Two Platoon moved out with their engines roaring. They moved over the bridge and through the Iraqi Police checkpoint. They stopped just short of the junction at Green 19 and the dismounts jumped out and started to clear the junction in the warm Basra sun. When they were halfway through it, they reported on the radio and we moved out. One Platoon moved first with Arnhem Company HQ and the Battle Group HQ following on. We moved down to just short of Green 19.

Two Platoon, seeing that we had caught up, moved off. Call sign 22 with the Warrior sergeant in command moved forward and as they did there was a massive explosion that ripped through the air just behind them. He quickly checked that no one was hurt and reported the contact over the radio and told the ops room that he had no casualties, and that the Warrior was still working. He also told the ops room that the device was in full view of the Iraqi Police checkpoint and that the insurgents could not have laid it without them seeing it.

With the report sent we pushed on and moved down and got to our holding position at Purple 4. It was just before 1400hrs, and we had to hold our position until the other troops got a confirmed sighting of our target. It was hot and our bodies were cooking in our Warriors with all our kit on getting baked in the blistering sun. We had to keep necking the frozen water just to keep ourselves from going down. They had us holding at Purple 4 and they also had the ISF holding on the other side of town about a mile away. The plan was that when he was confirmed at a certain location, we would go with both sets of troops cutting him off and trapping him.

At 1415hrs the radio kicked into life as a confirmed sighting of him in his white 4 x 4 jeep was sent. 'GO, GO, GO' was the call that came from the ops room over the radio. Arnhem Company Warriors roared as their engines kicked into action and we moved off going as fast as we could. We headed straight on at Yellow 7 and after a few meters his 4 x 4 pulled out in front of us.

Call sign 10 who had One Platoon's commander in the turret was at the front of Arnhem Warrior's, with Zero Charlie just behind him. We were flying down the street trying to catch him. The call came over the radio that the car was to be stopped using all necessary means. The gunner in call sign 10 got his sight onto the car and stamped on his firing pedal. We heard the shout of stoppage come over the radio and we answered back with a 'GET OUT OF OUR WAY' as our Warrior had a clean shot onto the car.

They were about to move out of the way when the ISF in their Hummies pulled out 10m to our front. They took the lead and after 50m we saw their M60 machine guns kick into action spitting out their deadly tracer rounds at the moving white car. The glass on the back of the car smashed everywhere as the bullets flew into it and the car banked right and smashed into the side of the building. The ISF pulled up behind the car and our Warrior pulled up at the side with what looked like two dead people in the back.

I watched with amazement as the two in the front jumped out. The bodyguard who was driving ran right down an alleyway with a volley of shots following him from the ISF that smacked into the wall just above his head. The commander of the JAM jumped out of the passenger's side of the car, with a pistol in his hand and as he turned left, he was struck down with a burst of bullets that stopped him in his tracks. He fell to the floor and lay dead next to his car. His car by this time was of fire and there were bangs going off all over the place as the ammunition and weapons in the back of their car exploded. The ISF troops went down the alleyway in chase of his bodyguard and his car exploded into flames as his petrol tank was set on fire. We looked out and could see his body burning with the intense heat. We could also smell him, which was not a nice experience.

The ISF and One Platoon pushed on moving to our right to try and cut off the bodyguard. Company HQ and Battalion HQ stayed by the burning car and burning bodies to control what was happening. Two Platoon where over to our left and their Warriors had taken up fire positions to try and offer everyone some protection. They soon spotted insurgents moving up on the rooftops and the ground as they came under contact from different locations. Every Warrior in their platoon was coming under gunfire as the word got around that we were on the ground. Their gunners opened fired with their chain guns, cutting down at least two insurgents and forcing some of the others to go to ground.

Back with call sign Zero Charlie we started to see movement on the rooftop and the top cover were placed up to try and offer some protection. The shout came from the back that an RPG team was spotted to our front near a red oil tank on a roof, I shouted back 'WHERE?' 'WATCH MY TRACER' was the cry I got back. The back of the Warrior was aloud with noise as his light machine gun kicked into action, I watched as his tracer flew through the air and smacked into one of the insurgents, knocking him off the roof. I spotted the RPG team and steadied my sight onto my first target and took over the fight. I fired and kept on firing until I had fired about 150 7.62mm tracer rounds from my chain gun. I hit as least one insurgent, who again had fallen off the roof and forced the others to go to ground. The wall around the oil tank was a complete mess and had crumpled away in many places.

We heard 'CONTACT' come over the radio from One Platoon as their Warriors came under RPG's and small arms fire. Call sign 12 with the Warrior sergeant in command spotted a firing point with three insurgents firing. One had an RPG launcher and the other two had AK-47 rifles. The gunner got his sight onto the targets as did the commander with his rifle from the turret. The driver, seeing the threat to him, jumped up in his seat and engaged them with ten rounds of 9mm from his pistol but being over 50m away he missed.

Back at Company HQ location all the Warriors were now under RPG and smalls arms fire. Call sign Zero Bravo with Frank in the gunner's seat spotted an insurgent location on his right. His turret spun around, and he quickly got the sights onto his target and stamped onto his firing pedal. His deadly tracer flew through the air and hit its target full whack in the chest, knocking him off his feet.

At Two Platoon's location call sign 20's gunner and one of the lads on top cover spotted two insurgents firing from behind a wall. The first man had an RPG launcher and the second had an AK-47 rifle. They both got their sights onto their targets and fired, hitting one and forcing the other to duck down behind the wall. Seeing this, the platoon commander told his gunner to switch to main armament. He stamped on the pedal and released his three 30mm rounds that smacked into the wall blowing it to bits but when he looked there was no sign of any body. The lucky twat must have crawled away just at the right time. There were RPG's and tracer rounds flying all over the place and the commander of Two Platoon kept up the tradition of coming close to getting his fucking head blown off. He popped his head up only to find an RPG warhead fly past him with a WHOOSH.

One Platoon was still under fire as well and their gunners and top covers were working hard to try and keep the insurgents' heads down who were trying to fire at them and the ISF at their location. In the back of call sign Zero Charlie, Wes was on top cover when he spotted three gunmen jump out in the alleyway. He brought his rifle up to his shoulder and got the sight onto the first one. They spotted him and tried to make a dash for cover. He fired with over twenty rounds of 5.56mm from his rifle with the rounds hitting his first target in the leg and quickly switching to his next but they were out of sight. He moved back to his first target only to see his legs disappear as the injured man crawled into cover.

At the same time, I shouted for the top cover to get down as our Warrior started to receive accurate single shots that were pinging off the metal. I shouted for all the lads to scan the ground through the Warrior sights and the driver shouted out that there was movement 50m to our front on a rooftop near a big sign of an Iraqi poster. I got my sights onto the rooftops and watched. For the first minuet there was no movement than I saw a head pop up and look at us. That was not enough evidence for me to open fire, so I kept on watching. His head came up again, but I could still not see a weapon. His head came up again but this time I saw the weapon come above the top of the wall he was at.

I stamped on my firing pedal and the 7.62mm tracer smacked into the wall forcing his head down. I kept on firing until the wall fell apart leaving a gap in it that I could see through. I switched from my chain gun to my 30mm cannon and steadied the sight. I stamped on my firing pedal. 'BANG, BANG, BANG.' The three rounds left my barrel and smashed into the wall. I did not see a body, but I did see his weapon fly through the air as the first round exploded on the rooftop. If he was behind the wall, I was quite sure that he was in no state to fire back anymore and the threat was gone.

Call sign 23 who had been under contact for nearly all the time we had been on the ground got the order over the radio to get ready to move out. He put his head up and had a look around when his head got covered in glass from one of his sights. He jumped down and had a look around as he tried to look through his left sight, he saw that he had something blocking in it. He jumped up only to find that he had an RPG warhead sticking out of it. The lucky bastard, it never exploded when it hit. If it had, it would have taken his head clean off.

We got the order to move and the whole company started to move out with RPGs and tracer rounds still flying all over the place. We broke out of the contact area and pushed on until we were out of the city. Within half an hour we were entering the COB on what had been one of the most aggressive afternoon we had. We had been in a full force-on-force battle with some of the most hardened insurgents we had ever fought. We were pretty lucky not to have people killed or injured.

We fuelled up and closed down and as we entered our camp, we got the confirmation over the radio that the main target Abu Qadir (Wissam Al Waili) was the person who had been killed with three of his aides. He had escaped the British Army for over three years but at last he was no longer a threat and had been taken out by the Iraqi Army. He was responsible for many deaths in that time. many being British forces and many being his own Iraqi people. At the O Group the OC passed on a well done from the Brigade Commander for what was one of the most successful operations of the tour.

That evening the insurgents hit us with three different indirect fire attacks the first attack contained just a single rocket with the second attack containing five rockets and the third attack containing three rockets. They all exploded away from the tented areas with no one being hurt. We got into bed that night hoping that with less than six days to go we might have done our last patrol.

We got up the next day and I moved over to the company office. Our hope of yesterday's patrol been our last were soon dashed as the company 2IC warned us off that we would be down at Bridge HQ that night on standby for a TST operation. The day was spent on sorting out the Warriors and packing our boxes with all the kit we were sending home. A lot of us left what we could for the lads coming in and hoped they could make use of it. Some of the lads gave the local Iraqis who worked in our camps some of the stuff to take home to their families.

That night the officers moved up to Brigade HQ and we were all on standby again. At midnight we got the good news that we were stood down and I went around and told the boys to close down the Warriors and get into bed. The next day was 27 May and we had four days to go. Once again, the 2IC informed us that we would be on standby for a TST operation that night and again we spent the day sorting ourselves out ensuring that come 2100hrs we were good to go. The officers moved to Brigade HQ again and we waited back in camp. Within an hour we got the call to crash out and we mounted up and moved forward to Brigade HQ. The officers were waiting, and we got briefed that we were deploying on a strike and search operation.

We moved out with One Platoon leading and with Company HQ following on with Two Platoon and Three Platoon bringing up the rear. We came out the front gate and headed towards the A Pod Bridge were we turned left and headed down the ramp. We then turned right and headed down the dirt track towards Green 20. At Green 20 we moved over the road and headed left towards Green 19. We were soon on the road heading from Green 19 towards Purple 1 when there was a massive explosion that hit the Warrior in front of us.

It was call sign 13 and they had taken the full force of the blast. We looked on and waited for the commander to report. Within a few seconds he reported that everyone was fine and that there were a few bits that had fallen off inside, but the Warrior was still working. Frank in the Warrior behind us spotted movement to his right and he noticed that they had weapons. He fired a volley of tracer from his chain gun, but the insurgents had already moved. We carried on moving and we were soon at the target area and the strike teams went in.

Within 30 minutes they had completed the strike and search and had moved out where they mounted back up. We headed out when one of Three Platoon's Warriors was just missed by a massive explosion that ripped through the night air but luckily for them missing their Warrior. As we moved out call sign 21 with the platoon sergeant in command moved to Purple 1 to try and offer some protection as we moved through. He soon had an RPG flying through the air with one exploding on his left-hand side of his Warrior. With only a little time to push in Iraq he was not taking any chances and lobbed a red phosphorous grenade that gave an instant smoke screen and covered the last of our Warriors through the junction.

We pushed on past Green 19 with a few mortar rounds dropping in and exploding on the other side of the road. With no one being hurt we just pushed on and moved back into the COB.

We refuelled and moved back to the tank park, on looking at call sign 13 Warrior it was noted that the IED had gone through the armour and passed between the driver and the gunner. They had been the luckiest fuckers around. Unlike the commander (Vanders), who recalled how it was his eighth time on tour that he had been IED'd (he was running out of people who wanted to go on patrol with him). We moved back into camp and sorted all the post operational paperwork out before grabbing some scoff and getting some sleep.

We got up in the afternoon and continued getting all the stuff ready for the handover. In the evening, the OC informed us that the next party from the Royal Welsh would be here the next day. It had about thirty people in it containing the OC and all his commanders, as well as some lads who would be taking over our Warriors. That evening the next party from the Royal Welsh got in at about 0200hrs and the first thing they had to do was take cover as the insurgents hit us with three rockets that exploded just past our camp.

Our lads who were on guard that night had to move and check an area before the all clear was given. As he passed the new arrivals he quietly said, 'Welcome to Iraq, it's fucking yours', with a wicked smile on his face. Once the all clear was given Carl showed them to their tents and they were soon on the floor again as we got hit with five rockets.

The next day was 28 May, and it was to be our last day operational as the last two days were to be used for handover. In the afternoon we got hit with three rockets but most of the company were out showing the new commanders the ground and how we entered the city. Their patrol went well and because they were not entering the city they managed not to get contacted. Once they came back in, we got told that we would be on standby for a TST operation that night.

The commander from both units went up to Brigade HQ at 2100hrs and we were all on standby back at camp. At 2300hrs we were crashed out and we mounted up and moved up to our meeting point. The officer came out and told us that we would be involved in a strike and search operation just past Green 18. Blenheim Company would move first, and secure Green 18 and Arnhem Company would push past and escort A Company to the target house.

We got to the front gate and Blenheim Company moved out and approached Green 18 from Yellow 2 Bravo. We followed on about 200m behind them. As they got to Yellow 2 Bravo their lead Warrior stopped as he noticed two heat sources in the middle of the road leading to Green 18. They deployed their lads, and they moved forward and noticed that the ground had been disrupted in two areas. They asked the ops room to confirm it with some surveillance equipment from one of the helicopters, and they came back and confirmed that he had the same signature as a possible IED.

We waited for about 20 minutes for a decision to be made and we got the call back that the operation was cancelled and the area to our front was to be placed out of bounds to all troops. We moved back in and could not believe that such a mad tour had come to an end with such a shit patrol. I was not arsed as it meant no one else had been hurt or killed and that we could handover and fuck off as soon as we could. We got in and closed down and you could see the joy in the lads faces as they walked around, hugging each other and shaking each other's hands. They had been through a lot, and they had every right to be proud of themselves. We closed down the Warriors and went and got some sleep.

We got up in the afternoon and worked down the tank park to ensure that everything was good to go. The insurgents reminded us that we were not out of danger yet as they attacked us twice with three rockets in each attack, but again they exploded near the airfield without anyone being hurt. In the evening, they hit us again with six rockets but this time they were close, and we all hugged our walls as they exploded just past our camp. The next day the OC was leaving a couple of days early to get his arm looked at back in the UK. An hour later the OC informed us that we were now stood down for the night and not needed down at Brigade HQ.

We spent the day handing over the Warriors and all of our equipment and stores. I handed all the ammo over to their CQMS as their CSM was not in until the next day with his company. It felt good to get it all out of the way. In the evening most of us went around to the welfare village. It had been a long time since we had had a night off and we enjoyed it with a bite to eat and a milkshake.

We woke up the next day happy as it was our last day in Basra. We had breakfast and then move to our boxes that were being search by the RMPs. They had to ensure that no one was taking any weapons back or smuggling fags or pills. Once done the ISO container was sealed and that was the last we would see them for six weeks until they arrived back in the UK.

We then moved to the cookhouse for a brief on our journey back and our decompression which was to be a day in Cyprus. Once all of this was done, we had our lunch and then we handed over our tents as the new lads moved in. I gave the lads some time at the welfare village to get their last bits and pieces. I had a chat with the new CSM as we did our handover. I gave him as much information as I could to help him and his company. In the afternoon we were at the welfare village, and we had to take cover twice as they fired in some rockets at the COB.

At 2000hrs we all met up at the guardroom and headed to the air head. We moved out and the lads cheered as we left our camp for the last time. At the air head we had all our bags scanned and off they went to the UK, as we would not need them in Cyprus. We got briefed and got told that our C-130 would be here about midnight to take us to Kuwait. We waited about and soon we got the call to move forward and board our coach. We had just got on the coach when the alarm went off and the air head staff shouted for everyone to get off and hit the deck as we were under attack. Two rockets hit the COB and exploded near the runway.

After 10 minutes we got told to board the coach and we made the short trip to our C-130 that was waiting with the engines running ready to go. We moved on and all sat down and did our seatbelts up. The back ramp was raised and all of a sudden, a bell inside started to ring as we got another four rockets from the insurgents. The air crew shouted for everyone to lie down flat. We all started to laugh, we were sitting on tons of fuel in a plane, and he was telling us to lie down. Within 10 minutes we were moving and there was a cheer from the lads as the plane took off and headed out of Iraqi airspace.

I just sat next to the 2IC (John) and shook his hand. The 2IC for me had been an amazing officer during this tour and a better friend. The way he stepped up as the OC on the ground for the last couple of months of the tour was a credit to how good he was. How he never got the Distinguished Service Order (DSO) for his time in command I will never know.

8

HOME

It was 1 June by the time we landed in our C-130 in Kuwait. It was about 0200hrs. We got a brief that our chartered flight from Kuwait to Cyprus would be at 0700hrs and we could get some food or some sleep until we were called for. Our holding base was a large US airbase. I told the lads to get some scoff as the Americans knew how to look after their soldiers. Most of the lads dropped their day sacks off and of we went towards the cookhouse.

It was nice to be able just to walk from A to B without our body armour or helmets on and without any danger of a rocket falling in and blowing you to pieces. We got to the cookhouse and walked inside. There were Stars and Stripes all over the place, but they knew how to eat. It was past two in the morning, and they still had burger bars, fry-ups, rice dishes, pasta dishes and all kinds on the go.

The lads were like kids in a candy shop. We sat there with our belly-buster burgers and fries, pasta and not forgetting our Mr Whippy ice creams all washed down with a massive cup of full fat Coke. We had our fill and as we were leaving, we spotted a freezer with ice pops and cones. I laughed to myself as we walked over to our tents like little kids sucking on an ice pop. We jumped on a bed for a couple of hours before we boarded a coach and headed towards our plane.

It took off and within a few hours we had landed in Cyprus. We got off the plane and boarded another coach that took us to a camp called Blood Hound Camp that was situated overlooking the Mediterranean Sea. They had a training team waiting for us that were responsible for our decompression. We got told that we had beds waiting for us that were already made up and when we got up in the morning not to make them as it would be sorted out and remade by the cleaners. They told us that after a bit of lunch we were going to get dropped off at the beach for the afternoon.

When we came back, we would get briefs on what to expect when we got home. After this we would have a BBQ where we would get a chance to have a beer and to let off some steam before we got home. The next day we would get dropped off at some sports fields in Happy Valley where we could play sports or chill out until our flight was ready. Sounded good to us so we moved over to our wooden blocks and dropped our day sacks off. Apart from leave it was going to be our first night in a bed for over seven months. We got out of our desert combats and put some shorts and a t-shirt on and some trainers or flip flops.

We walked down to the cookhouse and grabbed some scoff. It was good and there was a lot of it. After lunch we headed down to the beach and it was just nice to get into the sea and chill out. It had a floating island about 20m out and a lot of the lads swam out and just chatted away or fooled around chucking each other in. Some stayed on the beach playing football or volleyball or just sunbathed topping up their tan. It was a good afternoon, relaxed, chilled out and the weather was good.

Around 1700hrs we moved back to camp were we all sat down and got a brief. They started by showing us a video of what we had achieved during our seven-month tour. Then the padre stood up and told us how to handle going home after such a violent tour of duty. How things were going to be hard not just for us but for our families as well.

After the brief had finished, we moved outside where the BBQ was in full flow. We grabbed a beer for the first time in seven months. Most of the lads just got pissed and let off some steam. They had a dance off with all the new lads having to enter and also sang songs.

Some settled problems that they had with someone during the tour, but credit to Arnhem Company there was no fighting or people getting decked. Everyone just had a good time and let off some steam before they got home. Some of the lads got naked: do not ask me why, it is just a squaddie thing. By 0200hrs they were all tucked up in bed pissed up.

The next day we got up and one of the lads was getting a lot of stick as he was that pissed that night that he had shit and pissed the bed and just to make it a hat trick he had vomited up as well (he cleaned it up as he could not leave that for the cleaners). We had some breakfast and moved down to the sports fields. Half the boys just lay about trying to get over their hangover. Some of us had a game of football and then went for a swim in the sea. Just before midday they did some burgers for us before we put on our clean ironed combats and boarded our coaches. A lot of us had not been looking forward to decompression and thought it was going to be a waste of time but at the end of it we all agreed that it had been worthwhile. It was good to let of some steam and relax for 24 hours before we returned home.

We got to the airport, and I got a few bottles of Keo brandy in as they were really cheap in Cyprus. We were called forward and boarded our planes and within a few hours we had landed at Teesside Airport. Our families were asked to wait at the camp and meet us there. When we got off the plane there were no welcome home banners or anyone from the British public cheering us. We moved through the airport with people just looking on and you could not help feeling devalued. It hit home how much the country thought of our involvement in Iraq. At the same time, the British Army were just doing what our country was asking of us and they should have still been proud of us if not the war.

We got our bags and got on a coach and completed the short 20-minute trip to our camp. The National TV crew were there, and my coach pulled up first and I was the first off. My little girl Kirsty ran up and gave me a big hug. Lyn and Daniel soon joined us and we all just hugged each other. Marti was also there to meet us, and the good news was he had his sight back. We moved to the gym where I was asked to speak to the news crews from the BBC and ITV. They were trying their best to get us to make a comment about Tony Blair and to make us slip up about what we thought of Britain's involvement in Iraq. I just stood there and smiled and told them the truth about how glad we were to be home, and our thoughts were with the families and loved ones of the ones who had not returned or were recovering from their injuries.

Op Telic 9 was the most aggressive and violent tour of Iraq since and including the war. The British Army had 462 individual indirect fire attacks on the bases in and around the city with over 2,300 rockets or mortars being fired at us. That was more than all the other Op Telic added together. The troops of Op Telic 9 had taken part in 107 strike operations detaining 198 targets with 68 being interned. We had taken part in even more search operations with the following being found: 980 rockets or mortars, 282 weapons, 29 IEDs and 190 IED components, 135 RPG warheads and 175 grenades as well as tons of ammunition. We had done 754 convoys and covered enough ground to go around the world six and half times. We had claimed 340 dead enemy hits and had even dropped 500lb bombs on indirect fire teams. We had also carried out counter-IED ambushes with great success.

So, you have to ask yourself what we achieved for the local people of Basra City. Well, we improved their electricity from 11 hours a day to 18 hours a day. We improved their roads and helped them rebuild their date palm business. We spent over £60 million on improving their city and building up their schools. We helped train up their Army with them taking control of the Old State Building, Shatt Hotel, and Shibah Log Base and also handing them back Maysaan Province.

On a personal note, Op Telic 9 was at times the hardest time of my life. On the other hand, it was the highlight of my career. From a soldier's point of view, being involved in a full aggressive tour is something my career needed. I ticked everything I wanted to do as a professional infantry soldier and was tested to the full by a determined enemy. Being in a firefight with some of the bravest and well trained soldiers I have ever worked with was the biggest adrenaline rush I have ever had. On the other side seeing your friends getting blown to pieces and injured is a life changing event. It saddens you to the core watching someone's life slip away or having to pick up your dead friends. For myself and everyone who was on that tour, Op Telic 9 will become the signature tour of their career and something that bonds us together for life.

I do believe the Battalion command failed the officers and soldiers on the tour. Only a handful of minor bravery awards were given to the deployed force. The Recce Platoon commander and his 2IC should of received Military Crosses for the attack on Yellow Two Alpha and their amazing command. My driver Chris driving over the IED you could say the same and if you mention Sgt George Probert's actions with the injured lad from the RPG attack, I would even argue on another tour he would be recommended for a Victora Cross. This is just scratching the surface of a tour packed with outstanding gallantry from the first day to the last. I believe that because the tour was unpopular back at home and now everyone had eyes on Afghanistan it was all political. People in command had to be stronger, including myself.

Seven months before I considered us as a force for good and wanted to improve the way of life for the people of Iraq. By the end of the tour, I could not help to think who the hell are we!! The Iraqi people did not want us there or to be Western and what was wrong with their way of life? If that is what they were happy with, good for them. As a country it was pretty arrogant of us to think any different. I still believe that if we did not help their forces and police to become organised then this was an ideal ground to breed and train terrorists, which would have resulted in dozens of attacks on Western countries.

I said at the start of the book about the British Military having no end game, but as the tour went on and land and bases were handed back to the Iraqi to control, you can argue I was wrong and there was a plan in place, I just didn't see it from the tactical level.

But was it worth it? From Jamie Hancock to Corporal Jeremy Brook, twenty-nine souls had been lost on Op Telic 9, with eight of them being from our battalion. Kingsman Jamie Hancock, Sergeant Graham Hesketh, Kingsman Alex Green, Second Lieutenant Jonathan Carlos Bracho-Cooke, Kingsman Danny Wilson, Second Lieutenant Joanna York Dyer, Kingsman Adam James Smith, and Kingsman Alan Jones.

They all lost their lives serving for their Queen and country and paid with the ultimate sacrifice and the ones who were paying the price are their loved ones who were left behind and all the soldiers still trying to recover from their terrible injuries, but they should be proud. The so-called Generation Z who were serving in the British Army in Iraq and Afghanistan stepped up and performed just the same way the Falklands, Northern Ireland, and Balkans veterans did throughout the years. These young men and woman, like the veterans before them, have demonstrate today what is still great in Great Briton and them and their families should be proud of what they achieved.

This book is dedicated to the fallen, the injured, the soldiers and our supporting families.

Please follow Carl on his Author's Facebook Page for more information about his future books and competitions